YOU ARE BEING BETRAYED BY THE U.S. GOVERNMENT

SAM WRIGHT, JR.

authorHOUSE®

AuthorHouse™
1663 Liberty Drive, Suite 200
Bloomington, IN 47403
www.authorhouse.com
Phone: 1-800-839-8640

First published by AuthorHouse 1/31/2008

ISBN: 978-1-4343-6732-7 (sc)
ISBN: 978-1-4343-6731-0 (hc)

Library of Congress Control Number: 2008900946

Printed in the United States of America
Bloomington, Indiana

This book is printed on acid-free paper.

If any Government official, including the President, the Chief Justice, or any member of Congress, wishes to challenge ANYTHING in this book, then I will gladly defend what I have written in the forum of your choice.
I warn you — I'm bringing the Constitution.

We often hear that in these United States there is the "rule of law." The "rule of law" is supposed to protect the liberties and rights of citizens against arbitrary and abusive government power. In this book you will learn how unprotected you really are.

These provisions for the security of the rights of the citizen stand in the Constitution in the same connection and upon the same ground, as they regard his liberty and his property. It cannot be denied that both were intended to be enforced by the judiciary as one of the departments of the government established by that Constitution.

No man in this country is so high that he is above the law. No officer of the law may set that law at defiance with impunity. All the officers of the government, from the highest to the lowest, are creatures of the law, and are bound to obey it.

Courts of justice are established, not only to decide upon the controverted rights of the citizens as against each other, but also upon rights in controversy between them and the government.

Under our system the *people* . . . are the sovereign.

Justice Samuel F. Miller
Supreme Court of the United States
United States v. Lee   1882

TABLE OF CONTENTS

PREFACE

After *We the People* declared our independence and won the Revolutionary War, *We the People* no longer had a ruler. We became a self-governing People. *We the People* are the sovereigns in this country. Our sovereignty has never been surrendered to the Government. *We the People* are the rulers; the Government is not the ruler.

The supreme law of the land is our Constitution, not the will of any Governmental official or Department of the Government. In 1882 in the Supreme Court case of United States v. Lee, Mr. Justice Miller, referring to the Constitution, said,

"It is the supreme power in our system of government, and every man who by accepting office participates in its functions is only the more strongly bound to submit to that supremacy, and to observe the limitations which it imposes upon the exercise of the authority which it gives."

Our Constitution protects us, the People, against the Government exercising arbitrary or unlimited power because the Constitution is the only source of power for the Government, or any Branch or officer of it. In 1803 in the case of Marbury v. Madison, Mr. Chief Justice Marshall said, *"The very essence of civil liberty certainly consists in the right of every individual to claim the protection of the laws, whenever he receives an injury. One of the first duties of government is to afford that protection."* In spite of the Constitution, a citizen finds that the Government is not a protector, but a constant barrier to and offender of the citizen's rights. Congress, the Executive Branch, and the Judicial Branch have no existence outside the Constitution. The Government may not ever lawfully exercise any power that the

People do not delegate to the Government in the Constitution. The Government may not lawfully surpass the limits contained in the Constitution. All of the Departments, offices and officers in the Government exist to serve as the tools that *We the People* use **to govern ourselves**.

The Framers of the Constitution believed that rights not specified in the Constitution are insecure and they believed that if the Government could administer public affairs according to its will and without regard to the inherent Rights of a free People, or if the Government was unrestrained by any fundamental law, then the Government would disregard the liberties and Rights of *We the People* exposing us to the oppressions of arbitrary power. The Bill of Rights was adopted because the People could not rely upon the Government to restrain itself and to secure certain rights of the People against invasion. Every day Congress, the Executive Branch, and the Judicial Branch prove that the Framers of the Constitution were right!! Boy, were they right!!!! The Government proves time and again that the Rights that *are* specified in the Constitution *are not secure*!!!!!!!!! Each branch of the Government intentionally disregards the framework, the rules, the prohibitions, the limits on power, and the People's Rights in the Constitution.

We have passed from a time of guarded and protected constitutional rights into an era of willful Government disregard and disobedience of the Constitution. Each Branch of the Federal Government is ignoring the Rights and the principles in the Constitution. The behavior of officials in each Branch of the Government proves that when our Constitution becomes inconvenient for them, they simply ignore it.

In the annual message to Congress of December 6, 1910 William H. Taft is quoted as saying "**No man ought to have, as a matter of right, a review of his case by the Supreme Court. He should be satisfied by one hearing before a court of first instance and one review by a court of appeals.**" Mr. Taft does not point to any provision of the Constitution that supports his "no man ought to have, as a matter of right" or his "he should be satisfied." The reason he didn't point to any provision of the Constitution is because he couldn't. Mr. Taft's "no man ought to have, as a matter of right" and his "he should be satisfied" demonstrates a tyrannical attitude of Government officials that is still present in our Government today. It is not within the power of any person in this country to decide when another ought to be satisfied concerning the redress of grievances for a wrong that was suffered.

The Constitution is written the way it is in order to protect the minority from the majority and to protect the citizens from the Government. The Government cannot take the Rights in the Constitution away because the Government does not grant the Rights. The Constitution does not delegate to the Government the power to take Rights away. More and more people are becoming more and more fearful of the Government because the Government ignores the People's Rights. Considering the abuses the People have suffered and continue to suffer at the hands of the Government, the fear seems to be well founded.

When the Constitution assigns a specific duty our individual rights depend upon the performance of that duty. The President of the United States is the head of the Executive Branch. The President does not hold employees in the Departments in the Executive Branch accountable for obeying the Constitution and the law. We are not likely to get a President to admit this failure to perform his responsibility. We are likely to get the response that the President appoints persons to head those Departments and those persons are responsible for holding the employees in their Department accountable for obeying the Constitution and the law.

The persons appointed by the President to head the Departments in the Executive Branch do not hold employees in their Departments accountable for obeying the Constitution and obeying the law. The people appointed by the President are not likely to admit this failure to perform their responsibility. They are likely to tell us that subordinate officials in their Departments are responsible for holding the employees in their Department accountable for obeying the Constitution and the law.

The subordinate officials . . . It goes on and on! Each Government official in the Executive Branch will give us — I'm not responsible, it's someone else! I wonder if the majority of them have any idea just what the Constitution says. They should, considering the fact that each one of them took an oath to support and defend the Constitution. They probably don't remember taking the oath! The Executive Branch is out of control because Government officials are not held accountable for failing to support the Constitution. When Congress asks Government officials in the Executive Branch about the lack of accountability, the response is that they are going to *start* a plan to ensure accountability! How many times does Congress have to hear the same nonsense before they realize that it *is* nonsense? Hey, maybe we have discovered the problem! The problem could be that the members of Congress are not as intelligent as the Government officials in either of the other two Branches, so they are unable to tell when they are being fed a line of bull!! The Executive Branch is running amuck and fails to follow the rules and laws written by Congress. No one in the Executive Branch fears Congress. Why should they? Congress takes no action when it is perfectly clear to Congress that the Executive Branch is not upholding the Constitution or the laws.

Federal judges, including the Justices of the Supreme Court, have repeatedly issued decisions that ignore the Constitution and the laws written by Congress. We will see that Congress can remove Federal judges, but the threat of removal has not deterred Federal judges. Federal judges do as they please!! Why? Because Congress permits them to!!

Before the Constitution was completed, the People were extremely concerned that Federal judges would create law and ignore the Congress. Mr. Alexander Hamilton addressed the People's concerns in his Federalist No. 81. Mr. Hamilton told the People of New York that the supposed danger of judiciary encroachment on legislative authority was in reality a phantom because "particular miscontructions and contraventions of the will of the legislature may now and then happen; but they can never be so extensive as to amount to an inconvenience, or in any sensible degree to affect the order of the political system. This may be inferred with certainty, from the general nature of the judicial power, from the objects to which it relates, from the manner in which it is exercised, from its comparative weakness, and from its total incapacity to support its usurpations by force. And the inference is greatly fortified by the consideration of <u>the important constitutional check which the power</u> <u>of instituting impeachments in one part of the legislative body, and</u> <u>of determining upon them in the other, would give to that body upon</u> <u>the members of the judicial department. This is alone a complete</u> <u>security.</u> There can never be danger that the judges, by a series of deliberate usurpations on the authority of the legislature, would hazard the united resentment of the body intrusted with it, while this body was possessed of the means of punishing their presumption, by degrading them from their stations. While this ought to remove all apprehensions on the subject . . . Having now examined, and, I trust, removed the objections to the distinct and independent organization of the Supreme Court, I proceed . . ." The actions of Federal Judges, including the Justices of the Supreme Court, prove that the Peoples' fear concerning Federal judges was well founded and the encroachment by Federal judges on the authority of Congress became reality. Federal judges act contrary to the Constitution and the will of Congress on a regular basis — not now and then, as Mr. Hamilton conceded would be the limit of the Judiciary's contrary actions to the will of Congress. The Judiciary's encroachments are much more than an inconvenience. These encroachments result in the Rights of the People being trampled upon.

The Supreme Court is an officer of the law and cannot at its discretion sport away the vested rights of the people, but it selects the cases that it hears based on vague and arbitrary criteria. Nothing in our judicial system is more unconstitutional than the decisions of the Justices of the Supreme Court regarding the granting of a petition for a writ of certiorari. How can I make such a statement? That's an easy question to answer! The Justices do not use any firm standards to control the application of a writ of certiorari. If your case only concerns your constitutional rights, then the Justices will deny your petition for a writ of certiorari. Your constitutional rights get trashed and the Supreme Court couldn't care less! I've looked and I've researched and I've researched and I've looked and I can't find a single portion of the Constitution that even implies, much less says, that if the case involves only the constitutional rights of a single citizen the Supreme Court may choose not to hear the citizen's case. The Supreme Court's practice of selecting cases to review offends the Constitution. The constitution does not empower any court, or any part of the Government, with any discretion in the execution of its duties or responsibilities. It is the duty of the Supreme Court to attend to its constitutional obligations. The facts in this book show that the right of the People to secure a review of decisions of the inferior courts does not depend on any discretionary power of the Supreme Court.

The detrimental effect of the Supreme Court's practice of choosing which cases it will hear is far reaching and the practice weakens our entire judicial system. It is likely that many people do not bother to appeal to the Supreme Court, no matter what the law is or how badly they have been wronged. The statistics published by the Supreme Court prove that appealing to the Supreme Court is likely to be a waste of time and money. The per curiam decisions issued by the Federal Courts of Appeals and the Merit Systems Protection Board's (MSPB) "does not meet the criteria for review" decisions show that Federal Courts of Appeals and the Merit Systems Protection Board also chose which cases they will review. I telephoned the Clerk's Office at the Court of Appeals for the Fourth Circuit and asked a gentleman, who identified himself as Mark, two questions. First — why do Courts of Appeals issue per curiam decisions and second — why do Courts of Appeals issue decisions without a judge's signature? Mark's only response was that Courts of Appeals issue per curiam decisions when the judges believe that the case does not add anything to existing law. He could not explain why a decision is issued without a judge's signature. The explanation that Mark did give sounds just like one of the reasons that the Supreme Court uses to justify which cases it will hear.

The reason given by the Supreme Court is that the Justices of the Supreme Court must think that the case is of some national importance. Rule 10 of the Rules of the Supreme Court makes this point perfectly clear.

Rule 10. Considerations Governing Review on Certiorari

Review on a writ of certiorari is not a matter of right, but of judicial discretion. A petition for a writ of certiorari will be granted only for compelling reasons. The following, although neither controlling nor fully measuring the Court's discretion, indicate the character of the reasons the Court considers:

(a) a United States court of appeals has entered a decision in conflict with the decision of another United States court of appeals in the same important matter; has decided an important federal question in a way that conflicts with a decision by a state court of last resort; or has so far departed from the accepted and usual course of judicial proceedings, or sanctioned such a departure by a lower court, as to call for an exercise of this Court's supervisory power;

(b) a state court of last resort has decided an important federal question in a way that conflicts with the decision of another state court of last resort or of a United States court of appeals;

(c) a state court or a United States court of appeals has decided an important question of federal law that has not been, but should be, settled by this Court, or has decided an important federal question in a way that conflicts with relevant decisions of this Court.

A petition for a writ of certiorari is rarely granted when the asserted error consists of erroneous factual findings or the misapplication of a properly stated rule of law.

Did you notice how many times the word *important* is used? How do the Justices of the Supreme Court measure *important*? How do the Justices know what is of importance to us? After all, *We the People* are the nation. We elect none of the Justices. None of the Justices represent any segment of the people. The Justices do not have constituents. Try placing a telephone call to any of the Justices, you will not be put through. Ever heard any of the Justices asking the people to telephone and let them know just how we feel on a topic? Not once do the Justices consider our feelings or opinion on any issue before deciding that the issue is of no importance. How can any of the Justices know what is of importance to us, *We the People*? The obvious answer is – THEY CAN'T KNOW!

For the sake of argument, let's concede that the Justices *do* have a foolproof method for determining what is *important*. Let's further concede, for the sake of argument, that every person, entity, spirit, animal, and other life form in the universe thinks that the case that you have appealed to the Supreme Court is unimportant. Wouldn't matter!! Why? Simple. The Constitution does not base our Right to have our appeal heard by the Supreme Court on what anyone, including the Justices of the Supreme Court, thinks about the importance of the case. The Constitution does not base the Supreme Court's duties or responsibilities on how the Justices feel about anything. The word *important* is not used in the Constitution!! *We the People* are the rulers, not the Supreme Court. *We the People* wrote the Constitution, not the Supreme Court. The Supreme Court works for us. The duty of the Justices of the Supreme Court is to **follow** the Constitution, not to rewrite the Constitution for their personal benefit!! The Constitution says that the violation of your rights is enough basis for the Supreme Court to hear your case. As you will see, the facts show that the Justices of the Supreme Court say that the violation of your rights is not enough for you to have your case heard before the Supreme Court and the Justices routinely refuse to hear such cases. The facts also show that the Justices of the Supreme Court do not place much importance on whether our case was decided correctly by lower court judges. Obviously, the Supreme Court makes its own rules and doesn't function according to the Constitution!! What's worse is that during testimony before a congressional committee the Justices of the Supreme Court told members of Congress that the Justices do not function according to the Constitution. Then the Justices asked Congress for permission to continue to function outside of the Constitution and for permission to trash even more of our Rights, and Congress agreed!!!!!!!!

The judges on the Federal Courts of Appeals and the members of the Merit Systems Protection Board know, because of the statistics published by the Supreme Court, that the likelihood of the Supreme Court even hearing your case is remote. The chances of your case being returned to them by the Supreme Court is between slim and none. Should your case be returned to them, there would not be anything said about their decision not to review your case. There will be no penalty or punishment. So, judges on the Federal Courts of Appeals and the members of the Merit System Protection Board review only the cases they want and *We the People* suffer. Who should hold them accountable? The Constitution says that Congress should, but it certainly does not! The Federal Judiciary does not hold judges accountable! You certainly cannot hold judges accountable because the Supreme Court has said, in spite of the Constitution, that you may not sue the Government or a Federal judge because they both have immunity from your lawsuit! So, Federal judges are free to do as they please, and this is supposed to be for the good of us — *We the People*!!

The Supreme Court's caseload is high and will remain high for many reasons. The facts show that some of the obvious reasons for the huge numbers of cases appealed to the Supreme Court are:

Judges in the inferior courts fail to do the job for which *We the People* pay each one of them very well.

The Supreme Court does not require the judges in the lower courts to follow its decisions.

Judges in the inferior courts are permitted to repeatedly issue decisions that are contrary to the Constitution and the law.

Judges in the Courts of Appeals rubber stamp decisions that are contrary to the Constitution and the law.

The Federal Judiciary does not police itself.

Congress does not police the Federal Judiciary.

Judges are permitted to remain in that sacred office when they do not uphold the Constitution or demonstrate good behavior.

I will show you at least six Supreme Court Justices and thirteen judges, Judges Ellis, Wilkins, Williams, Michael, Ervin, Luttig, Motz, Sullivan, Robinson, Silberman, Henderson, Tatel, and Wald, who do not faithfully or impartially discharge and perform their duties. It is highly unlikely that these judges are alone in their behavior. The Constitution demands removal for such behavior. These judges are still judges because Congress permits them to remain! Any federal judge who does not examine the law before issuing a decision in a case has not upheld his oath or supported the Constitution and should be removed by Congress, yet Congress never even imposes a penalty! When Federal judges create law or issue decisions that are contrary to the Constitution or the laws passed by Congress, the members of Congress do not take any action to protect our rights, or whatever action Congress took is so ineffectual it is the same as no action.

The Constitution gives only Congress the power to make rules for the Government and the power to make laws necessary for the functioning of the Government. Congress is our only defense against oppressive Government officials. Congress is our watchdog for the store (the store being our Rights). A Congress that failed to attend to its responsibilities and then failed to watch how the Supreme Court used the writ of certiorari started the domino effect of discretionary review. Not only is Congress not watching the store, Congress has in effect given the Executive and Judicial Branches the keys to the store and then left town! Congress has passed its watchdog responsibilities off to the Executive and Judicial Branches. Congress, in effect, expects the other two Branches to watch themselves. Want proof? The facts in this book show that Senator Kennedy said, in reply to a letter that complains that the District of Columbia Courts are unconstitutional, that he does not get involved in another person's legal matters. Also, the members of Congress' two Committees on the Judiciary showed no interest in the unconstitutional behavior of the District of Columbia Courts. The members of both the House and Senate Committees on the Judiciary failed to act in the face of the affirmative duty to act that is established by the oath they took to uphold the Constitution. Each member of both Committees on the Judiciary that failed to act should submit his or her resignation immediately! Will they? Not a chance! Each one is too busy . . . . taking our money. Congress leaves us at the mercy of the power mad Government officials in the other two branches of Government. There are no longer checks and balances because Congress does not perform its watchdog function. Congress allows:

- the courts to issue per curiam decisions.

- the MSPB to issue its "does not meet the criteria for review."

- the courts of appeals to uphold the MSPB's "does not meet the criteria for review when the courts of appeals cannot possibly know what the decision means.

- the courts to establish immunities for the Government even though that is the function of Congress.

- the courts to establish the deliberative-process privilege and administrative exhaustion doctrine in violation of the Constitution.

- judges who do not uphold the Constitution and are not of good behavior to remain judges.

Congress does not have an established procedure to find out when a judge does not faithfully or impartially discharge and perform their duties.

Each member of Congress takes an oath. They give their word to God and us. Every day the members of Congress ignore their oaths and their Constitutional responsibilities. Congress looks the other way while the Executive and Judicial Branches trash our rights. Congress passively accepts the lies and unresponsive answers given by Government officials in the other two Branches. For three decades, the Executive Branch has not complied with the civil rights laws and Congress permits the Executive Branch to continue to break the law. Congress has taken no action to protect our rights. Congress ignores requests to correct Government behavior and Congress refuses to require the Government to conform to the Constitution. Congress does not act in accordance with the Constitution.

We the People have the right to cause our Government officials to leave their positions in Government and *We the People* entrusted Congress with the responsibility of removing any Government official. You remember Congress —those people who beg us to elect them to the Senate and the House of Representatives so they can make sure the Constitution is upheld and also protect our Rights and protect us from the power wielding Government officials in the Executive and Judiciary Branches. The members of Congress simply must follow the Constitution. We pay the members of Congress an excellent salary to follow the Constitution and protect our Rights from power wielding Government officials, yet they still betray us. Each member of the Senate and the House of Representatives has a contract with America — **IT'S CALLED THE CONSTITUTION!!!!!!**

Webster's Collegiate Dictionary, Tenth Edition, defines *politician* as: (1) a person experienced in the art or science of government; (2) one actively engaged in conducting the business of a government; (3) a person engaged in party politics as a profession; (4) a person primarily interested in political office for selfish or other narrow usually short-sighted reasons. The business of our Government does not involve an art or science, but it requires the ability to read — the Constitution. To be actively engaged in conducting the business of our Government, a member of Congress must follow the Constitution. Now we are left with only two definitions that may apply to the majority of our politicians. Pick the one you think most describes our politicians. Feel comfortable?

George Mason, one of the Framers of our Constitution, believed that the House of Representatives was closest to the people and most responsive to their will, and that the popular election of the members of the House of Representatives was "the only security for the rights of the people." Well, history and the House of Representatives show that the House of Representatives is little, if any, security for the rights of the people.

The Declaration of Independence follows this Preface. There are some parts in bold print. Here are those parts:

> **We hold these truths to be self-evident, . . . that they are endowed by their Creator with certain unalienable Rights . . . the pursuit of Happiness . . . That to secure these rights, Governments are instituted among Men, deriving their just powers from the consent of the governed . . . That whenever any Form of Government becomes destructive of these ends, it is the Right of the People to alter or**

to abolish it . . . But when a long train of abuses and usurpations, pursuing invariably the same Object evinces a design to reduce them under absolute Despotism, it is their right, it is their duty, to throw off such Government, and to provide new Guards for their future security . . . for the sole purpose of fatiguing them into compliance . . . obstructed the Administration of Justice . . . For protecting them, by a mock Trial, from Punishment . . . For depriving us in many cases, of the benefits of Trial by Jury . . . For taking away our Charters, abolishing our most valuable Laws, and altering fundamentally the Forms of our Governments . . . In every stage of these Oppressions We have Petitioned for Redress . . . Our repeated Petitions have been answered only by repeated injury. . . whose character is thus marked by every act which may define a Tyrant, . . .

It is impossible to pursue Happiness (**the pursuit of Happiness**) when the Government is constantly ignoring the Constitution (**For taking away our Charters, abolishing our most valuable Laws, and altering fundamentally the Forms of our Governments**). The Government prevents itself from being corrected by the People, and protects Government officials from prosecution by creating the unconstitutional defenses of sovereign, absolute and qualified immunity (**evinces a design to reduce them under absolute Despotism**) and the investigations performed by the Government into wrongdoing by Government officials rarely culminates in punishment for the wrongdoer (**For protecting them, by a mock Trial, from Punishment**). Whenever a citizen manages to actually try a case against the Government, the Government drags it on, and on, and on, and on, and on, **for the sole purpose of fatiguing them** (the citizen) **into compliance**. During legal proceedings, Government officials and attorneys purposefully lie (**obstructed the Administration of Justice**). The Government retaliates against people who blow the whistle on Government wrongdoing (**Our repeated Petitions have been answered only by repeated injury**). A very strong argument can be made to support the idea that the Government has developed the characteristics of a Tyrant and is destructive to the ends for which it was established (**whose character is thus marked by every act which may define a Tyrant**). If it has done so, then it is the right of the People to alter or even abolish it (**it is the Right of the People to alter or to abolish it, and to provide new Guards for their future security**).

We are going to examine the Constitution and the operation of each Branch of the Government. We will compare the Government's operation against what the Constitution mandates. Our journey through the Constitution and our examination of the Government's behavior will show us that the Government (the Congress, the Executive Branch and the Judicial Branch) consistently disregards the Constitution, it acts beyond the authority granted in the Constitution, it does not function according to the Constitution, and it routinely disregards the Rights of the People. It purposefully prevents the People from exercising their constitutional Rights and it acts as though it is the ruler of the People instead of the tool by which *We the People* govern ourselves. The officials who wield power in the Government cannot be trusted to administer our government according to the Constitution. *We the People* are subjected to monumental abuses as a result.

Every citizen of this country has a personal stake in our Government's unconstitutional conduct. The Constitution is this nation's fundamental law. It is the only authority used to determine how the Government is required to operate. In declaring what shall be the supreme law of the land, the Constitution first mentions itself. It *organizes* the Government, it *delegates* powers from the People to be used by the Government, it *defines* and *limits* the powers of the Government, and it protects the minority against the majority. The entire operation of the Government is controlled by the Constitution. The Constitution defines the rules that **control** Government officials who wield power and under which the Government **MUST** operate. The Constitution controls every act, law or decision made by each member of the House of Representatives, by each member of the Senate, by the President and Vice President of the United States, every Federal judge, including the Justices of the Supreme Court, every Government agency established by Congress, and every employee of the Government. We will use some other documents to make the Constitution's meaning clear. When you read the word Government, I will be referring to the United States Government. The word Constitution, without a State name, will refer to the Constitution of the United States.

We are taught that (1) we live under the Constitution, (2) our Rights are protected by the Constitution, and (3) the Constitution contains checks and balances for the operation of the Government. No Government official may perform any official act without some authority in the Constitution! If it can be otherwise, then the Constitution is merely a piece of paper and it has no power. What would be the purpose of defining and limiting the powers of the Government and what purpose would it serve to include definitions and limitations in the Constitution, if the limits imposed in the Constitution may, at any time, be disregarded by the Government? If the limits in the Constitution do not confine the Government, then there is no distinction between a Government with limited powers and a Government with unlimited powers.

At the beginning of some sections of this book, you will find portions of the Constitution or the Declaration of Independence or laws of the United States that are applicable to that discussion. Following this preface is our Declaration of Independence. Before we move on, I'm going to suggest that you read the entire document. I am going to ask you to at least read the portions that are in bold print. Those portions will be especially applicable to our discussions. After you read our Constitution and Declaration of Independence we will be begin our journey with the Federal Judiciary. See you there!

CONSTITUTION OF THE UNITED STATES OF AMERICA

Preamble

We the People of the United States, in Order to form a more perfect Union, establish Justice, insure domestic Tranquility, provide for the common defence, promote the general Welfare, and secure the Blessings of Liberty to ourselves and our Posterity, do ordain and establish this Constitution for the United States of America.

Article. I.

Section. 1.
All legislative Powers herein granted shall be vested in a Congress of the United States, which shall consist of a Senate and House of Representatives.

Section. 2.
The House of Representatives shall be composed of Members chosen every second Year by the People of the several States, and the Electors in each State shall have the Qualifications requisite for Electors of the most numerous Branch of the State Legislature.

No Person shall be a Representative who shall not have attained to the Age of twenty five Years, and been seven Years a Citizen of the United States, and who shall not, when elected, be an Inhabitant of that State in which he shall be chosen.

Representatives and direct Taxes shall be apportioned among the several States which may be included within this Union, according to their respective Numbers, which shall be determined by adding to the whole Number of free Persons, including those bound to Service for a Term of Years, and excluding Indians not taxed, three fifths of all other Persons. The actual Enumeration shall be made within three Years after the first Meeting of the Congress of the United States, and within every subsequent Term of ten Years, in such Manner as they shall by Law direct. The Number of Representatives shall not exceed one for every thirty Thousand, but each State shall have at Least one Representative; and until such enumeration shall be made, the State of New Hampshire shall be entitled to chuse three, Massachusetts eight, Rhode-Island and Providence Plantations one, Connecticut five, New-York six, New Jersey four, Pennsylvania eight, Delaware one, Maryland six, Virginia ten, North Carolina five, South Carolina five, and Georgia three.

When vacancies happen in the Representation from any State, the Executive Authority thereof shall issue Writs of Election to fill such Vacancies.

The House of Representatives shall chuse their Speaker and other Officers; and shall have the sole Power of Impeachment.

Section. 3.
The Senate of the United States shall be composed of two Senators from each State, chosen by the Legislature thereof for six Years; and each Senator shall have one Vote.

Immediately after they shall be assembled in Consequence of the first Election, they shall be divided as equally as may be into three Classes. The Seats of the Senators of the first Class shall be vacated at the Expiration of the second Year, of the second Class at the Expiration of the fourth Year, and of the third Class at the Expiration of the sixth Year, so that one third may be chosen every second Year; and if Vacancies happen by Resignation, or otherwise, during the Recess of the Legislature of any State, the Executive thereof may make temporary Appointments until the next Meeting of the Legislature, which shall then fill such Vacancies.

No Person shall be a Senator who shall not have attained to the Age of thirty Years, and been nine Years a Citizen of the United States, and who shall not, when elected, be an Inhabitant of that State for which he shall be chosen.

The Vice President of the United States shall be President of the Senate, but shall have no Vote, unless they be equally divided.

The Senate shall chuse their other Officers, and also a President pro tempore, in the Absence of the Vice President, or when he shall exercise the Office of President of the United States.

The Senate shall have the sole Power to try all Impeachments. When sitting for that Purpose, they shall be on Oath or Affirmation. When the President of the United States is tried, the Chief Justice shall preside: And no Person shall be convicted without the Concurrence of two thirds of the Members present.

Judgment in Cases of Impeachment shall not extend further than to removal from Office, and disqualification to hold and enjoy any Office of honor, Trust or Profit under the United States: but the Party convicted shall nevertheless be liable and subject to Indictment, Trial, Judgment and Punishment, according to Law.

Section. 4.
The Times, Places and Manner of holding Elections for Senators and Representatives, shall be prescribed in each State by the Legislature thereof; but the Congress may at any time by Law make or alter such Regulations, except as to the Places of chusing Senators.

The Congress shall assemble at least once in every Year, and such Meeting shall be on the first Monday in December, unless they shall by Law appoint a different Day.

Section. 5.

Each House shall be the Judge of the Elections, Returns and Qualifications of its own Members, and a Majority of each shall constitute a Quorum to do Business; but a smaller Number may adjourn from day to day, and may be authorized to compel the Attendance of absent Members, in such Manner, and under such Penalties as each House may provide.

Each House may determine the Rules of its Proceedings, punish its Members for disorderly Behaviour, and, with the Concurrence of two thirds, expel a Member.

Each House shall keep a Journal of its Proceedings, and from time to time publish the same, excepting such Parts as may in their Judgment require Secrecy; and the Yeas and Nays of the Members of either House on any question shall, at the Desire of one fifth of those Present, be entered on the Journal.

Neither House, during the Session of Congress, shall, without the Consent of the other, adjourn for more than three days, nor to any other Place than that in which the two Houses shall be sitting.

Section. 6.

The Senators and Representatives shall receive a Compensation for their Services, to be ascertained by Law, and paid out of the Treasury of the United States. They shall in all Cases, except Treason, Felony and Breach of the Peace, be privileged from Arrest during their Attendance at the Session of their respective Houses, and in going to and returning from the same; and for any Speech or Debate in either House, they shall not be questioned in any other Place.

No Senator or Representative shall, during the Time for which he was elected, be appointed to any civil Office under the Authority of the United States, which shall have been created, or the Emoluments whereof shall have been encreased during such time; and no Person holding any Office under the United States, shall be a Member of either House during his Continuance in Office.

Section. 7.

All Bills for raising Revenue shall originate in the House of Representatives; but the Senate may propose or concur with Amendments as on other Bills.

Every Bill which shall have passed the House of Representatives and the Senate, shall, before it become a Law, be presented to the President of the United States: If he approve he shall sign it, but if not he shall return it, with his Objections to that House in which it shall have originated, who shall enter the Objections at large on their Journal, and proceed to reconsider it. If after such Reconsideration two thirds of that House shall agree to pass the Bill, it shall be sent, together with the Objections, to the other House, by which it shall likewise be reconsidered, and if approved by two thirds of that House, it shall become a Law. But in all such Cases the Votes of both Houses shall be determined by yeas and Nays, and the Names of the Persons voting for and against the Bill shall be entered on the Journal of each House respectively. If any Bill shall not be returned by the President within ten Days (Sundays excepted) after it shall have been presented to him, the Same shall be a Law, in like Manner as if he had signed it, unless the Congress by their Adjournment prevent its Return, in which Case it shall not be a Law.

Every Order, Resolution, or Vote to which the Concurrence of the Senate and House of Representatives may be necessary (except on a question of Adjournment) shall be presented to the President of the United States; and before the Same shall take Effect, shall be approved by him, or being disapproved by him, shall be repassed by two thirds of the Senate and House of Representatives, according to the Rules and Limitations prescribed in the Case of a Bill.

Section. 8.

The Congress shall have Power To lay and collect Taxes, Duties, Imposts and Excises, to pay the Debts and provide for the common Defence and general Welfare of the United States; but all Duties, Imposts and Excises shall be uniform throughout the United States;

To borrow Money on the credit of the United States;

To regulate Commerce with foreign Nations, and among the several States, and with the Indian Tribes;

To establish an uniform Rule of Naturalization, and uniform Laws on the subject of Bankruptcies throughout the United States;

To coin Money, regulate the Value thereof, and of foreign Coin, and fix the Standard of Weights and Measures;

To provide for the Punishment of counterfeiting the Securities and current Coin of the United States;

To establish Post Offices and post Roads;

To promote the Progress of Science and useful Arts, by securing for limited Times to Authors and Inventors the exclusive Right to their respective Writings and Discoveries;

To constitute Tribunals inferior to the supreme Court;

To define and punish Piracies and Felonies committed on the high Seas, and Offences against the Law of Nations;

To declare War, grant Letters of Marque and Reprisal, and make Rules concerning Captures on Land and Water;

To raise and support Armies, but no Appropriation of Money to that Use shall be for a longer Term than two Years;

To provide and maintain a Navy;

To make Rules for the Government and Regulation of the land and naval Forces;

To provide for calling forth the Militia to execute the Laws of the Union, suppress Insurrections and repel Invasions;

To provide for organizing, arming, and disciplining, the Militia, and for governing such Part of them as may be employed in the Service of the United States, reserving to the States respectively, the Appointment of the Officers, and the Authority of training the Militia according to the discipline prescribed by Congress;

To exercise exclusive Legislation in all Cases whatsoever, over such District (not exceeding ten Miles square) as may, by Cession of particular States, and the Acceptance of Congress, become the Seat of the Government of the United States, and to exercise like Authority over all Places purchased by the Consent of the Legislature of the State in which the Same shall be, for the Erection of Forts, Magazines, Arsenals, dock-Yards, and other needful Buildings;--And

To make all Laws which shall be necessary and proper for carrying into Execution the foregoing Powers, and all other Powers vested by this Constitution in the Government of the United States, or in any Department or Officer thereof.

Section. 9.
The Migration or Importation of such Persons as any of the States now existing shall think proper to admit, shall not be prohibited by the Congress prior to the Year one thousand eight hundred and eight, but a Tax or duty may be imposed on such Importation, not exceeding ten dollars for each Person.

The Privilege of the Writ of Habeas Corpus shall not be suspended, unless when in Cases of Rebellion or Invasion the public Safety may require it.

No Bill of Attainder or ex post facto Law shall be passed.

No Capitation, or other direct, Tax shall be laid, unless in Proportion to the Census or enumeration herein before directed to be taken.

No Tax or Duty shall be laid on Articles exported from any State.

No Preference shall be given by any Regulation of Commerce or Revenue to the Ports of one State over those of another; nor shall Vessels bound to, or from, one State, be obliged to enter, clear, or pay Duties in another.

No Money shall be drawn from the Treasury, but in Consequence of Appropriations made by Law; and a regular Statement and Account of the Receipts and Expenditures of all public Money shall be published from time to time.

No Title of Nobility shall be granted by the United States: And no Person holding any Office of Profit or Trust under them, shall, without the Consent of the Congress, accept of any present, Emolument, Office, or Title, of any kind whatever, from any King, Prince, or foreign State.

Section. 10.
No State shall enter into any Treaty, Alliance, or Confederation; grant Letters of Marque and Reprisal; coin Money; emit Bills of Credit; make any Thing but gold and silver Coin a Tender in Payment of Debts; pass any Bill of Attainder, ex post facto Law, or Law impairing the Obligation of Contracts, or grant any Title of Nobility.

No State shall, without the Consent of the Congress, lay any Imposts or Duties on Imports or Exports, except what may be absolutely necessary for executing it's inspection Laws: and the net Produce of all Duties and Imposts, laid by any State on Imports or Exports, shall be for the Use of the Treasury of the United States; and all such Laws shall be subject to the Revision and Controul of the Congress.

No State shall, without the Consent of Congress, lay any Duty of Tonnage, keep Troops, or Ships of War in time of Peace, enter into any Agreement or Compact with another State, or with a foreign Power, or engage in War, unless actually invaded, or in such imminent Danger as will not admit of delay.

Article. II.

Section. 1.

The executive Power shall be vested in a President of the United States of America. He shall hold his Office during the Term of four Years, and, together with the Vice President, chosen for the same Term, be elected, as follows:

Each State shall appoint, in such Manner as the Legislature thereof may direct, a Number of Electors, equal to the whole Number of Senators and Representatives to which the State may be entitled in the Congress: but no Senator or Representative, or Person holding an Office of Trust or Profit under the United States, shall be appointed an Elector.

The Electors shall meet in their respective States, and vote by Ballot for two Persons, of whom one at least shall not be an Inhabitant of the same State with themselves. And they shall make a List of all the Persons voted for, and of the Number of Votes for each; which List they shall sign and certify, and transmit sealed to the Seat of the Government of the United States, directed to the President of the Senate. The President of the Senate shall, in the Presence of the Senate and House of Representatives, open all the Certificates, and the Votes shall then be counted. The Person having the greatest Number of Votes shall be the President, if such Number be a Majority of the whole Number of Electors appointed; and if there be more than one who have such Majority, and have an equal Number of Votes, then the House of Representatives shall immediately chuse by Ballot one of them for President; and if no Person have a Majority, then from the five highest on the List the said House shall in like Manner chuse the President. But in chusing the President, the Votes shall be taken by States, the Representation from each State having one Vote; A quorum for this purpose shall consist of a Member or Members from two thirds of the States, and a Majority of all the States shall be necessary to a Choice. In every Case, after the Choice of the President, the Person having the greatest Number of Votes of the Electors shall be the Vice President. But if there should remain two or more who have equal Votes, the Senate shall chuse from them by Ballot the Vice President.

The Congress may determine the Time of chusing the Electors, and the Day on which they shall give their Votes; which Day shall be the same throughout the United States.

No Person except a natural born Citizen, or a Citizen of the United States, at the time of the Adoption of this Constitution, shall be eligible to the Office of President; neither shall any Person be eligible to that Office who shall not have attained to the Age of thirty five Years, and been fourteen Years a Resident within the United States.

In Case of the Removal of the President from Office, or of his Death, Resignation, or Inability to discharge the Powers and Duties of the said Office, the Same shall devolve on the Vice President, and the Congress may by Law provide for the Case of Removal, Death, Resignation or Inability, both of the President and Vice President, declaring what Officer shall then act as President, and such Officer shall act accordingly, until the Disability be removed, or a President shall be elected.

The President shall, at stated Times, receive for his Services, a Compensation, which shall neither be increased nor diminished during the Period for which he shall have been elected, and he shall not receive within that Period any other Emolument from the United States, or any of them.

Before he enter on the Execution of his Office, he shall take the following Oath or Affirmation:--"I do solemnly swear (or affirm) that I will faithfully execute the Office of President of the United States, and will to the best of my Ability, preserve, protect and defend the Constitution of the United States."

Section. 2.
The President shall be Commander in Chief of the Army and Navy of the United States, and of the Militia of the several States, when

called into the actual Service of the United States; he may require the Opinion, in writing, of the principal Officer in each of the executive Departments, upon any Subject relating to the Duties of their respective Offices, and he shall have Power to grant Reprieves and Pardons for Offences against the United States, except in Cases of Impeachment.

He shall have Power, by and with the Advice and Consent of the Senate, to make Treaties, provided two thirds of the Senators present concur; and he shall nominate, and by and with the Advice and Consent of the Senate, shall appoint Ambassadors, other public Ministers and Consuls, Judges of the supreme Court, and all other Officers of the United States, whose Appointments are not herein otherwise provided for, and which shall be established by Law: but the Congress may by Law vest the Appointment of such inferior Officers, as they think proper, in the President alone, in the Courts of Law, or in the Heads of Departments.

The President shall have Power to fill up all Vacancies that may happen during the Recess of the Senate, by granting Commissions which shall expire at the End of their next Session.
Section. 3.
He shall from time to time give to the Congress Information of the State of the Union, and recommend to their Consideration such Measures as he shall judge necessary and expedient; he may, on extraordinary Occasions, convene both Houses, or either of them, and in Case of Disagreement between them, with Respect to the Time of Adjournment, he may adjourn them to such Time as he shall think proper; he shall receive Ambassadors and other public Ministers; he shall take Care that the Laws be faithfully executed, and shall Commission all the Officers of the United States.

Section. 4.
The President, Vice President and all civil Officers of the United States, shall be removed from Office on Impeachment for, and Conviction of, Treason, Bribery, or other high Crimes and Misdemeanors.

Article III.

Section. 1.

The judicial Power of the United States shall be vested in one supreme Court, and in such inferior Courts as the Congress may from time to time ordain and establish. The Judges, both of the supreme and inferior Courts, shall hold their Offices during good Behaviour, and shall, at stated Times, receive for their Services a Compensation, which shall not be diminished during their Continuance in Office.

Section. 2.

The judicial Power shall extend to all Cases, in Law and Equity, arising under this Constitution, the Laws of the United States, and Treaties made, or which shall be made, under their Authority; — to all Cases affecting Ambassadors, other public Ministers and Consuls; — to all Cases of admiralty and maritime Jurisdiction; — to Controversies to which the United States shall be a Party; — to Controversies between two or more States; — between a State and Citizens of another State; — between Citizens of different States; — between Citizens of the same State claiming Lands under Grants of different States, and between a State, or the Citizens thereof, and foreign States, Citizens or Subjects.

In all Cases affecting Ambassadors, other public Ministers and Consuls, and those in which a State shall be Party, the supreme Court shall have original Jurisdiction. In all the other Cases before mentioned, the supreme Court shall have appellate Jurisdiction, both as to Law and Fact, with such Exceptions, and under such Regulations as the Congress shall make.

The Trial of all Crimes, except in Cases of Impeachment, shall be by Jury; and such Trial shall be held in the State where the said Crimes shall have been committed; but when not committed within any State, the Trial shall be at such Place or Places as the Congress may by Law have directed.

Section. 3.

Treason against the United States, shall consist only in levying War against them, or in adhering to their Enemies, giving them Aid and Comfort. No Person shall be convicted of Treason unless on the Testimony of two Witnesses to the same overt Act, or on Confession in open Court.

The Congress shall have Power to declare the Punishment of Treason, but no Attainder of Treason shall work Corruption of Blood, or Forfeiture except during the Life of the Person attainted.

Article. IV.

Section. 1.

Full Faith and Credit shall be given in each State to the public Acts, Records, and judicial Proceedings of every other State. And the Congress may by general Laws prescribe the Manner in which such Acts, Records and Proceedings shall be proved, and the Effect thereof.

Section. 2.

The Citizens of each State shall be entitled to all Privileges and Immunities of Citizens in the several States.

A Person charged in any State with Treason, Felony, or other Crime, who shall flee from Justice, and be found in another State, shall on Demand of the executive Authority of the State from which he fled, be delivered up, to be removed to the State having Jurisdiction of the Crime.

No Person held to Service or Labour in one State, under the Laws thereof, escaping into another, shall, in Consequence of any Law or Regulation therein, be discharged from such Service or Labour, but shall be delivered up on Claim of the Party to whom such Service or Labour may be due.

Section. 3.

New States may be admitted by the Congress into this Union; but no new State shall be formed or erected within the Jurisdiction of any other State; nor any State be formed by the Junction of two or more States, or Parts of States, without the Consent of the Legislatures of the States concerned as well as of the Congress.

The Congress shall have Power to dispose of and make all needful Rules and Regulations respecting the Territory or other Property belonging to the United States; and nothing in this Constitution shall be so construed as to Prejudice any Claims of the United States, or of any particular State.

Section. 4.

The United States shall guarantee to every State in this Union a Republican Form of Government, and shall protect each of them against Invasion; and on Application of the Legislature, or of the Executive (when the Legislature cannot be convened), against domestic Violence.

Article. V.

The Congress, whenever two thirds of both Houses shall deem it necessary, shall propose Amendments to this Constitution, or, on the Application of the Legislatures of two thirds of the several States, shall call a Convention for proposing Amendments, which, in either Case, shall be valid to all Intents and Purposes, as Part of this Constitution, when ratified by the Legislatures of three fourths of the several States, or by Conventions in three fourths thereof, as the one or the other Mode of Ratification may be proposed by the Congress; Provided that no Amendment which may be made prior to the Year One thousand eight hundred and eight shall in any Manner affect the first and fourth Clauses in the Ninth Section of the first Article; and that no State, without its Consent, shall be deprived of its equal Suffrage in the Senate.

Article. VI.

All Debts contracted and Engagements entered into, before the Adoption of this Constitution, shall be as valid against the United States under this Constitution, as under the Confederation.

This Constitution, and the Laws of the United States which shall be made in Pursuance thereof; and all Treaties made, or which shall be made, under the Authority of the United States, shall be the supreme Law of the Land; and the Judges in every State shall be bound thereby, any Thing in the Constitution or Laws of any State to the Contrary notwithstanding.

The Senators and Representatives before mentioned, and the Members of the several State Legislatures, and all executive and judicial Officers, both of the United States and of the several States, shall be bound by Oath or Affirmation, to support this Constitution; but no religious Test shall ever be required as a Qualification to any Office or public Trust under the United States.

Article. VII.

The Ratification of the Conventions of nine States, shall be sufficient for the Establishment of this Constitution between the States so ratifying the Same.

The Word, "the," being interlined between the seventh and eighth Lines of the first Page, the Word "Thirty" being partly written on an Erazure in the fifteenth Line of the first Page, The Words "is tried" being interlined between the thirty second and thirty third Lines of the first Page and the Word "the" being interlined between the forty third and forty fourth Lines of the second Page.

Attest William Jackson Secretary

Done in Convention by the Unanimous Consent of the States present the Seventeenth Day of September in the Year of our Lord one thousand seven hundred and Eighty seven and of the Independence of the United States of America the Twelfth In witness whereof We have hereunto subscribed our Names,

G°. Washington
Presidt and deputy from Virginia

Delaware
Geo: Read
Gunning Bedford jun
John Dickinson
Richard Bassett
Jaco: Broom

North Carolina
Wm. Blount
Richd. Dobbs Spaight
Hu Williamson

Georgia
William Few
Abr Baldwin

Massachusetts
Nathaniel Gorham
Rufus King

Pennsylvania
B Franklin
Thomas Mifflin
Robt. Morris
Geo. Clymer
Thos. FitzSimons
Jared Ingersoll
James Wilson
Gouv Morris

South Carolina
J. Rutledge
Charles Cotesworth Pinckney
Charles Pinckney
Pierce Butler

Maryland
James McHenry
Dan of St Thos. Jenifer
Danl. Carroll

Virginia
John Blair
James Madison Jr.

New Hampshire
John Langdon
Nicholas Gilman

Connecticut
Wm. Saml. Johnson
Roger Sherman

New Jersey
Wil. Livingston
David Brearley
Wm. Paterson
Jona Dayton

New York
Alexander Hamilton

Amendment I

Congress shall make no law respecting an establishment of religion, or prohibiting the free exercise thereof; or abridging the freedom of speech, or of the press, or the right of the people peaceably to assemble, and to petition the Government for a redress of grievances.

Amendment II

A well regulated Militia, being necessary to the security of a free State, the right of the people to keep and bear Arms, shall not be infringed.

Amendment III

No Soldier shall, in time of peace be quartered in any house, without the consent of the Owner, nor in time of war, but in a manner to be prescribed by law.

Amendment IV

The right of the people to be secure in their persons, houses, papers, and effects, against unreasonable searches and seizures, shall not be violated, and no Warrants shall issue, but upon probable cause, supported by Oath or affirmation, and particularly describing the place to be searched, and the persons or things to be seized.

Amendment V

No person shall be held to answer for a capital, or otherwise infamous crime, unless on a presentment or indictment of a Grand jury, except in cases arising in the land or navel forces, or in the Militia, when in actual service in time of War or public danger; nor shall any person be subject for the same offense to be twice put in jeopardy of life or limb, nor shall be compelled in any criminal case to be a witness against himself, nor be derived of Life, liberty, or property, without due process of law; nor shall private property be taken for public use without just compensation.

Amendment VI

In all criminal prosecutions, the accused shall enjoy the right to a speedy and public trial, by an impartial jury of the State, and district wherein the crime shall have been committed, which district shall have been previously ascertained by law, and to be informed of the nature and cause of the accusation, to be confronted with the witnesses against him, to have compulsory process for obtaining witnesses in his favor, and to have the assistance of counsel for his defence.

Amendment VII

In Suits at common-law, where the value in controversy shall exceed twenty dollars, the right of trial by jury shall be preserved, and no fact tried by a jury shall be otherwise re-examined in any Court of the United States, than according to the rules of the common-law.

Amendment VIII

Excessive bail shall not be required, nor excessive fines imposed, nor cruel and unusual punishments inflicted.

Amendment IX

The enumeration in the Constitution of certain rights shall not be construed to deny or disparage others retained by the people.

Amendment X

The powers not delegated to the United States by the Constitution, nor prohibited by it to the States, are reserved to the States respectively, or to the people.

Amendment XI

The Judicial power of the United States shall not be construed to extend to any suit in law or equity, commenced or prosecuted against one of the United States by Citizens of another State, or by Citizens or Subjects of any Foreign State.

Amendment XII

The Electors shall meet in their respective states, and vote by ballot for President and Vice President, one of whom, at least, shall not be an inhabitant of the same state with themselves; they shall name in their ballots the person voted for as President, and in distinct ballots the person voted for as Vice President, and they shall make distinct lists of all persons voted for as President, and of all persons voted for as Vice-President, and of the number of votes for each, which lists they shall sign and certify, and transmit sealed to the seat of the government of the United States, directed to the President of the Senate, — The President of the Senate shall, in the presence of the Senate and House of representatives, open all the certificates and the votes shall then be counted; — The person having the greatest number of votes for President, shall be the President, if such number be a majority of the whole number of Electors appointed; and if no person have such majority, then from the persons having the highest numbers not exceeding three on the list of those voted for as President, the House of Representatives shall choose immediately, by ballot, the President. But in choosing the President, the votes shall be taken by states, the representation from each state having one vote; a quorum for this purpose shall consist of a member or members from two-thirds of the states, and a majority of all the states shall be necessary to a choice. [And if the House of Representatives shall not choose a President whenever the right of choice shall devolve upon them, before the fourth day of March next following, then the Vice President shall act as President, as in the case of the death or other constitutional disability of the President] The person having the greatest number of votes as Vice President, shall be the Vice President, if such number be majority of the whole number of Electors appointed, and if no person have a majority, then from the two highest numbers on the list, the Senate shall choose the Vice President; a quorum for the purpose shall consist of two-thirds of the whole number of Senators, and a majority of the whole number shall be necessary to a choice. But no person constitutionally ineligible to the office of President shall be eligible to that of Vice President of the United States.

Amendment XIII

Section 1. Neither slavery nor involuntary servitude, except as a punishment for crime whereof the party shall have been duly convicted, shall exist within the United States, or any place subject to their jurisdiction.
Section 2. Congress shall have power to enforce this article by appropriate legislation.

Amendment XIV

Section 1. All persons born or naturalized in the United States and subject to the jurisdiction thereof, are citizens of the United States and of the State wherein they reside. No State shall make or enforce any law which shall abridge the privileges or immunities of citizens of the United States; nor shall any State deprive any person of life, liberty, or property, without due process of law; nor deny to any person within its jurisdiction the equal protection of the laws.
Section 2. Representatives shall be apportioned among the several States according to their respective numbers, counting the whole number of persons in each State, excluding Indians not taxed. But when the right to vote at any election for the choice of electors for President and Vice President of the United States, Representatives in Congress, the Executive and Judicial officers of a State, or the members of the Legislature thereof, is denied to any of the male inhabitants of such State, being twenty-one years of age, and citizens of the United States, or in any way abridged, except for participation in rebellion, or other crime, the basis of representation therein shall be reduced in the proportion which the number of such male citizens

shall bear to the whole number of male citizens twenty-one years of age in such State.

Section 3. No person shall be a Senator or representative in Congress, or elector of President and Vice President, or hold any office, civil or military, under the United States, or under any State, who, having previously taken an oath, as a member of Congress, or as an officer of the United States, or as a member of any State legislature, or as an executive or judicial officer of any State, to support the Constitution of the United States, shall have engaged in insurrection or rebellion against the same, or given aid or comfort to the enemies thereof. But Congress may by a vote of two-thirds of each House, remove such disability.

Section 4. The validity of the public debt of the United States, authorized by law, including debts incurred for payment of pensions and bounties for services in suppressing insurrection or rebellion, shall not be questioned. But neither the United States nor any State shall assume or pay any debt or obligation incurred in aid of insurrection or rebellion against the United States, or any claim for the loss or emancipation of any slave; but all such debts, obligations and claims shall be held illegal and void.

Section 5. Congress shall have power to enforce, by appropriate legislation, the provisions of this article.

Amendment XV

Section 1. The right of citizens of the United States to vote shall not be denied or abridged by the United States or by any State on account of race, color, or previous condition of servitude.

Section 2. Congress shall have power to enforce this article by appropriate legislation.

Amendment XVI

Congress shall have power to lay and collect taxes on incomes, from whatever source derived, without apportionment among the several States, and without regard to any census or enumeration.

Amendment XVII

The Senate of the United States shall be composed of two Senators from each State, elected by the people thereof, for six years; and each Senator shall have one vote. The electors in each State shall have the qualifications requisite for electors of the most numerous branch of the State legislatures.

When vacancies happen in the representation of any State in the Senate, the executive authority of such State shall issue writs of election to fill the vacancies by election as the legislature may direct.

This amendment shall not be so construed as to affect the election or term of any Senator chosen before it becomes valid as part of the Constitution.

Amendment XVIII

Section 1. After one year from the ratification of this article the manufacture, sale, or transportation of intoxicating liquors within, the importation thereof into, or the exportation thereof from the United States and all territory subject to the jurisdiction thereof for beverage purposes is hereby prohibited.

Section 2. Congress and the several States shall have concurrent power to enforce this article by appropriate legislation.

Section 3. This article shall be inoperative unless it shall have been ratified as an amendment to the Constitution by the legislatures of the several States, as provided in the Constitution, within seven years from the date of the submission hereof to the States by Congress.

Amendment XIX

The right of citizens of the United States to vote shall not be denied or abridged by the United States or by any State on account of sex. Congress shall have power to enforce this article by appropriate legislation.

Amendment XX

Section 1. The terms of the President and Vice President shall end at noon on the 20th day of January, and the terms of Senators and Representatives at noon on the 3d day of January, of the years in which such terms would have ended if this article had not been ratified; and the terms of their successors shall then begin.

Section 2. Congress shall assemble at least once in every year, and such meeting shall begin at noon on the 3d day of January, unless they shall by law appoint a different day.

Section 3. If, at the time fixed for the beginning of the term of the President, the President elect shall have died, the Vice President elect shall become President. If a President shall not have been chosen before the time fixed for the beginning of his term, or if the President elect shall have failed to qualify, then the Vice President elect shall act as President until a President shall have qualified; and Congress may by law provide for the case wherein neither a President elect nor a Vice President elect shall have qualified, declaring who shall then act as President, or the manner in which one who is to act shall be selected, and such person shall act accordingly until a President or Vice President shall have qualified.

Section 4. Congress may by law provide for the case of the death of any of the persons from whom the House of Representatives may choose a President whenever the right of choice shall have devolved upon them, and for the case of the death of any of the persons from whom the Senate may choose a Vice President whenever the right of choice shall have devolved upon them.

Section 5. Sections 1 and 2 shall take effect on the 15th day of October following the ratification of this article.

Section 6. This article shall be inoperative unless it shall have been ratified as an amendment to the Constitution by the legislatures of three fourths of the several States within seven years from the date of its submission.

Amendment XXI

Section 1. The eighteenth article of amendment to the Constitution of the United States is hereby repealed.
Section 2. The transportation or importation into any State, Territory, or possession of the United States for delivery or use therein of intoxicating liquors, in violation of the laws thereof, is hereby prohibited.
Section 3. This article shall be inoperative unless it shall have been ratified as an amendment to the Constitution by conventions in the several States, as provided in the Constitution, within seven years from the date of the submission hereof to the States by Congress.

Amendment XXII

Section 1. No person shall be elected to the office of the President more than twice, and no person who has held the office of President, or acted as President, for more than two years of a term to which some other person was elected President shall be elected to the office of the President more than once. But this Article shall not apply to any person holding the office of President, or acting as President, during the term within which this Article becomes operative from holding the office of President or acting as President during the remainder of such term.
Section 2. This article shall be inoperative unless it shall have been ratified as an amendment to the Constitution by the legislatures of three fourths of the several States within seven years from the date of its submission to the States by Congress.

Amendment XXIII

Section 1. The District constituting the seat of Government of the United States shall appoint in such manner as Congress may direct:
    A number of electors of President and Vice President equal to the whole number of Senators and Representatives in Congress to which the District would be entitled if it were a State, but in no event more than the least populous State; they shall be in addition to

those appointed by the States, but they shall be considered, for the purposes of the election of President and Vice President, to be electors appointed by a State; and they shall meet in the District and perform such duties as provided by the twelfth article of amendment.

Section 2. Congress shall have power to enforce this article by appropriate legislation.

Amendment XXIV

Section 1. The right of citizens of the United States to vote in any primary or other election for President or Vice President, for electors for President or Vice President, or for Senator or Representative in Congress, shall not be denied or abridged by the United States or any State by reason of failure to pay any poll tax or other tax.

Section 2. Congress shall have power to enforce this article by appropriate legislation.

Amendment XXV

Section 1. In case of the removal of the President from office or of his death or resignation, the Vice President shall become President.

Section 2. Whenever there is a vacancy in the office of the Vice President, the President shall nominate a Vice President who shall take office upon confirmation by a majority vote of both Houses of Congress.

Section 3. Whenever the President transmits to the President pro tempore of the Senate and the Speaker of the House of Representatives his written declaration that he is unable to discharge the powers and duties of his office, and until he transmits to them a written declaration to the contrary, such powers and duties shall be discharged by the Vice President as Acting President.

Section 4. Whenever the Vice President and a majority of either the principal officers of the executive departments or of such other body as Congress may by law provide, transmit to the President pro tempore of the Senate and the Speaker of the House of Representatives their written declaration that the President is unable to discharge the powers and duties of the office as Acting President.

Thereafter, when the President transmits to the President pro tempore of the Senate and the Speaker of the House of Representatives his written declaration that no inability exists, he shall resume the powers and duties of his office unless the Vice President and a majority of either the principal officers of the executive department or of such other body as Congress may by law provide, transmit within four days to the President pro tempore of the Senate and the Speaker of the House of Representatives their written declaration that the President is unable to discharge the powers and duties of his office. Thereupon Congress shall decide the issue, assembling within forty-eight hours for that purpose if not in session. if Congress, within twenty-one days after receipt of the latter written declaration, or, if Congress is not in session, within twenty-one days after Congress is required to assemble, determines by two-thirds vote of both Houses that the President is unable to discharge the powers and duties of his office, the Vice President shall continue to discharge the same as Acting resident, otherwise, the President shall resume the powers and duties of his office.

Amendment XXVI

Section 1. The right of citizens of the United States, who are eighteen years of age or older, to vote shall not be denied or abridged by the United States or by any State on account of age.
Section 2. Congress shall have power to enforce this article by appropriate legislation.

Amendment XXVII

No law varying the compensation for the services of the Senators and Representatives shall take effect, until an election of representatives shall have intervened.

THE DECLARATION OF INDEPENDENCE

When in the Course of human events, it becomes necessary for one people to dissolve the political bands which have connected them with another, and to assume among the Powers of the earth, the separate and equal station to which **the Laws of Nature and of Nature's God entitle them**, a decent respect to the opinions of mankind requires that they should declare the causes which impel them to the separation.

We hold these truths to be self-evident, that all men are created equal, that **they are endowed by their Creator with certain unalienable Rights**, that among these are Life, Liberty, and the pursuit of Happiness. **That to secure these rights, Governments are instituted among Men**, deriving their just powers from the consent of the governed, **That whenever any Form of Government becomes destructive of these ends, it is the Right of the People to alter or to abolish it, and to institute new Government, laying its foundation on such principles and organizing its powers in such form, as to them shall seem most likely to effect their Safety and Happiness**. Prudence, indeed, will dictate that Governments long established should not be changed for light and transient causes; and accordingly all experience hath shown, that mankind are more disposed to suffer, while evils are sufferable, than to right themselves by abolishing the forms to which they are accustomed. But **when a long train of abuses and usurpations, pursuing invariably the same Object evinces a design to reduce them under absolute Despotism, it is their right, it is their duty, to throw off such Government, and to provide new Guards for their future security**. Such has been the patient sufferance of these Colonies; and such is now the necessity which constrains them to alter their former Systems of Government. The history of the present King of Great Britain is **a history of repeated injuries and usurpations, all having in direct object the establishment of an absolute Tyranny** over these States. To prove this, let Facts be submitted to a candid world.

He has refused his Assent to Laws, the most wholesome and necessary for the public good.

He has forbidden his Governors to pass Laws of immediate and pressing importance, unless suspended in their operation till his Assent should be obtained; and when so suspended, he has utterly neglected to attend to them.

He has refused to pass other Laws for the accommodation of large districts of people, unless those people would relinquish the right of Representation in the Legislature, a right inestimable to them and formidable to tyrants only.

He has called together legislative bodies at places unusual, uncomfortable, and distant from the depository of their Public Records, for the sole purpose of fatiguing them into compliance with his measures.

He has dissolved Representative Houses repeatedly, for opposing with manly firmness his invasions on the rights of the people.

He has refused for a long time, after such dissolutions, to cause others to be elected; whereby the Legislative Powers, incapable of Annihilation, have returned to the People at large for their exercise; the State remaining in the mean time exposed to all the dangers of invasion from without, and convulsions within.

He has endeavoured to prevent the population of these States; for that purpose obstructing the Laws of Naturalization of Foreigners; refusing to pass others to encourage their migration hither, and raising the conditions of new Appropriations of Lands.

He has obstructed the Administration of Justice, by refusing his Assent to Laws for establishing Judiciary Powers.

He has made Judges dependent on his Will alone, for the tenure of their offices, and the amount and payment of their salaries.

He has erected a multitude of New Offices, and sent hither swarms of Officers to harass our People, and eat out their substance.

He has kept among us, in times of peace, Standing Armies without the Consent of our legislature.

He has affected to render the Military independent of and superior to the Civil Power.

He has combined with others to subject us to a jurisdiction foreign to our constitution, and unacknowledged by our laws; giving his Assent to their acts of pretended legislation:

For quartering large bodies of armed troops among us:

For protecting them, by a mock Trial, from Punishment for any Murders which they should commit on the Inhabitants of these States:

For cutting off our Trade with all parts of the world:

For imposing taxes on us without our Consent:

For depriving us in many cases, of the benefits of Trial by Jury:

For transporting us beyond Seas to be tried for pretended offences:

For abolishing the free System of English Laws in a neighbouring Province, establishing therein an Arbitrary government, and enlarging its Boundaries so as to render it at once an example and fit instrument for introducing the same absolute rule into these Colonies:

For taking away our Charters, abolishing our most valuable Laws, and altering fundamentally the Forms of our Governments:

For suspending our own Legislature, and declaring themselves invested with Power to legislate for us in all cases whatsoever.

He has abdicated Government here, by declaring us out of his Protection and waging War against us.

He has plundered our seas, ravaged our Coasts, burnt our towns, and destroyed the lives of our people.

He is at this time transporting large armies of foreign mercenaries to compleat the works of death, desolation and tyranny, already begun with circumstances of Cruelty & perfidy scarcely paralleled in the most barbarous ages, and totally unworthy the Head of a civilized nation.

He has constrained our fellow Citizens taken Captive on the high Seas to bear Arms against their Country, to become the executioners of their friends and Brethren, or to fall themselves by their Hands.

He has excited domestic insurrections amongst us, and has endeavoured to bring on the inhabitants of our frontiers, the merciless Indian Savages, whose known rule of warfare, is an undistinguished destruction of all ages, sexes and conditions.

In every stage of these Oppressions We have Petitioned for Redress in the most humble terms: **Our repeated Petitions have been answered only by repeated injury**. A Prince, **whose character is thus marked by every act which may define a Tyrant,** is unfit to be the ruler of a free People.

Nor have We been wanting in attention to our British brethren. We have warned them from time to time of attempts by their legislature to extend an unwarrantable jurisdiction over us. We have reminded them of the circumstances of our emigration and settlement here. We have appealed to their native justice and magnanimity, and we have conjured them by the ties of our common kindred to disavow these usurpations, which, would inevitably interrupt our connections and correspondence. They too have been deaf to the voice of justice and of consanguinity. We must, therefore, acquiesce in the necessity, which denounces our Separation, and hold them, as we hold the rest of mankind, Enemies in War, in Peace Friends.

We, therefore, the Representatives of the United States of America, in General Congress, Assembled, appealing to the Supreme Judge of the world for the rectitude of our intentions, do, in the Name, and by Authority of the good People of these Colonies, solemnly publish and declare, That these United Colonies are, and of Right ought to be Free and Independent States; that they are Absolved from all Allegiance to the British Crown, and that all political connection between them and the State of Great Britain, is and ought to be totally dissolved; and that as Free and Independent States, they have full Power to levy War, conclude Peace, contract Alliances, establish Commerce, and to do all other Acts and Things which Independent States may of right do. And for the support of this Declaration, with a firm reliance on the Protection of Divine Providence, we mutually pledge to each other our Lives, our Fortunes and our sacred Honor.

I BELIEVE I CAN DO ANYTHING I WANT

OR

THE FEDERAL JUDICIARY

Article III of the Constitution
The Judges, both of the supreme and inferior Courts,
shall hold their Offices during good Behaviour

Article VI of the Constitution

The Senators and Representatives before mentioned, and the
Members of the several State Legislatures, and all executive and
judicial Officers, both of the United States and of the several States,
shall be bound by Oath or Affirmation, to support this Constitution

Article III of the Constitution says that judges hold their office **only during good behavior**. A judge's appointment is not necessarily for a lifetime. Judges are appointed, paid a salary, and have a responsibility to apply the law. Article VI of the Constitution requires all judicial officers to take an oath or affirmation to support the Constitution. Title 28 of the United States Code, Part I, Chapter 21, Section 453 requires each justice or judge of the United States to take the following oath: "I,   , do solemnly swear (or affirm) that I will administer justice without respect to persons, and do equal right to the poor and to the rich, and that I will faithfully and impartially discharge and perform all the duties incumbent upon me as   according to the best of my abilities and understanding, agreeably to the Constitution and laws of the United States. So help me God."

Before a judge may apply the law in a case, the judge must determine the law that is applicable to the case. If a judge does not know which law applies in a case, then a judge has the responsibility to research the law to find out which law does apply.

A part of deciding a case is issuing a decision in the case. Our federal judges issue decisions in cases without knowing or researching the law that is applicable to the case, or the judge knows the law and purposefully does not apply the applicable law. For instance, in 1997, a case was filed in Federal court in Alexandria, Virginia (case no. CA 97-312-A) requesting an injunction against the Department of Justice. The case alleges that the Department of Justice exceeded its authority when it decided to represent a Government attorney, who was accused of misconduct in a complaint filed with the New York Bar Association. The Department of Justice is only authorized by Congress to represent Government employees in *litigation*. The proceedings before the New York Bar Association do not fall within the definition of *litigation*. Assistant U.S. Attorney Richard Parker argued that the Department of Justice's decision to represent the Government attorney could not be challenged in Federal court because the Government had not waived sovereign immunity. The presiding judge, T.S. Ellis, III, said that the Department of Justice could not be sued because it is a part of the Government and the Government has sovereign immunity unless Congress has expressly waived sovereign immunity. Judge Ellis dismissed the case against the Government. The case was appealed. Filing an appeal is not free! The cost for filing an appeal in this case was $105.00! The Court of Appeals refused to reverse Judge Ellis' decision. The three judge panel (Judges Wilkins, Williams, and Michael) at the Court of Appeals (case no. 97-1575) said in a per curiam opinion that Judge Ellis' decision was correct because the person bringing the suit did not establish that the Government had waived sovereign immunity.

Assuming for the moment that the Government has sovereign immunity, the question that the judges must answer in this case is, "did Congress waive sovereign immunity?" It is not the responsibility of the citizen to tell the judge what the law is. It is the judge's job to research the law and determine if the Government has waived sovereign immunity. The fact of the matter is, in this case the Government **has** waived sovereign immunity. Title 5, Part I, Chapter 7, Section 702 of the United States Code reads: "A person suffering legal wrong because of agency action, or adversely affected or aggrieved by agency action within the meaning of a relevant statute, is entitled to judicial review thereof. **An action in a court of the United States seeking relief other than money damages** and stating a claim that an agency or an officer or employee thereof acted or failed to act in an official capacity or under color of legal authority **shall not be dismissed nor relief therein be denied on the ground that it is against the United States** or that the United States is an indispensable party. The United States may be named as a defendant

36

in any such action, and a judgment or decree may be entered against the United States: Provided, That any mandatory or **injunctive decree** shall specify the Federal officer or officers (by name or by title), and their successors in office, personally responsible for compliance. Nothing herein (1) affects other limitations on judicial review or the power or duty of the court to dismiss any action or deny relief on any other appropriate legal or equitable ground; or (2) confers authority to grant relief if any other statute that grants consent to suit expressly or impliedly forbids the relief which is sought." This section of the United States Code makes it clear that, in the circumstances of the case mentioned above, Congress waived any sovereign immunity that the Government might have. The four judges involved either do not know the law, did not research the law, or know the law and purposefully did not apply the law.

As you can see, four judges failed to perform the job for which they are paid and failed to uphold their oath. Because of a lying Assistant U.S. Attorney and four Federal judges, who failed to keep their oath, the case was dismissed. Even when Congress waives the mystical sovereign immunity, federal judges prevent a citizen from correcting the unconstitutional behavior of the Government!

In many cases, our federal courts issue "per curiam" opinions or decisions. Per curiam opinions or decisions are opinions or decisions that are not signed by a judge and the author of the opinion or decision is not identified. QUESTION - If a judge decides a case, then what reason could there be for a judge not signing the decision or opinion he issues? ANSWER -There can be NO *good* reason for any decision issued by a judge not being signed by that judge. Signing the decision is a duty that judges take an oath to faithfully perform and that is exactly what *We the People* pay each one of them to do! If the decision comes from a judge, then the decision would have a judge's signature on it. Obviously, a per curiam decision is not issued by a judge.

In a case (case no. 98-1380) before a three judge panel (Judges Ervin, Luttig, and Motz) of the Court of Appeals for the Fourth Circuit, a per curiam decision was given. Pay close attention! There is going to be a quiz! The Court of Appeals for the Fourth Circuit is located in Richmond, Virginia. According to the Clerk's Office at the Court of Appeals for the Fourth Circuit, Judges Ervin, Luttig, and Motz stopped sitting on **June 5, 1998**. That means that the three judges left the courthouse in Richmond, Virginia and went to their separate home buildings across the state of Virginia. Any decisions issued while the judges are not sitting have to be sent to the courthouse in Richmond, Virginia. To get a decision to the courthouse a judge has to send it, mail it, fax it, take it, have someone take it (you get the idea), etc. to the courthouse.

The per curiam decision in this case was issued on **June 10, 1998** — 1 . . 2 . . 3 . . 4 . . 5 days after the judges stopped sitting. One of the three judges had to send, mail, fax, telephone, take, or have someone take the decision to the courthouse in Richmond. A judge would necessarily have to sign the decision. How else is anyone at the courthouse in Richmond to know that the decision is indeed the decision of a single judge or a combination of the judges. Time for the quiz! QUESTION - Why would a judge's signature not be on the decision? Take your time. Well, not toooo much time! Clock is ticking. All right here is my answer. A judge did not sign the decision because none of the three judges reviewed this case, decided this case, or issued the decision in this case! Clearly, this is not good behavior on the part of any of the three judges, but each one will continue to be a judge and continue to receive that salary *We the People* pay them!

Here is another example of the attitude that **I CAN DO ANYTHING I WANT**. A seventeen-count case was filed against the Government (case number CA95-1406-A) in Federal court in Alexandria, Virginia. Once again Judge T. S. Ellis, III is involved. Judge Ellis summarily dismissed fifteen of the counts and awarded summary judgment to the Government on the remaining two counts. Judge Ellis' decisions were appealed to the Court of Appeals. The decision from the Court of Appeals contains the following statement: "We have reviewed the record and the district court's opinions and find no reversible error. Accordingly, we affirm on the reasoning of the district court." Judges Hal, Murnaghan, and Phillips supposedly decided the appeal. The reference to the district court means Judge Ellis. Guess what? None of the judges signed the decision. Once again, the decision issued was a per curiam decision. Surprised? I bet you aren't!

It is impossible for Judges Hal, Murnaghan, and Phillips to have independently reviewed this case and each judge come to the decision that Judge Ellis did not make any reversible errors (reversible error is a mistake made by a judge that caused harm to one of the parties) in his decisions. Now I'll tell you why it is impossible. Without getting into all the details of what Judge Ellis said, **Judge Ellis did not give any reason at all for dismissing one of the counts**. It is impossible for Judges Hal, Murnaghan, and Phillips each to have reviewed the record and missed this most important point. In order to affirm Judge Ellis' decision, based on Judge Ellis' reasoning, each judge would need to know the reason given by Judge Ellis and agree with it. Until Judges Hal, Murnaghan, and Phillips find each reason given by Judge Ellis for dismissing each count they can hardly affirm Judge Ellis' decision based on Judge Ellis' reasoning. We have found three more judges who do not faithfully discharge and perform their duties yet they are still federal judges.

Collusion between judges and the attorneys in the U.S. Attorney's office is not uncommon. Here is an example. In combined civil cases against the United States Department of Labor, numbers 96-2456 and 96-1722, filed in the United States District Court for the District of Columbia, Judge Emmet G. Sullivan decided to refer the cases to Magistrate Judge Deborah Robinson for a **Report and Recommendation**. After receiving the cases, Magistrate Robinson **ordered** the Assistant U.S. Attorney to file a motion to dismiss, or, in the alternative, for summary judgment. The Assistant U.S. Attorney did as Magistrate Robinson ordered and then Magistrate Robinson granted the motions. Magistrate Robinson sent the cases back to Judge Sullivan and Judge Sullivan dismissed the lawsuits!

The problems here are these. The cases were referred to Magistrate Robinson for a *Report and Recommendation*. We all know what the words report and recommendation mean. Simply put, Magistrate Robinson was to give Judge Sullivan a narrative of the cases with her suggestions on what should be done. When your boss tells you to go to one of the company's stores and give him a report and recommendation would you go to the store and then issue decisions based on how you think things ought to be? I cannot find any authority that permits Magistrate Robinson to **order** the Assistant U.S. Attorney to file a motion! I also cannot find any authority that permits Magistrate Robinson to rule on the motion to dismiss, or, in the alternative, for summary judgment when Judge Sullivan did not request or authorize Magistrate Robinson to make any rulings. Judge Sullivan simply asked Magistrate Robinson for a report and recommendation.

The filing of motions is up to the parties or the parties' attorneys involved in a case. A party must have grounds to file a motion. This means the party must have a justifiable reason for filing a motion. If a party does not have a justifiable reason for filing a motion, then the judge can punish the party or the party's attorney. If a party doesn't wish to file a motion, then that party does not have to. Thus, the filing of a motion is **practicing law**. When Magistrate Robinson decided on her own that the Government would be best served by the filing of a motion, decided what motion the Government should file, and then ordered the Government to file the motion, Magistrate Robinson began representing the Government. At that stage in the case Magistrate Robinson began practicing law!

Title 28 of the United States Code, Part I, Chapter 21, Section 431 reads "Any **justice or judge** appointed under the authority of the United States **who engages in the practice of law is guilty of a high misdemeanor**." Article II, Section 4 of the Constitution says, "The President, Vice President and **all civil Officers of the United States, shall be removed from Office on Impeachment for, and Conviction of,** Treason, Bribery, or **other high Crimes and Misdemeanors**." The Constitution makes a high misdemeanor an impeachable offense for all civil Officers of the United States. Magistrate Judges are civil Officers of the United States. Magistrate Judge Robinson's practice of law makes her guilty of a high misdemeanor.

On some occasions Federal judges have even argued a case for the Government. Arguing the Government's case **IS** practicing law! I wonder just when the next removal hearing for a Federal judge will be held? Soon? Well, there are no removal hearings scheduled for any Federal judges and I haven't found one member of Congress who has taken any steps to stop or correct any of this. Obviously, no member of Congress cares!

After the appeal was filed in the above case, Assistant U.S. Attorney Brian J. Sonfield filed a document in the United States Court of Appeals for the District of Columbia. The relevant part of the document reads,

In that Order, the District Court did not reach the merits of appellee's arguments but merely denied appellee's motions pending the anticipated filing by appellant of an amended complaint. See March 28, 1996 Order of the Honorable Emmet G. Sullivan. Appellant filed no such amended complaint, and the District Court directed appellee to refile its dispositive motions. See Report & Recommendation of United States Magistrate Judge Deborah A. Robinson (attached as Exhibit 1 to appellee's Motion for Summary Affirmance), at 1 & n.1. Under the local rules, the District Court was free to refer appellee's dispositive motions to the magistrate judge for hearing and recommendation. See Local Rule 504(a)(5).

Question time! Do the statements "Appellant filed no such amended complaint, and the District Court directed appellee to refile its dispositive motions" and "Under the local rules, the District Court was free to refer appellee's dispositive motions to the magistrate judge for hearing and recommendation. See Local Rule 504(a)(5)" lead you to believe that the Government's motions were in place at the time that Judge Sullivan referred the cases to the Magistrate Judge Robinson? The fact is **there were no dispositive motions referred by Judge Sullivan to Magistrte Judge Robinson**! Remember that Magistrate Robinson ordered the filing of the motion **AFTER** she received the cases!! Also, the order issued by Judge Sullivan denying the Government's motions says absolutely nothing about the motions being denied **pending the anticipated filing of an amended complaint**. This is a blatant attempt by Assistant U.S. Attorney Sonfield to mislead the judges at the Court of Appeals regarding just what really did happen in the district court. I contacted Assistant U.S. Attorney Sonfield and he had no comment regarding his behavior other than he and I disagree on the case. Mr. Sonfield

41

should be punished for such behavior, but he won't be! Such behavior by Assistant U.S. Attorneys is the norm, not the exception. Federal judges permit Government attorneys to lie without punishment and to ignore the rules and the deadlines established for use in Federal court.

Now we will examine a case that was appealed to the United States Court of Appeals for the District of Columbia Circuit. In this appeal a citizen sues a person who is a Government official. However, the Government official was not sued in his official capacity. The citizen is the appellant and the Government is the appellee. The body of the decision reads:

No. 98-5141 September Term, 1997
94cv02000

BEFORE: Wald, Silberman, and Henderson, Circuit Judges

O R D E R

Upon consideration of the motion for summary affirmance and the opposition thereto; and the cross-motion for entry of default, which the court construes as a motion for summary reversal, the opposition thereto, and the reply, it is

ORDERED that the motion for summary affirmance be granted substantially for the reasons stated by the magistrate judge's report and recommendation filed March 5, 1998, as adopted by the district court in its March 31, 1998 order. The merits of the parties' positions are so clear as to warrant summary action. See Taxpayers Watchdog, Inc. v. Stanley, 819 F.2d 294, 297 (D.C.Cir. 1987) (per curiam); Walker v. Washington, 627 F.2d 541 (D.C. Cir.) (per curiam), cert. denied, 449 U.S. 994 (1980). It is

FURTHER ORDERED that the motion for summary reversal be denied. Magistrate judges "may hear and determine any pretrial motion" at the request of the district court. See D.D.C. Local Rule 503(a). The Justice Department has authority to provide representation to federal employees sued in their individual capacities when providing legal counsel would be in the interest of the United States. See 28 C.F.R. § 50.15(a).

The Clerk is directed to withhold issuance of the mandate herein until seven days after disposition of any timely petition for rehearing. See D.C.Cir. Rule 41.

Per Curiam
(There are three sets of initials are written here. Those initials are PW, LHS, and KLH)

The major problem with this decision is — **THERE ARE NO FACTS IN THIS DECISION TO SUPPORT THE DECISION.** Let me explain further. A motion for summary affirmance is a request that the judges issue a ruling that says that the district court's decision is correct. Supposedly, these three judges decided "that the motion for summary affirmance be granted substantially for the reasons stated by the magistrate judge's report and recommendation filed March 5, 1998, as adopted by the district court in its March 31, 1998 order." This is the same as these judges only saying that the magistrate judge is correct. Well, the magistrate judge might be correct, but judges in the courts of appeals are required to explain **WHY** the magistrate judge is correct, because Congress passed a law that requires them to list the reasons for their decisions. The use of the words "substantially for the reasons stated by the magistrate judge's report and recommendation" does not explain *which reasons.* These judges do not explain, as required by law, why the magistrate judge's reasons are correct.

These judges simply say, "the merits of the parties' positions are so clear as to warrant summary action." What are the merits of the parties' positions? Don't know do you? That's because the judges don't explain what the merits of the parties' positions are. They deny the motion for summary reversal, but they don't say why. Lastly, two statements are included for no apparent purpose. The first statement is "Magistrate judges 'may hear and determine any pretrial motion' at the request of the district court." So what? This decision does not say that the judges found that the district court requested the magistrate judge to hear and determine any pretrial motion! The second statement is "The Justice Department has authority to provide representation to federal employees sued in their individual capacities when providing legal counsel would be in the interest of the United States." Once again, so what? This decision does not say that the judges found that the Justice Department was properly representing this Government official sued in his individual capacity, nor does this decision say that the judges found that the United States has any interest at all in this case!

This order does not say that the judges reviewed the record from the court below. Without reviewing the record of exactly what happened in the court below, it is impossible for the judges to know to grant the Government's motion for summary affirmance, or to grant the citizen's motion for summary reversal, or to deny both motions. How can these judges know which decision to make or which side is correct concerning what happened in the court below without reading the record of what happened in the court below? The obvious answer is they can't know! They didn't let "getting the facts" stand in the way of ruling for the Government and against the citizen. This is **NOT GOOD BEHAVIOR!**

Let's examine another case. This case, no. 98-5170, was also before the United States Court of Appeals for the District of Columbia Circuit. A citizen appeals the district court judge's decision. The citizen is the appellant and the Government is the appellee. Judges Laurence Silberman, Karen Henderson, and David Tatel were the judges who supposedly decided this appeal. The body of the decision in this appeal reads:

O R D E R

Upon consideration of appellee's motion for summary affirmance; and appellant's verified motion for summary judgment, which is being treated as a motion for summary reversal, and the opposition thereto, it is

ORDERED that appellee's motion for summary affirmance be granted and the motion for summary reversal be denied. The merits of the parties' positions are so clear as to warrant summary action. See Taxpayers Watchdog, Inc. v. Stanley, 819 F.2d 294, 297 (D.C.Cir. 1987)(per curiam); Walker v. Washington, 627 F.2d 541, 545 (D.C.Cir.)(per curiam), cert. denied, 449 U.S. 994 (1980).

Appellant has not demonstrated that the challenged government action deprived him of a liberty or property interest that is protected by the due process clause of the Fifth Amendment. See Brock v. Roadway Express, Inc., 481 U.S. 252, 260 (1987). Nor has appellant demonstrated that the district court abused its discretion in granting appellee's motion for leave to file out of time. See LoSacco v. City of Middletown, 71 F.3d 88, 93 (2d Cir. 1995). Further, the district court correctly held that it lacked subject matter jurisdiction to review the General Counsel's decision not to issue unfair labor practice complaints. See Turgeon v. FLRA, 677 F.2d 937, 940 (D.C.Cir. 1982). Finally, appellant's request for information from appellee was properly construed as a request for information under the Freedom of Information Act ("FOIA"), see, e.g., NLRB V. Sears, Roebuck & Co., 421 U.S. 321, 143 n. 10 (1975), and appellant has not challenged the applicability of the FOIA exemptions cited by the district court. See Ryan v. Bentsen, 12 F.3d 245, 249 n.5 (D.C.Cir. 1993)(court need not decide issues not raised by parties on appeal).

The Clerk is directed to withhold issuance of the mandate herein until seven days after disposition of any timely petition for rehearing. See D.C.Cir. Rule 41.

Per Curiam
(There are three sets of initials are written here. Those initials are
LHS, KLH, PW)

The first paragraph of this order declares that the only documents considered before issuing this order were the Government's (appellee's) motion for summary affirmance and the citizen's (appellant's) verified motion for summary judgment. Once again, the record from the district court was not considered. The citizen's motion was verified which means the citizen's motion is sworn to, is the equivalent of an affidavit and is, therefore, evidence. The Government's motion is not verified and is, therefore, not evidence. So, the only evidence before the judges at the Court of Appeals was from the citizen. We know judges are required to rule based on the evidence before them and we know what evidence Judges Silberman, Henderson, and Tatel had before them before issuing this order. Now, let's carefully examine this order.

The first and second sentences start by saying, "Appellant has not demonstrated" and "Nor has appellant demonstrated." The appeals process is provided so that a party *can demonstrate* that a lower court committed errors. A party is not required to prove that errors occurred **before** the appeal is heard. If that were the case, then there would be no need for an appeal process!

The third sentence declares that the district court "correctly held that it lack subject matter jurisdiction." The fourth sentence declares, "appellant's request for information from appellee was properly construed as a request for information under the Freedom of Information Act ("FOIA")." Remember, the only evidence before Judges Silberman, Henderson, and Tatel is the citizen's motion. The citizen's motion does not say that the district court correctly held that it lack subject matter jurisdiction. Nor does the citizen's motion say that appellant's request for information from appellee was properly construed as a request for information under the Freedom of Information Act. Lastly, this order says, "The merits of the parties' positions are so clear as to warrant summary action." Black's Law Dictionary definition of **merits** is **the word as a legal term is to be regarded as referring to the strict legal rights of the parties**. How can the merits of the Government's position be so clear as to warrant a decision in favor of the Government when there is no evidence before the judges to support the Government's position?

The judges did not have the record from the district court and the citizen's motion does not say that the Government is correct, so how could the judges have reached the conclusions in this order? Guess what? The Government's motion says all of these things! I see you are perplexed. "But the Government's motion is not evidence of anything," you exclaim. "That's true," I respond. "But judges are required to rule on the evidence," you exclaim. "That's true," I respond. "Then how can these judges . . ." Before you can finish your next question I interject, "The judges favor the Government and as you can see they don't let the facts or the evidence get in their way!" "Obviously," is your final response.

The three sets of initials at the bottom of this decision are noteworthy. Let's speculate, shall we? If either Judge Silberman or Judge Henderson, or Judge Tatel ordered someone, like their law clerk or secretary, to type this decision, then the author would be identified and that judge's signature block would be at the bottom of this decision. However, no judge's signature block is at the bottom of this decision. So, continuing our speculation, this is likely — a law clerk was assigned this case, that law clerk read through the motions filed by the citizen and the Government, that law clerk knows that the judges favor the Government, that law clerk's good performance rating depends on eliminating cases from the judges' workload, that law clerk wrote a memorandum accompanied by this decision and sent it to each judge, and each judge simply initial the bottom of this decision. Whatever is the case, the three sets of initials do not match the names of the judges who supposedly decided the case! I wonder just how the Court of Appeals can explain this! Neither Judge Silberman, nor Judge Henderson, nor Judge Tatel read anything or considered any of the documents in this case. These judges certainly did not rule based on the facts or any evidence! Of that we can be sure because they told us so!

Let's look at another order from the United States Court of Appeals for the District of Columbia Circuit. In case No. 98-5141, a per curiam decision was issued by Judges Patricia M. Wald, Laurence Silberman, and Karen Henderson. The body of the decision reads:

BEFORE: Wald, Silberman and Henderson, Circuit Judges

ORDER

Upon consideration of appellant's petiiton for rehearing filed August 13, 1998, it is

ORDERED that the petition be denied.

Per Curiam

FOR THE COURT:
Mark J. Langer, Clerk

BY:
Linda Jones
Deputy Clerk

This per curiam order tells us a lot! This per curiam order has a signature block for the court clerk instead of a signature block for one of the three judges, and someone signed for the clerk. Now, if the court clerk can put his signature block on an order issued by one, two or three judges and have someone sign for the court clerk, then why can't a judge put his signature block on the order issued by that judge and have someone sign for that judge? If someone can sign for the court clerk who is signing for the judges, then surely the signature block for the judge responsible for the decision can be put on the order, but it isn't! Either none of the judges issued this decision, or no judge wants to be held responsible for it!!!

Here is one last decision from the United States Court of Appeals for the District of Columbia Circuit.

No. 98-5182

September Term, 1998
94cv02456
95cv01722

BEFORE: Silberman, Henderson, and Tatel, Circuit Judges

ORDER

Upon consideration of appellee's motion for summary affirmance or, in the alternative, to dismiss appeal as untimely; and appellant's motion for summary reversal, and the opposition thereto, it is

ORDERED that the motion to dismiss be denied. See Lauderdale County Sch. Dist. V. Enterprise Consol. Sch. Dist., 24 F.3d 671, 682 (5ᵗʰ Cir. 1994); Huston v. Mitchell, 908 F.2d 275, 277 (8ᵗʰ Cir. 1990). It is

FURTHER ORDERED that the motion for summary affirmance be granted and the motion for summary reversal be denied. The merits of the parties' positions are so clear as to warrant summary action. See Taxpayers Watchdog, Inc. v. Stanley, 819 F.2d 294, 297 (D.C.Cir. 1987) (per curiam); Walker v. Washington, 627 F.2d 541 (D.C. Cir.) (per curiam), cert. denied, 449 U.S. 994 (1980). Substantially for the reasons stated in the magistrate judge's report and recommendation filed February 18, 1998, as adopted by the district court in its March 31, 1998 order, appellant's claims under the Rehabilitation Act and Freedom of Information Act were properly dismissed.

In addition, because the district court did not reach the merits of the dispositive motions in its March 28, 1996 order, the doctrine of res judicata does not apply to bar appellee's renewed dispositive motion. See Montana v. United States, 440 U.S. 147, 153 (979)(res judicata requires final judgment on the merits). Furthermore, the June 13, 1997 order was properly issued by the magistrate judge in accordance with Local Rule 503(a), and the district court did not abuse its discretion in declining to enter a default judgment against appellee. See 10A Wright & Miller, Federal Practice and Procedure, Civil § 2702 at ¶. 178-80 (1998)("[W]hen the government's default is due to a failure to plead . . . the court typically will refuse to enter a default or, if a default is entered, it will be set aside."); see also Fed. R. Civ. P. 55(e). Moreover, this court is without jurisdiction to review the Virginia court's transfer decision. See Starnes v. McGuire, 512 F.2d 918, 924 (D.C. Cir. 1974)(en banc).

With respect to appellant's claims of retaliation under Title VII, 42 U.S.C. § 2000-3, even assuming he was able to establish a prima facie case of retaliation, he has failed to raise a material question of fact that appellee's claimed reasons for the actions taken were pretextual or otherwise not true. See <u>Texas Dep't of Community Affairs v. Burdine</u>, 450 U.S. 248, 256 (1981).

The Clerk is directed to withhold issuance of the mandate herein until seven days after disposition of any timely petition for rehearing. See D.C. Cir. Rule 41.

Per Curiam
(There are three sets of initials are written here. Those initials are LHS, KLH, and PW)

Let's start with the amazing fact that the three sets of initials written at the bottom of this decision do not agree with the names of the judges assigned to the appeal! Once again, the judges fail to provide the facts to support (1) the denial of the motion to dismiss, (2) the denial of the motion for summary reversal, (3) the statement that the merits of the parties' positions are so clear as to warrant summary action, (4) the statement that appellant's claims under the Rehabilitation Act and Freedom of Information Act were properly dismissed, (5) the statement that the doctrine of res judicata does not apply, (6) the statement that the June 13, 1997 order was properly issued by the magistrate judge, or (7) the statement that appellant has failed to raise a material question of fact that appellee's claimed reasons for the actions taken were pretextual or otherwise not true.

It is important to note that the first paragraph says, "Upon consideration of appellee's motion for summary affirmance or, in the alternative, to dismiss appeal as untimely; and appellant's motion for summary reversal, and the opposition thereto." Once again, the judges at the Court of Appeals did not consider the record of what happened in the lower court before they rendered this decision. Without considering the record of what happened in the lower court, it is impossible for the judges at the Court of Appeals to know that (1) the doctrine of res judicata does not apply, (2) appellant failed to raise a material question of fact that appellee's claimed reasons for the actions taken were pretextual or otherwise not true, (3) appellant's claims under the Rehabilitation Act and Freedom of Information Act were properly dismissed, and (4) the June 13, 1997 order was properly issued by the magistrate judge.

We can see a pattern of disgraceful behavior on the part of judges in the courts of appeals. Judges render decisions that are not based on the facts or the evidence. They simply rule for the Government! Decisions contain the initials of judges not assigned to the case. Decisions do not contain the signature or name of the judge issuing the decision. Judges fail to provide the facts that are the basis of their decisions. Congress refuses to watch them and the Supreme Court refuses to review or reverse their decisions.

Bombshell coming!! In appeal number 98-5141 the decision says that the appeal was before Judges **Wald**, Silberman, and Henderson. In appeal numbers 98-5170 and 98-5182 the decision says that the appeal was before Judges Silberman, Henderson, and **Tatel**. Judges Silberman and Henderson were the only two judges involved in all three appeals. **The three sets of initials on all three decisions appear to be the same!** There is something rotten here! This brings forth a lot of questions. We cannot get satisfactory answers to any of the questions though. Mr. Robert Bonner, an employee in the clerk's office at the United States Court of Appeals for the District of Columbia Circuit, advised me that no records or recordings are made of the meetings, conferences, discussions, or whatever between the judges. We can't really know or find out what goes on in the courts of appeals. Surprised? I am! Congress ought to be surprised and outraged!

The federal judiciary is not policed by itself or by Congress. That is to say that no person or committee reviews the actions or decisions of federal judges to be certain that judges are upholding their sacred oath and trust and if a judge is not upholding his or her oath, then action is taken to remove the judge. The Newsletter of the Federal Courts, Volume 30, Number 7, July 1998, reports that during subcommittee hearings held by the House Judiciary Subcommittee on Courts and Intellectual Property in June 1998, Representative Howard Coble asked Judge William Terrell Hodges what the Federal Judiciary is doing about judges who fail to recuse themselves from cases concerning companies in which the judge has stock. The same volume of the Newsletter of the Federal Courts reports that Judge Hodges responded to the question by saying that the Federal Judiciary has taken measures to be certain judges are aware of their responsibilities. Sounds like one politician talking to other politicians!! The question was not has the Federal Judiciary taken steps to be certain judges are aware of the responsibility to recuse themselves from cases concerning companies in which the judge has stock. The question was **what are you doing about judges who fail to recuse themselves**. Obviously, the answer to the question is "nothing!!"

If any judge is unaware of the responsibility to recuse him or herself from a case concerning a company in which the judge has stock, then the judge has not been trained well. Poor training of judges by the federal judiciary would make it impossible to receive justice in the federal courts. But Judge Hodges did not say judges were not being properly trained, or judges are not trained regarding when recusal is appropriate. If the subcommittee is genuinely concerned about what the federal judiciary is doing about judges who fail to recuse themselves from cases concerning companies in which the judge has stock, then the members of the subcommittee would have found the response given by Judge Hodges to be entirely unacceptable. The reason Judge Hodges' response is unacceptable is judges **are already aware** of their responsibility regarding recusal!!

The federal judiciary has a complaint process that may be used by anyone who has a complaint against a judge. A person who wishes to file a complaint against a judge submits a written complaint outlining the facts to the Judicial Council. The federal judiciary pretends to investigate the complaint. Let's take a look at what happened in an actual complaint. In 1997, Judicial Complaint 97-16 was filed against Judge Emmet G. Sullivan, United States District Court for the District of Columbia. The essence of this judicial misconduct complaint is two acts of misconduct by Judge Sullivan. The person filing the complaint with the Judicial Counsel wrote,

1. If Judge Sullivan can provide the Judicial Council with a rationale for refusing to rule on the validity of Magistrate Judge Robinson's June 13 Order, then Judge Sullivan and I have a disagreement. If Judge Sullivan cannot give a rationale for this behavior, then he is guilty of misconduct; and

2. If Judge Sullivan can provide the Judicial Council with a rationale for refusing to set a new deadline by which Magistrate's Judge Robinson will be required to issue her report and recommendation pursuant to Judge Sullivan's own May 1 Order, then Judge Sullivan and I have a disagreement. If Judge Sullivan cannot give a rationale for this behavior, then he is guilty of misconduct.

In summary, Judge Sullivan's August 28 pro forma rulings, i.e., a) NOT to rule on a transparently unlawful ruling of the magistrate while continuing to rely upon it in the face of an unopposed motion challenging the validity of said unlawful ruling and, additionally, b) subverting Judge Sullivan's own May 1 Order are utterly devoid of logic; the total absence of rationale for this behavior is inescapable to any objective person. If such judicial misconduct as has been exposed by this judicial complaint is tolerated, there is no legal right that a Judge Sullivan cannot arbitrarily deny. In this particular circumstance, if the judicial misconduct of Judge Sullivan is condoned by the Judicial Council, then the pursuit of truth becomes a sham in the D. C. Circuit and justice is averted indefinitely.

This appears to be a well-grounded complaint concerning judicial misconduct. After all judges ARE REQUIRED to have a rationale for EACH and EVERY decision (including a decision to postpone a decision or a decision not to decide on an issue) in a case. If a judge has a rationale, then it should be easy for the judge to give that rationale! The complaint implies that the judge cannot have any rationale for his action, inaction or decisions. We judge a person's mental competence, not on whether the person has a rationale for his or her actions but on how sound the person's rationale is. If a judge has no rationale for an action, inaction, or decision, then the judge may not be mentally competent enough to be a judge! If a judge is not mentally competent, then the basis exists for removal of the judge. Without a rationale for a decision, a judge is certainly guilty of judicial misconduct.

Judge Sullivan did not provide the Judicial Council with his rationale and the Judicial Council did not compel Judge Sullivan to give his rationale. The Judicial Council dismissed this complaint of judicial misconduct. The reason used by the Judicial Council for dismissing this complaint is that the complaint is not in conformity with Title 28 of the United States Code, Section 372(c)(1). Let's see what that section of the United States Code says! That section of the United States Code reads, "Any person alleging that a circuit, district, or bankruptcy judge, or a magistrate, has engaged in conduct prejudicial to the effective and expeditious administration of the business of the courts, or alleging that such a judge or magistrate is unable to discharge all the duties of office by reason of mental or physical disability, may file with the clerk of the court of appeals for the circuit a written complaint containing a brief statement of the facts constituting such conduct. In the interests of the effective and expeditious administration of the business of the courts and on the basis of information available to the chief judge of the circuit, the chief judge may, by written order stating reasons therefor, identify a complaint for purposes of this subsection and thereby dispense with filing of a written complaint."

We have a complaint filed with the Judicial Council that alleges that a judge does not have any rationale for his action, inaction or decision. Having no rationale indicates that the judge may be mentally incompetent. Any one of these is prejudicial to the effective and expeditious administration of the business of the courts. After reading the section of the United States Code given by the Judicial Council, we see that the complaint **does** conform to the United States Code. Filing the complaint regarding Judge Sullivan's judicial misconduct accomplished absolutely nothing! Judge Sullivan is left on the bench to continue issuing decisions without having any rationale or without having to give his rationale!

Inferior courts fail to follow the rules promulgated by the Supreme Court. For example, Congress passed a law, Title 28, Part I, Chapter 21, Section 452 of the United States Code, and the Supreme Court wrote a rule, Rule 77 of the Federal Rules of Civil Procedure, that the district courts are to be deemed always open for the filing of any papers. This means that each district court is required by law and direction of the Supreme Court to have some method to permit the filing of papers after normal business hours. However, according to the Clerk's Office in the District Court in Alexandria, Virginia, there are many district courts that do not have any means for the filing of papers after normal business hours. The District Court in Alexandria, Virginia is one of the courts which does not comply with the law or the direction given by the Supreme Court. Neither Congress nor the Supreme Court (1) knows which federal courts comply with the law or the rules, (2) has a method in place in order to be made aware when federal courts do not comply with the law or the rules, or (3) takes corrective action when courts do not comply with the law or the rules.

The United States is divided into twelve federal circuits. Each federal circuit has at least one district court and one court of appeals. In the Federal courts, the district court is the first stop to begin a lawsuit. Many decisions from the district courts contain the phrase "the law in this circuit is." All federal district courts and all federal courts of appeals are suppose to decide cases based on the Constitution or the laws passed by Congress. Federal law does not change from state to state (except when a federal decision is based on a state law and for the purpose of this discussion we will assume that no state law is involved). The federal law in each federal circuit ought to be the same. If two federal circuits disagree on what the law is or should be, then those Courts of Appeals should ask the Supreme Court to decide the issue. After all, the Supreme Court was established to decide with finality what the federal law is. Instead, each Court of Appeals stays with its decision. A citizen has to pay another fee, appeal to the Supreme Court, and ask the Supreme Court to clear up the conflict between the Courts of Appeals. When the Supreme Court refuses to hear the case, as it often does, the conflict remains. At that point, who knows what the federal law is? It is impossible to render justice to any citizen under federal law when the Federal courts cannot agree on what the federal law is. It is impossible for the citizens to know what the federal law is when the federal courts cannot agree on what the law is!! I guess *We the People* better start checking before we travel from state to state and find out what the federal law is on the other side of the state line because it just might be different!

THE
SUPREME
COURT

THE SUPREME COURT TAKES POWER NOT GRANTED TO IT

OR

SOVEREIGN, ABSOLUTE, QUALIFIED, AND GOVERNMENT CONTRACTOR IMMUNITIES ARE UNCONSTITUTIONAL

From the Declaration of Independence

We hold these truths to be self-evident, that all men are created equal, that they are endowed by their Creator with certain unalienable Rights, that among these are Life, Liberty, and the pursuit of Happiness. **That to secure these rights, Governments are instituted among Men, deriving their just powers from the consent of the governed. That whenever any Form of Government becomes destructive of these ends, it is the Right of the People to alter or to abolish it**,

Article I of the Constitution

All legislative Powers herein granted shall be vested in a Congress of the United States, **which shall consist of a Senate and House of Representatives**.

They shall in all Cases, except Treason, Felony and Breach of the Peace, **be privileged from** Arrest during their Attendance at the Session of their respective Houses, and in going to and returning from the same; and for any Speech or Debate in either House, **they shall not be questioned in any other Place.**

To make all Laws which shall be necessary and proper for carrying into Execution the foregoing Powers, and all other Powers vested by this Constitution in the Government of the United States, or in any Department or Officer thereof.

Article III of the Constitution

The judicial power of the United States, shall be vested in one supreme court, and in such inferior courts as the Congress may from time to time ordain and establish.

Article VI of the Constitution

This Constitution, and the Laws of the United States which shall be made in Pursuance thereof; and all Treaties made, or which shall be made, under the Authority of the United States, **shall be the supreme Law of the Land; and the Judges in every State shall be bound thereby**, any Thing in the Constitution or Laws of any State to the Contrary notwithstanding.

Amendment I to the Constitution

Congress shall make no law respecting an establishment of religion, or prohibiting the free exercise thereof; or abridging the freedom of speech, or of the press; or **the right of the people** peaceably to assemble, and **to petition the Government for a redress of grievances**.

Amendment IX to the Constitution

The enumeration in the Constitution, of certain rights, **shall not be construed to deny or disparage** others retained by the people.

Amendment X to the Constitution

The powers not delegated to the United States by the Constitution, not prohibited by it to the States, **are reserved to the States respectively, or to the people**.

Amendment XIV

All persons born or naturalized in the United States and subject to the jurisdiction thereof, are citizens of the United States . . .

The Government is a government of expressed and limited powers, and all powers from the People not delegated to the Government are retained by the People and by the States. The First Amendment to the Constitution contains a series of rights. The definition of a series is — a number of things of the same kind in a row or following one after the other in succession. In the First Amendment there are a number of things of the same kind (Rights) following one after the other in succession. Reflect on what you were taught in grammar and you will remember that one of the uses of a comma is to separate things in a series. The phrases in the First Amendment which contain the Rights are separated by a comma. The last phrase in the series is joined to the rest of the phrases by the word and. The First Amendment establishes the following rights: (1) <u>freedom of religion</u>, (2) <u>freedom of speech</u>, (3) <u>freedom of the press</u>, (4) <u>the right to peaceably assemble</u>, and (5) <u>the right to petition the government for a redress of grievances</u>.

In the case of Edwards v. South Carolina decided by the Supreme Court on February 25, 1963, Mr. Justice Steward acknowledges in the opinion of the Court that the right "to petition the Government for a redress of grievances" is a separate right. In this opinion Mr. Justice Steward writes, "South Carolina infringed the petitioners' constitutionally protected rights of free speech, free assembly, and freedom to petition for redress of their grievances. It has long been established that these First Amendment freedoms are protected . . . " The First Amendment forbids the making of any law that restricts any of the Rights listed. The last phrase in the series of Rights — the right to petition the government for a redress of grievances — makes it clear that every citizen has the constitutionally protected Right to **petition** the Government for a **redress** of **grievances**. It is one of our most comprehensive Rights; and one of the ways the Constitution guards against Government abuses, in order to prevent Government officials who are vested with authority from becoming oppressors.

So that we can understand completely and exactly what is being protected by the phrase "to petition the Government for a redress of grievances" we need to get the definitions for the words petition, redress, and grievance. Black's Law Dictionary defines:

> **petition** as a formal written application to a court requesting judicial action on a certain matter.
> **redress** as satisfaction for an injury or damages sustained.

63

> **grievance** as an injury, injustice or wrong which gives ground for complaint.

Because the definition of the word grievance contains the word complaint let's get the definition of the words complaint and complainant. Black's Law Dictionary defines:

> **complaint** as a pleading which sets forth a claim for relief.
> **complainant** as one who applies to the courts for legal redress by filing a complaint.

The definition of the word petition tells us that a petition can be a document other than a sheet of paper with lots of signatures on it. A citizen's formal written application to a court requesting judicial action on a certain matter (a **petition**) that sets forth a claim for relief and satisfaction for an injury (**redress**), injustice or wrong sustained (**grievance**) *is the filing of a lawsuit*. Now we see completely and exactly what right is being protected by the last phrase in the series in the First Amendment. The constitutionally protected right to petition the Government for a redress of grievances includes our right to file a lawsuit against the Government. Want proof? Since this country was born, a person who files a lawsuit or complaint has been referred to as a petitioner. The person bringing the lawsuit is referred to as the petitioner in the following Supreme Court cases: United States v. Clarke, Vitarelli v. Seaton, Butz v. Economou, Data Processing Service v. Camp, Malley v. Briggs. Want more proof? Ok, one of the first governing documents that *We the People* used was the Articles of Confederation. I knew you would remember that the Articles of Confederation preceded our Constitution. Here is portion of Article IX of the Articles of Confederation:

The United States in Congress assembled shall also be the last resort on appeal in all disputes and differences now subsisting or that hereafter may arise between two or more States concerning boundary, jurisdiction, or any other cause whatever; which authority shall always be exercised in the manner following: — Whenever the legislative or executive authority or lawful agency of any State in controversy with another shall present a *petition* to Congress *stating the matter in question and praying for a hearing*, notice thereof shall be given by order of Congress to the legislative or executive authority of the other State in controversy, and a day assigned for the appearance of the parties by their lawful agents, who shall then be directed to appoint, by joint consent, commissioners or judges to constitute a court for hearing and determining the matter in question; but if they cannot agree, Congress shall name three persons out of each of the United States, and from the list of such persons each party shall alternately strike out one, the petitioners beginning, until the number shall be reduced to thirteen . . .

In the Articles of Confederation, a State presented its appeal of a dispute against another State in the form of a *petition* stating *the matter in question and praying for a hearing.* The filing of a petition stating the matter in question and praying for a hearing is the same as the filing of a lawsuit and asking for a trial! Want still more proof? Ok, keep in mind that we separated from Great Britain. In the 1803 case of Marbury v. Madison, Mr. Chief Justice Marshall said, "In Great Britain the king himself is sued in the respectful form of a *petition,* and he never fails to comply with the judgment of his court."

The filing of a lawsuit by a citizen is only **one** method of petitioning the Government for a redress of grievances. There are several other methods for petitioning the Government for a redress of grievances that may be better known to you. For instance, the carrying of a picket-sign outside a Government building or having your relatives, friends, and neighbors sign a document showing that they all agree on a particular subject and then mailing the document to a Government official are methods of petitioning the Government.

The First Amendment protects **all** of the methods that a citizen may use to petition the Government for a redress of grievances because the First Amendment prohibits any law restricting the Right to petition the Government for a redress of grievances by stating "Congress shall make no law . . . abridging . . . the right of the people . . . to petition the Government for a redress of grievances." Congress is the only Government body granted law-making power by the Constitution. If Congress is prevented from making a law, then no law can be made.

The Supreme Court established sovereign immunity in the case of Chisholm v. Georgia in 1793, absolute immunity for judges in the case of Bradley v. Fisher in 1872, absolute immunity for prosecutors in the case of Yaselli v. Goff in 1927, and qualified immunity for Government officials in the case of Procunier v. Navarette in 1978. Sovereign, absolute, and qualified immunity are not based on the Constitution or any laws passed by Congress. They are the result of the personal views of Supreme Court Justices based on what the Justices believe the law *should* be — **not what the law actually is**.

The Justices of the Supreme Court use "the common-law" as a basis for these immunities. Common-law originated in England. It is not based on the Constitution or any laws passed by Congress. The Supreme Court adopted these immunities because the Justices on the Supreme Court believe that these immunities are necessary (1) for the proper functioning of the Government and (2) to protect the Government and Government officials from lawsuits filed by citizens to redress grievances against the Government or Government officials.

The Constitution is the supreme law of the land. The power to decide what laws or immunities are necessary for the proper functioning of the Government, with some exceptions to that power, is specifically **given to Congress** in Article I of the Constitution. The Constitution delegates **the administration of justice** and **the application** of the law of the land to the federal courts. The Constitution does not grant any federal judge the power to decide what laws or immunities are necessary for the proper functioning of the Government. Federal judges, including the Justices on the Supreme Court, may not exercise the power of law making because they are not granted any law making authority in the Constitution. Deciding what is and what is not going to be a law of the United States is a law making function and the law making function belongs to Congress.

In the cases of Pulliam v. Allen, Volume 466 of the United States Reports, page 529, Pierson v. Ray, Volume 386 of the United States Reports, pages 554-555, and Tenney v. Brandhove, Volume 341 of the United States Reports page 367 the Supreme Court uses the following rationale to explain common-law immunities: "Our cases have proceeded on the assumption that common-law principles of legislative and judicial immunity were incorporated into our judicial system and that they should not be abrogated absent clear legislative intent to do so." The first question is "by who, or by what and when were these common-law principles of legislative and judicial immunities incorporated into our judicial system?" The second question is "were these immunities incorporated into our judicial system by lawful authority?" The Supreme Court doesn't tell us who, what, or when regarding the incorporation of these immunities into our judicial system.

Did you get the most important point in the Supreme Court quote above? I missed it until about the sixth or seventh time I read it. Here it is — have proceeded on the **assumption**! The Justices of the Supreme Court based a decision of monumental importance not on a fact or even an inference, but on an **assumption**. They do not need to assume at all. The Constitution is right there for them to read! In fact, the Constitution prevents the Justices of the Supreme Court from assuming! Remember that the Constitution says that it is the supreme law of the land! Justice requires that cases be decided based on the **law** and the **facts**! There is no assuming!

The common-law principles of legislative and judicial immunity **ARE NOT** part of the Constitution or the laws of the United States. If the Constitution incorporated any of those common-law principles, then we would find wording in the Constitution similar to "such parts of the common-law . . . as did form the law of . . . on the nineteenth day of April, one thousand seven hundred seventy-five . . ." The New York State Constitution has just such wording in it and it was in existence before the Constitution! The Commonwealth of Virginia, in the Code of Virginia, Title 1, Chapter 2, Section 1-10, also incorporated the common-law into its law by stating "The common law of England, insofar as it is not repugnant to the principles of the Bill of Rights and Constitution of this Commonwealth, shall continue in full force within the same, and be the rule of decision, except as altered by the General Assembly." The Framers could have included the wording from either the New York State Constitution or the Code of Virginia in the Constitution. They chose not to. In Article VI of the Constitution, the Framers included a provision for all debts and engagements entered into *before* the Constitution to be valid under the Constitution, as under the Confederation. The Framers could have included similar wording regarding the common-law. They chose not to. The Constitution does not incorporate any common-law principles of immunity.

Congress has not incorporated any common-law immunities into the laws of this country. The common-law immunities referred to by the Justices of the Supreme Court were incorporated by Justices of the Supreme Court, but the Constitution does not grant the Justices of the Supreme Court the power to incorporate common-law immunities or anything else into the laws of the United States. Therefore, lawful authority did not incorporate the common-law immunities incorporated by the Justices of the Supreme Court. Thus, the common-law immunities granted to the Government by the Supreme Court are unconstitutional. It is that simple!

The common-law immunities granted to the Government by the Supreme Court are all based on how things **WERE** in England **BEFORE** the Constitution! We must remember that the Constitution says that the Constitution is the supreme law of **this** country, so, that pretty well takes care of the old laws from England being supreme here. Before the Supreme Court can establish any immunity based on the common-law, the Constitution or a law passed by Congress must incorporate the common-law into the federal law. Supreme Court Justice Brandeis points out in the 1938 case of Erie R. v. Tompkins **there is no federal common-law**. Obviously, federal judges cannot base decisions on something that does not exist! The Constitution requires federal judges to uphold the Constitution and the laws of the United States. Without any support in the Constitution or in the laws of the United States, federal judges, including the Justices of the Supreme Court, are without any authority or basis for sovereign, absolute, and qualified immunity.

In the case of Marbury v. Madison, Mr. Chief Justice Marshall makes it clear that sovereign, absolute, and qualified immunities cannot be based on common-law and that these immunities do not exist in the United States. He said,

"Is it to be contended that where the law in precise terms, directs the performance of an act, in which an individual is interested, the law is incapable of securing obedience to its mandate? Is it on account of the character of the person against whom the complaint is made? Is it to be contended that the heads of departments are not amenable to the laws of their country? Whatever the practice on particular occasions may be, the theory of this practice will certainly never be maintained. No act of the legislature confers so extraordinary a privilege, nor can it derive countenance from the doctrines of the common law."

"If one of the heads of departments commits any illegal act, under color of his office, by which an individual sustains an injury, it cannot be pretended that his office alone exempts him from being sued in the ordinary mode of proceeding, and being compelled to obey the judgment of the law."

In the 1793 Supreme Court case of Chisholm v. Georgia, Volume 2 of the United States Reports, page 419, Mr. Justice Wilson said,

"If then it be true, that the sovereignty of the nation is in the people of the nation, and the residuary sovereignty of each State in the people of each State, it may be useful to compare these sovereignties with those in Europe, that we may thence be enabled to judge, whether all the prerogatives which are allowed to the latter, are so essential to the former. There is reason to suspect that some of the difficulties which embarrass the present question, arise from inattention to differences which subsist between them.

It will be sufficient to observe briefly, that the sovereignties in Europe, and particularly in England, exist on feudal principles. That system considers the Prince as the sovereign, and the people as his subjects; it regards his person as the object of allegiance, and excludes the idea of his being on an equal footing with a subject, either in a Court of Justice or elsewhere. That system contemplates him as being the fountain of honor and authority; and from his grace and grant derives all franchises, immunities and privileges; it is easy to perceive that such a sovereign could not be amenable to a Court of Justice, or subjected to judicial control and actual constraint. It was of necessity, therefore, that suability became incompatible with such sovereignty. Besides, the Prince having all the Executive powers, the judgment of the Courts would, in fact, be only monitory, not mandatory to him, and a capacity to be advised, is a distinct thing from a capacity to be sued. The same feudal ideas run through all their jurisprudence, and constantly remind us of the distinction between the Prince and the subject. No such ideas obtain here; at the Revolution, the sovereignty devolved on the people; and they are truly the sovereigns of the country, but they are sovereigns without subjects and have none to govern but themselves; the citizens of America are equal as fellow citizens, and as joint tenants in the sovereignty.

From the differences existing between feudal sovereignties and Governments founded on compacts, it necessarily follows that their respective prerogatives must differ. Sovereignty is the right to govern; a nation or State-sovereign is the person or persons in whom that resides. In Europe the sovereignty is generally ascribed to the Prince; here it rests with the people; there, the sovereign actually administers the Government; here, never in a single instance; our Governors are the agents of the people, and at most stand in the same relation to their sovereign, in which regents in Europe stand to their sovereigns. Their Princes have personal powers, dignities, and pre-eminences, our rulers have none but official; nor do they partake in the sovereignty otherwise, or in any other capacity, than as private citizens."

In the 1816 Supreme Court case of Martin v. Hunter's Lessee, Volume 14 of the United States Reports, page 304, Mr. Justice Story said,

"The constitution of the United States was ordained and established, not by the states in their sovereign capacities, but emphatically, as the preamble of the constitution declares, by 'the people of the United States.' There can be no doubt that it was competent to the people to invest the general government with all the powers which they might deem proper and necessary; to extend or restrain these powers according to their own good pleasure, and to give them a paramount and supreme authority. As little doubt can there be, that the people had a right to prohibit to the states the exercise of any powers which were, in their judgment, incompatible with the objects of the general compact; to make the powers of the state governments, in given cases, subordinate to those of the nation, or to reserve to themselves those sovereign authorities which they might not choose to delegate to either. The constitution was not, therefore, necessarily carved out of existing state sovereignties, nor a surrender of powers already existing in state institutions, for the powers of the states depend upon their own constitutions; and the people of every state had the right to modify and restrain them, according to their own views of the policy or principle. On the other hand, it is perfectly clear that the sovereign powers vested in the state governments, by their respective constitutions, remained unaltered and unimpaired, except so far as they were granted to the government of the United States. These deductions do not rest upon general reasoning, plain and obvious as they seem to be. They have been positively recognized by one of the articles in amendment of the constitution, which declares, that 'the powers not delegated to the United States by the constitution, nor prohibited by it to the states, are reserved to the states respectively, or to the people.' The government, then, of the United States, can claim no powers which are not granted to it by the constitution, and the powers actually granted, must be such as are expressly given, or given by necessary implication."

In plain simple English, Justice Wilson and Justice Story said that Kings and Princes have sovereignty, but here *We the People* have the sovereignty; and the Government and Government officials do not have sovereign immunity.

An examination of the Declaration of Independence and the Constitution make it clear that it is the Right of the people to **alter** (correct) **destructive** (unconstitutional) government. The Constitution explicitly guarantees, in the First Amendment, that each citizen will always have the Right and the opportunity to have his grievance against the Government heard. A United States citizen's Right to sue the Government for wrongs committed is a right retained by the People that has never been surrendered to the Government. Mr.

71

Justice Matthews, in the case of Yick Wo v. Hopkins in 1855, said "**Sovereignty** itself is, of course, not subject to law, for it **is the author and source of law**; but in our system, while sovereign powers are delegated to the agencies of government, <u>sovereignty itself remains with the people</u>, by whom and for whom all government exists and acts." Thus, when a citizen of the United States sues the Government, the Constitution forbids the Government from using the defense of sovereign immunity. Sovereign immunity, when exercised as a defense by the Government to a suit brought by a citizen of the United States who petitions the Government for a redress of grievances, inhibits the exercise of the constitutionally protected Right of a citizen to petition for a redress of grievances. At the very least, sovereign immunity dictates and limits how citizens may petition the Government for redress of grievances. The First Amendment to the Constitution also forbids dictating and limiting how citizens may petition the Government for redress of grievances.

Federal judges require an express waiver of sovereign immunity by Congress before a citizen may bring a lawsuit against the Government. In effect, Federal judges are saying that Congress must first give its permission before a citizen may file a lawsuit against the Government. Before Congress may waive sovereign immunity, there must be something that grants the Government sovereign immunity. As we have seen, there is nothing in the Constitution or federal law that provides a grant of sovereign immunity. It is the expressed will of the People of the United States, stated plainly and specifically in the First Amendment to the Constitution of the United States, that a citizen can sue the Government.

Federal judges, by requiring that Congress must first give its permission before a citizen may bring a lawsuit against the Government for a redress of grievances, have built upon a foundation not present in, and indeed contrary to, the Constitution. Assistant United States Attorneys go into federal courts on behalf of the Government and advocate sovereign immunity. The argument is nothing more than a request by the Government to be allowed to continue the Government's unconstitutional behavior.

In the case of Imbler v. Pachtman, Volume 424 of the United States Reports pages 422 and 423, the Supreme Court states that "public policy" requires absolute and qualified immunity for some Government officials. The "public policy" referred to by the Supreme Court is not found in the Constitution and it is not established in any law written by Congress. The Constitution grants the elected members of Congress the power to decide what "public policy" is. Congress has never established any such "public policy." In order to establish absolute and qualified immunity for certain Government officials, Justices of the Supreme Court simply decided what the public policy is for our country. The Justices of the Supreme Court are not granted the power to decide what public policy is and then decide cases based on their own concept of what that public policy requires. According to the Constitution, the Supreme Court's functions are to decide cases based on what *is* in the Constitution and to interpret the laws <u>based on what Congress has already written</u>. It is the duty of the Justices of the Supreme Court to subordinate their own personal views and to subordinate their own ideas of what legislation is wise and what is not.

Why hasn't Congress established such a public policy, you might ask? Well, that's simple. Congress might want to establish such a "public policy," or Congress might not want to, but regardless how Congress feels about it, **the First Amendment prevents Congress from establishing such a "public policy!"** "Congress shall make no law . . . abridging . . . the right of the people . . . to petition the Government for a redress of grievances." Establishing such a "public policy" would abridge (restrict) the right of the people to petition the Government for a redress of grievances. The Framers decided that these immunities are not necessary for the Government to fulfill its governmental functions.

In Article I, Section 6, the Constitution grants members of Congress *limited immunity* (they are in all cases, except treason, felony and breach of the peace, privileged from arrest during their attendance at, and in going to and from, the session of their respective houses, and they cannot be questioned in any place other than their respective House for any speech or debate in either House). Obviously, the Framers of the Constitution knew how to grant immunities to the Government. The Framers could have granted the Government or any Government official any immunity they saw fit. However, they decided that sovereign, absolute, and qualified immunities are not necessary for the Government. The implementation of immunity defenses by Federal judges for the Government, or for Government officials, to suits brought against the Government by citizens of the United States has caused a tear in the cloth that is the foundation of this nation and infringes on a citizen's constitutional rights and freedoms.

Now would be a good time to address what is known as the government contractor defense. The Supreme Court has established that government contractors are shielded from liability. Let me give you an example. You may have seen a movie about an Air Force Captain who dies in a F-16 and his widow sues General Dynamics — the manufacturer of the F-16. There was a jury trial and the jury awarded money damages to the widow. The Court of Appeals overturned the jury's award and ruled that the widow could not sue General Dynamics because General Dynamics has government contractor immunity.

This immunity for government contractors was established by federal judges based on the reasoning that when a government contractor acts under the authority and direction of the Government, the government contractor shares the sovereign immunity of the Government. As we have seen, there is no sovereign immunity for the Government to protect it from a lawsuit by a citizen of the United States. Obviously, when a citizen of the United States sues a government contractor, a government contractor cannot use an immunity that does not exist to defeat the lawsuit! The government contractor immunity does not have its foundation in the Constitution or in any law passed by Congress. Once again, federal judges have decided what *they* think *should* be law and they have failed to interpret what *is* the law. Federal judges, in establishing the government contractor defense, have exercised authority beyond that granted to them in the Constitution. Our journey into the Constitution has taught us that anything, including the government contractor immunity, contrary to the Constitution and anything done contrary to the Constitution is not the law of the land. The government contractor immunity (or the government contractor defense) was established by federal judges contrary to the Constitution, therefore, the government contractor immunity is unconstitutional, and it cannot be the law of the United States.

The only purposes served by sovereign, absolute, qualified, and government contractor immunity are to (1) subject citizens to the abuses possible when Government officials enjoy unbridled discretion, (2) exert unlawful pressure on citizens not to go forward with grievances against the Government, (3) create a barrier behind which malicious Government officials go undetected and unpunished, and (4) allow Government officials to commit, perpetuate, condone, and conceal unlawful acts.

The Department of Justice does not protect the People's interests, as it should, by prosecuting offending Government officials. Rather, the Department of Justice rushes to defend Government officials guilty of a variety of unlawful behavior. The Government simply protects its unconstitutional behavior by throwing up the sovereign immunity shield — all in the name of good efficient government. Such behavior from the Government is not for the benefit of the People. The founders of our nation rebelled and threw off just such a government.

In order for any of the immunities discussed above to be constitutional, the Constitution must grant Federal judges the power to create laws and the power to decide what immunities are necessary for the proper execution of the powers vested in the Government or in any department or officer thereof. Of course, this is not so. To bring the Government into accord with the Constitution, Congress must declare that the First Amendment prohibits the Government from using the defense of sovereign immunity against suits brought by citizens and that the Constitution vests Congress and not Federal judges with the authority to establish any immunities necessary for Government officials.

In 1998 a lawsuit (CA 98-277-A) was filed by a citizen of the United States against the Government in federal court in Alexandria, Virginia challenging the constitutionality of (1) the Government's sovereign immunity when a citizen sues the Government, (2) the Supreme Court's discretionary review, and (3) the constitutionality of the Judiciary Act of 1925 (the Supreme Court's discretionary review and the Judiciary Act of 1925 are discussed separately in subsequent sections). The Government filed a motion to have the lawsuit dismissed. The citizen filed a response to the Government's motion and Chief Judge Claude M. Hilton issued a decision dismissing the lawsuit. Judge Hilton's reasons for dismissing the lawsuit are: (1) the citizen does not have the right to bring the lawsuit, (2) the citizen has not suffered any injury as a result of the Government's actions, and (3) the Government has sovereign immunity. An appeal was filed and the Court of Appeals issued a decision that upholds Judge Hilton's decision.

We will now take a look into the guts of this lawsuit. We need to look at a copy of the papers filed in this lawsuit against the Government. First, the lawsuit:

COMPLAINT

COMES NOW, your Plaintiff and hereby submits this Complaint to declare unconstitutional, null, and void the Federal Tort Claims Act, the doctrine of sovereign immunity, the Act of March 3, 1891, ch. 517, 26 Stat. 826, the Act of February 13, 1925, ch. 229, 43 Stat. 936, and any other laws that grant the Supreme Court of the United States discretion to perform the duties assigned to it in the Constitution of the United States. In support thereof, Plaintiff alleges as follows:

NATURE OF ACTION

This action arises under the Constitution of the United States, Article I, Article III, the First Amendment, and the Tenth Amendment, and seeks to have the the Federal Tort Claims Act, the Act of February 13, 1925, ch 229, 43 Stat. 936 (also known as the Judiciary Act of 1925), the Act of March 3, 1891, ch. 517, 26 Stat. 826, each and every law, or relevant part thereof, that grants to the Supreme Court of the United States the discretion to decide to perform or not to perform the duties assigned to it in the Constitution of the United States, and the doctrine of sovereign immunity, insofar as the Federal Government is permitted to assert the defense of sovereign immunity against an action by a citizen of the United States, declared unconstitutional, null and void.

This is a class complaint. The class is so numerous that joinder of all members is impracticable, there are questions of law or fact common to the class, the claims or defenses or the representative parties are typical of the claims or defenses of the class, and the agent of the class will fairly and adequately protect the interests of the class. The prosecution of separate actions by individual members of the class would create a risk of inconsistent or varying adjudications with respect to individual members of the class which would create the risk of inconsistent national law and the defendant has acted or refused to act on grounds generally applicable to the class, thereby making appropriate relief with respect to the class as a whole.

The class includes, but is not limited to, all citizens of the United States that have (1) instituted an action against the United States and in that action the United States successfully defended against the action because of the doctrine of sovereign immunity, or (2) had a petition for a writ of certerori denied by the Supreme Court of the United States since 1925.

JURISDICITON

This Court maintains jurisdiction pursuant to 28 U.S.C. § 1331.

VENUE

Venue is proper in this Court pursuant to the provisions of 28 U.S.C. § 1391.

I

1. Plaintiff is an adult citizen of the Commonwealth of Virginia and the United States of America.
2. Plaintiff filed a complaint for a preliminary restraining order and for a temporary and permanent injunction naming the Attorney General of the United States (in her official capacity) as defendant.
3. The Attorney General of the United States asserted the doctrine of sovereign immunity as a defense to Plaintiff's complaint.
4. Plaintiff's complaint was dismissed with prejudice because of the doctrine of sovereign immunity.
5. The doctrine of sovereign immunity, insofar as the Federal Government asserts the defense against citizens of the United States, is repugnant to the First and Tenth Amendments to the Constitution of the United States.
6. Plaintiff, and others similarly situated, have suffered injury in fact as a result of the doctrine of sovereign immunity being asserted by the Federal Government.

II

7. Plaintiff filed a petition for a writ of certiorari in the Supreme Court of the United States.

8. Plaintiff asserts in his petition for a writ of certiorari that courts inferior to the Supreme Court issued decisions in his case that conflict with decisions issued by the Supreme Court.

9. Plaintiff's petition for a writ of certiorari is without opposition.

10. Plaintiff's petition for a writ of certiorari was denied.

11. The Supreme Court's denial of Plaintiff's petition for a writ of certiorari is based on the authority granted by an act or acts that are repugnant to the Constitution of the United States.

12. The Supreme Court's denial of Plaintiff's petition for a writ of certiorari denied Plaintiff rights secured to him by the Federal Constitution.

13. Plaintiff, and others similarly situated, have suffered injury in fact as a result of the Supreme Court's refusal to supervise inferior courts.

14. Plaintiff, and others similarly situated, have suffered injury in fact as a result of the Supreme Court's denial of a petition for a writ of certiorari that alleges that inferior courts have issued decisions contrary to the decisions of the Supreme Court.

III

15. The Supreme Court interfered with the operations of the legislative branch during the legislative process involving the Act of February 13, 1925 (also known as the Judiciary Act of 1925), ch. 229, 43 Stat. 936.

16. The Supreme Court may not exercise a legislative function.

17. The Supreme Court may not usurp the legislative function.

18. Congress delegated its legislative powers to the Supreme Court.

19. Congress may not delegate its legislative powers to the Supreme Court.

20. The Act of February 13, 1925, ch. 229, 43 Stat. 936 is repugnant to the Constitution of the United States.

21. Plaintiff's petition for a writ of certiorari would have been an appeal as of right but for the Act of February 13, 1925, ch. 229, 43 Stat. 936.

22. Plaintiff, and others similarly situated, have suffered injury in fact as a result of the Act of February 13, 1925, ch. 229, 43 Stat. 936.

23. The acts and decisions described herein have been applied in such a way as to deny constitutional rights.

24. The acts in question are unconstitutional and void in providing for the discretionary review by the Supreme Court of decisions of inferior Courts that contradict decisions issued by the Supreme Court.

25. The Federal Tort Claims Act abridges the right of the people to petition the Government for a redress of grievances, and therefore, offends the First Amendment to the Constitution of the United States.

26. The acts and decisions described herein are repugnant to the Constitution and offend Article I, and/or Article III, and/or the First Amendment, and/or the Tenth Amendment.

WHEREFORE, plaintiff, and all others similarly situated, pray that the doctrine of sovereign immunity when asserted by the United States as a defense against an action brought by a citizen of the United States, the Federal Tort Claims Act, the Act of February 13, 1925, ch. 229, 43 Stat. 936 (also known as the Judiciary Act of 1925), and the Act of March 3, 1891, ch 517, 26 Stat. 826, and any other laws that grant the Supreme Court of the United States discretion to perform the duties assigned to it in the Constitution of the United States be declared unconstitutional, null, and void and not the law of the land, and all petitions for a writ of certiorari that allege that courts inferior to the Supreme Court of the United States have issued decisions contrary to decisions issued by the Supreme Court of the United States that have been denied be reconsidered, and all petitions for a writ of certiorari that have been denied by the Supreme Court that would have been appeals as of right be reconsidered as appeals as of right, and all cases brought by citizens of the United States against the United States that have been dismissed against the United States because of the United States' sovereign immunity be reinstated, and award Plaintiff fees, costs and expenses.

The citizen appropriately swears to this complaint, so it is the equivalent of an affidavit and, therefore, is evidence.

Next, the Government's motion to dismiss the lawsuit (footnotes have been omitted):

UNITED STATES' MOTION TO DISMISS

This is a declaratory action in which the pro se plaintiff seeks to have well-established statutory and case law declared unconstitutional. Specifically, plaintiff seeks on behalf of an undefined class to have the concept of sovereign immunity abolished, and the Federal Tort Claims Act, the Judiciary Act of 1925 and its predecessor statute, and any other laws that grant the Supreme Court of the United States discretion declared unconstitutional. He further seeks to have substantially all cases for which the Supreme Court has denied certiorari since 1925 — together with all cases ever that have ever dismissed for non-waiver of sovereign immunity — reinstated.

Because the plaintiff has suffered no injury, he lacks the requisite standing to bring this case. Moreover, he fails to assert any basis for jurisdiction, other than 28 U.S.C. § 1331, and fails to cite an applicable waiver of sovereign immunity pursuant to which the Court may adjudicate this action. In fact, he cannot do so, since the government has not waived sovereign immunity in this instance. Accordingly, this Court lacks subject matter jurisdiction and this case should be dismissed.

Background

This action stems from a previous matter in which plaintiff filed a complaint with the New York legal licensing authorities against a Federal Aviation Administration (FAA) attorney, Mary McCarthy. In that complaint, the plaintiff alleged that Ms. McCarthy behaved unethically in some fashion while representing the FAA in a case where the plaintiff, a non-attorney, represented a co-worker before the Merit Service Protection Board (MSPB). When the Department of Justice defended Ms. McCarthy before the licensing board, the plaintiff filed suit to temporarily restrain and preliminarily enjoy it from representing her, although he had no personal stake in either the outcome of the MSPB matter or the outcome of the investigation of Ms. McCarthy by the New York licensing authorities. This court denied the plaintiff's motion, and dismissed the suit with prejudice for lack of subject matter jurisdiction on the grounds that the government had not waived sovereign immunity. The Fourth Circuit Court of Appeals affirmed the ruling and the Supreme Court denied the plaintiff's petition for writ of certiorari.

The United States respectfully contends that this case should be dismissed because the plaintiff lacks standing to bring this action. Plaintiff has sustained no injury, or at the very most, only an abstract injury that does not confer upon him the ability to obtain the sweeping relief he seeks. Moreover, plaintiff's claims are barred since the government has not waived sovereign immunity. Plaintiff does not allege any waiver of sovereign immunity in his complaint, nor would this case fall within the immunity waivers provided in the Federal Tort Claims Act (FTCA), 28 U.S.C. § 1334, 2671, et. seq., the Administrative Procedures Act (APA), 5 U.S.C. § 701, et seq., or the Little Tucker Act, 28 U.S.C. § 1346(a)(2). Thus, this case should be dismissed for lack of subject matter jurisdiction.

Argument

A. Plaintiff Lacks Standing to Bring this Suit

Article III, § 2 of the Constitution, conferred upon federal courts the jurisdiction to hear only matters involving "Cases or Controversies." To satisfy this "case or controversy" requirement, courts have long held that a plaintiff bringing an action in the federal courts must have standing to bring that action. Lujan v. Defenders of Wildlife, 504 U.S. 555, 559-60 (1992). Thus, the doctrine of standing is a central concept in federal jurisprudence and must be considered at the outset of any action to avoid turning the judiciary into a "forum [for the airing of] generalized grievances about the conduct of government" for which the legislative and executive branches are better suited. Flast v. Cohen, 392 U.S. 83, 106 (1968).

The standing doctrine has three essential components: injury, causation and redressability. Marshall v. Meadows, 105 F.3d 904, 906 (4thCir. 1997). In order to have standing in federal court, a plaintiff must show:

> (1) he has suffered an actual or threatened injury, Valley Forge Christian College v. American United for Separation of Church

> and State, 454 U.S. 464, 472 (1982); (2) a causal connection
> between the injury complained of and the challenged action,"
> Simon v. Eastern Kentucky Welfare Rights Organization, 426
> U.S. 26, 41 (1976); and (3) the injury can be redressed by a
> favorable decision, id. At 38, 43.

Marshall at 906. See also Lujan, 504 U.S. at 560.

In this case, the plaintiff cannot satisfy any of these elements. The sole "injury" that the plaintiff alleges is the dismissal of his previous case because the government had not waived sovereign immunity. Complaint at ¶ 6. He further implies, without benefit of any specific evidence to support his implication, that had that dismissal not been affirmed by the Fourth Circuit Court of Appeals and had the Supreme Court not denied his petition for certiorari, he would otherwise have prevailed on the merits of his case. However, the plaintiff cannot show that he would have won his appeal but for the doctrine of sovereign immunity. Moreover, he cannot show that he was harmed in any way by the Supreme Court's denial of his petition for certiorari. Further, he has not alleged, nor can he show, that any other person he seeks to represent as part of a class action was in fact injured as a result of sovereign immunity being asserted in their cases, or by a denial of certiorari by the Supreme Court. As such, any injury that plaintiff or the class that he seeks to represent has incurred is merely abstract or hypothetical.

However, an abstract injury is insufficient to confer standing upon a litigant. In Schlesinger v. Reservists Committee to Stop the War, 418 U.S. 208 (1974), the Supreme Court held that an organization of current and former military members lacked standing as citizens to bring a class action against the Secretary of Defense in order to strike Members of Congress from the military Reserve rolls, to secure a permanent injunction, and to reclaim all pay that the Members had received while in the Reserves.

> The very language of respondent's complaint . . . reveals
> that it is nothing more than a matter of speculation whether
> the claimed nonobservance of that Clause deprives citizens
> of the faithful discharge of the legislative duties of reservist
> Members of Congress. And that claimed nonobservance,
> standing alone, would adversely affect only the generalized

interest of all citizens in constitutional governance, and that
is an abstract injury.

418 U.S. at 217 (emphasis added).

Here, the plaintiff seeks to have this Court declare that the
doctrine of sovereign immunity and the ability of the Supreme Court
to grant or deny petitions for certiorari are unconstitutional, without
ever showing that he or the class is directly harmed. This is exactly
the type of claim the court in Schlesinger determined was barred
from being heard in federal court.

However, even if plaintiff could show some type of attenuated
injury to satisfy the first element of the standing requirements, he
utterly fails to show any causation or redressability. Without a
showing that he would have prevailed had his case not been barred
by sovereign immunity or had the Supreme Court considered it, the
plaintiff cannot show that his alleged injury was in fact caused by the
allegedly unconstitutional practice of writ of certiorari or the doctrine
of sovereign immunity. See Simon v. Eastern Kentucky Welfare
Rights Organization, Inc., 426 U.S. at 42-3 (no standing where "it
is purely speculative whether the denials of service specified in
the complaint fairly can be traced to [the governmental action at
issue].").

Further, plaintiff's alleged injury cannot be redressed by the
remedy he seeks in this case. The remedy he seeks is to have the
Supreme Court hear his case. Even if it were to do so and if it were
to rule in favor of the plaintiff, there would be no remedy. In that
action, plaintiff sought to keep the government from representing
Ms. McCarthy before the state licensing authorities in a grievance
matter that plaintiff had filed. That grievance matter has now been
concluded.

In Steel Company v. Citizens for a Better Environment, ___ U.S.
___, 118 S.Ct. 1003 (1998), an association of individuals interested
in environmental protection sued a small manufacturing company
under the Emergency Planning and Community Right-to-Know Act
of 1986 (EPCRA), alleging the manufacturing company had failed to
filed requisite environmental release and hazardous chemical forms.
The association relied upon a provision of EPCRA that provided
that any citizen could bring suit to enforce the act provided certain

procedures were met. However, the Supreme Court determined that the association did not have standing to bring the suit because "[n]one of the specific items of relief sought, and none that we can envision as 'appropriate' under the general request would serve to reimburse respondent for losses caused by the late reporting." Id. at ___, 118 S.Ct. at 1018. The Court further found that the civil penalties provided by statute would not be payable to the association, but would instead be payable to the U.S. Treasury, so by requesting the penalties, the association was not seeking remediation of its own injury, but "vindication of the rule of law — the 'undifferentiated public interest' in faithful execution of EPCRA." Id. citing Lujan, supra.

> This will not suffice. . . . it is [not] enough that respondent will be fratified by seeing petitioner punished for its infractions and that the punishment will deter the risk of future harm. . . . By the mere bringing of his suit, every plaintiff demonstrates his belief that a favorable judgment will make him happier. But although a suitor may derive great comfort and joy from the fact that the United States Treasury is not cheated, that a wrongdoer gets his just deserts, or that the nation's law are faithfully enforced, that psychic satisfaction is not an acceptable Article III remedy because it does not redress a cognizable Article III injury.

Id. at ___, 118 S.Ct. 1018-19. In the instant case, plaintiff has suffered no cognizable Article III injury. The remedy he seeks will not remediate his own injury: the New York licensing authorities have already heard and decided his grievance against Ms. McCarthy. Instead, the only benefit the plaintiff could achieve is the gratification that he won. Gratification alone does not remedy the alleged injury. "Relief that does not remedy the injury suffered cannot bootstrap a plaintiff into federal court: that is the very essence of the redressabilty requirement." Id. at ___, 118 S.Ct. 1019. Thus, this Court is unable to redress any of his grievances, and plaintiff lacks standing to bring this suit.

B. There is No Waiver of Sovereign Immunity Pursuant to Which Plaintiff May Bring this Suit.

1. Waivers of Sovereign Immunity Are Strictly Construed

Notwithstanding plaintiff's protestations that the doctrine of sovereign immunity is repugnant to the First and Tenth Amendments to the Constitution of the United States, Complaint at I.5., it is the law of the land. The doctrine of sovereign immunity pre-dates the Constitution, and was affirmed in the earliest Supreme Court cases. Chisholm v. Georgia, 2 U.S. (2 Dall.) 419, 1 L.Ed. 440 (1793). The doctrine has been continuously upheld on logical and practical grounds as well. See, Kawananakoa v. Polyblank, 205 U.S. 349 (1907); United States v. Mitchell, 445 U.S. 535 (1980).

The consent of the United States to be sued cannot be implied, but must be unequivocally expressed and strictly construed. United States v. Testan, 424 U.S. 392, 399 (1976); Mitchell, 445 U.S. at 538; United States v. Nordic Village, 503 U.S. 30 (1992); Lane v. Pena, 518 U.S. 187 (1996). If such consent is found, it is strictly construed against the person seeking to sue the government. Research Triangle Institute v. Board of Governors of the Federal Reserve System, 132 F.3d 985 (4thCir. 1997). In Research Triangle, the Fourth Circuit held that the general rule in all such cases is that "with regard to the federal government and its instrumentalities, sovereign immunity is presumed . . . any statutory waiver is strictly construed, with all ambiguities resolved in favor of the sovereign." Id. at 987.

Congress has the constitutional right to condition its waiver of immunity in any way it pleases. United States v. Sherwood, 312 U.S. 584, 586 (1941) ("the terms of [Congress'] consent to be sued in any court define the court's jurisdiction to entertain that suit."). Accordingly, even after a plaintiff has overcome the presumption of sovereign immunity and found an express Congressional waiver, he must strictly adhere to any and all conditions and procedures that Congress deems fit to attach to the waiver. Id.

2. Plaintiff Fails to State an FTCA Claim

There are several statutes under which a plaintiff may sue the United States. One of the most widely invoked is the Federal Torts Claims Act (FTCA), 28 U.S.C. § 1346. 2671, et. seq., which provides a limited waiver of sovereign immunity. United States v. Orleans,

425 U.S. 807 (1976). In enacting the FTCA, Congress consented to liability for:

> money damages, accruing on and after January 1, 1945, for injury or loss of property, or personal injury or death caused by the negligent or wrongful act or omission of any employee of the Government while acting within the scope of his office or employment, under circumstances where the United States, if a private person, would be liable to the claimant in accordance with the law of the place where the act or omission occurred.

28 U.S.C. § 1346(b). Thus, Congress waived sovereign immunity under the FTCA only for (i) money damages (ii) for injury or loss of property (iii) caused by the negligent or wrongful acts or omissions of a federal employee acting within the course or scope of his employment; and (iv) the act or omission constituted a violation of the law of the state within which the act or omission occurred. In the instant case, none of these elements are met. Id.

Plaintiff does not seek monetary damages in this litigation. Moreover, he does not claim an injury to his person or any loss of property. He does not allege that the injuries that he claims he has suffered were caused by the negligent or wrongful acts or omissions of a federal employee. And, the court's dismissing his case based upon sovereign immunity and the Supreme Court's denial of his petition of certiorari in no way constitutes a violation of Virginia, or any other state, law. Thus, plaintiff cannot show what there has been a waiver of sovereign immunity under the FTCA.

3.   Plaintiff Fails to State an APA Claim

The Administrative Procedure Act (APA), 5 U.S.C. § 702, authorizes a plaintiff to sue the United States for "relief other than money damages." Although Plaintiff seeks declaratory relief in this action, he does not state a cause of action which could be properly brought under the APA. Section 702 only authorizes a suit when a plaintiff has "suffered legal wrong because of agency action or [been] adversely affected by agency action within the meaning of a relevant statute. . . ." Plaintiff complains that the harm he suffered is a result of Congress's passing statutes and the courts dismissing, or refusing to consider, his case in accordance with those statutes. However, neither Congress or the Supreme Court are "agencies" within the meaning of the APA. Sections 551(1) and 701(b)(1) of the APA state that "agency . . . does not include (A) Congress; [or] (B) the courts of the United States. . . ." See J.H. Miles & Co. v. Brown, 910 F.Supp. 1138 (E.D.Va. 1995). Thus, because there has been no agency action to review, the APA does not apply.

    4. Plaintiff Fails to State a Little Tucker Act Claim.

28 U.S.C. § 1346(a)(2), also known as the Little Tucker Act, provides a waiver of sovereign immunity for district courts to hear lawsuits for:

> [a]ny other civil action or claim against the United States, not exceeding $10,000 in amount, founded upon the Constitution, or any Act of Congress, or any regulation of an executive department, or any express or implied contract with the United States . . .

Id. However, "the [Little Tucker] Act has long been construed as authorizing only actions for monetary judgments and not suits for equitable relief against the United States". Richardson v. Morris, 409 U.S. 464-65 (1971) citing United States v. Jones, 131 U.S. 1 (1889). See also, Bowen v. Massachusetts, 487 U.S. 879 (1988); Randall v. United States, 95 F.3d 339 (4th Cir. 1996).

    In the instant case, plaintiff has only sought equitable relief. He has not sought monetary damages. Therefore, he cannot bring this claim under the Little Tucker Act.

C. The Doctrine of Sovereign Immunity and the Acts of Congress of Which Plaintiff Complains are Constitutional.

    Even assuming, arguendo, that the plaintiff has standing to bring this case, and assuming that he can identify some statute that waives sovereign immunity and granting this court subject matter jurisdiction, plaintiff's case still fails on it merits. As previously mentioned, the doctrine of sovereign immunity was affirmed in the earliest Supreme Court cases. Chisholm v. Georgia, 2 U.S. (2 Dall.) 419, 1 L.Ed. 440 (1793). Moreover, the doctrine has been continuously upheld. See, Kawananakoa v. Polyblank, 205 U.S. 349 (1907), United States v. Mitchell, 445 U.S. 535 (1980).

In addition, the certiorari process is constitutional as well. The Constitution provides: "[I]n all [cases arising under the Constitution or under the Laws of the United States] the supreme Court shall have appellate Jurisdiction as to Law and Fact, with such Exceptions, and under such Regulations as Congress shall make." Article III, Section 2 (emphasis added). Congress excepted certain cases from the appellate process pursuant to this constitutional provision when it passed the Judiciary Act of 1925, as well as its predecessor statute. Congress's actions in limiting the cases that were required to be heard by the Supreme Court were thus within the limitations that the framers of the Constitution envisioned.

Finally, 28 U.S.C. 1651(a) states that "[t]he Supreme Court, and all courts established by Act of Congress, may issue all writs necessary or appropriate in aid of their respective jurisdictions and agreeable to the usages and principles of law." This language has been held to include the writ of certiorari. United States Alkali Export Association v. California Alkali Export Association, 325 U.S. 196 (1945). Thus, the certiorari process is constitutional.

Conclusion

For the reasons set forth above, this Court should dismiss this case with prejudice.

The Government's motion **IS NOT** sworn to and therefore it is not evidence.

Now, the citizen's response to the Government's motion to dismiss:

PLAINTIFF'S RESPONSE TO UNITED STATES' MOTION TO DISMISS

Defendant's counsel argues that plaintiff needs to (1) assert a basis for jurisdiction other than 28 U.S.C. § 1331 and (2) cite an applicable waiver of sovereign immunity. The instant case alleges that certain federal statutes and the doctrine of sovereign immunity, insofar as the Federal Government is permitted to assert the defense of sovereign immunity against an action by a citizen of the United States, are unconstitutional. Therefore, 28 U.S.C. § 1331, which grants federal courts jurisdiction over claims founded upon the Federal Constitution, is the only basis that need be asserted for jurisdiction. A citation to an applicable waiver of sovereign immunity is not obligatory in the case at bar because the Federal Government may not assert the defense of sovereign immunity in an action that alleges federal statutes or federal conduct is unconstitutional. Whether the statutory law is well-established is not a relevant consideration when addressing the issue of the statutory law's constitutionality.

Defendant's counsel also argues that plaintiff lacks standing to bring this suit and plaintiff must show (1) he has suffered an actual or threatened injury, (2) a causal connection between the injury complained of and the challenged action, and (3) the injury can be redressed by a favorable decision. Plaintiff has satisfied each of these components in the complaint. Complaint at ¶ 1, 6, 13, 14, 22, 23, and 25. Further, any time the United States Government acts contrary to the Constitution of the United States, we the people have the constitutional right, indeed the duty, to correct unconstitutional government. A citizen's right to correct unconstitutional government is a right retained under Amendments I and IX of the Constitution of the United States.

Defendant's counsel nakedly and contradictorily asserts, in the unsworn and unsupported memorandum of points and authorities in support of defendant's motion to dismiss, that the sole injury that the plaintiff alleges is the dismissal of his previous case because the government had not waived sovereign immunity and that plaintiff has suffered no injury, or at the very most, only an abstract injury. The complaint, in ¶¶ 13, 14, and 22, clearly alleges injuries. Plaintiff's complaint, that is the equivalent of an affidavit because the complaint is verified in accordance with 28 U.S.C. § 1746, alleges in paragraphs 6, 13, 14, and 22 that plaintiff and others similarly situated have suffered injury in fact. Plaintiff need not prove any injury at this time because defendant's counsel's assertions are nothing more than unsupported conjecture. Further, the liberal pleading requirements of Rule 8 of the Federal Rules of Civil Procedure do not require plaintiff to prove anything in the complaint. Legions of case law find the complaint sufficient opposition to an unsupported motion.

Government counsel assumes too much and has no support for any of the naked assertions. Defendant's counsel incorrectly assumes that the instant case is based entirely on a previous matter regarding

Mary McCarthy and the New York legal licensing authorities and that plaintiff filed a petition for writ of certiorari in the Mary McCarthy matter. Government counsel attempts to support her erroneous assumptions with a citation to 118 S.Ct. 171 in footnote 3 on page 2 of the memorandum of points and authorities. The instant case is not based entirely on the McCarthy matter and plaintiff did not file a petition for writ of certiorari in the McCarthy matter. The allegation, in paragraph 7 of the complaint, that the Supreme Court denied plaintiff's petition for writ of certiorari concerned a matter that in no way involves McCarthy. If defendant's counsel had performed an inquiry reasonable under the circumstances, then defendant's counsel would know that the caption of the case in the McCarthy matter is Wright v. Reno. The caption of the case cited at 118 S.Ct. 171 is not Wright v. Reno.

Government counsel asserts that if the Supreme Court were to hear plaintiff's previous case and if it were to rule in favor of the plaintiff, there would be no remedy. However, if, in fact, the Supreme Court were to hear plaintiff's previous case and if it were to rule in favor of the plaintiff, the remedy could be an award of **$4,800,000.00, back pay with interest, attorney's fees, disbursements and costs, medical fees, lost benefits, promotion, differentials, and overtime**. These remedies will suffice to remediate plaintiff's injuries.

Defendant's position seems to be that the doctrine of sovereign immunity can be unconstitutional under the First and Tenth Amendments to the Constitution of the United States and it can also be the law of the land. Nothing that is repugnant to the Constitution of the United States can be the law of the land. The fact that the doctrine of sovereign immunity predates the Federal Constitution is irrelevant. The allegation in the complaint is not the date that the doctrine of sovereign immunity began, but that the doctrine of sovereign immunity, insofar as the Federal Government is permitted to assert the defense of sovereign immunity against an action by a citizen of the United States, is unconstitutional.

Defendant argues that Congress may exclude certain cases from the appellate jurisdiction of the Supreme Court and relies on Article III, Section 2 of the Federal Constitution. Plaintiff agrees that Article III, Section 2 of the Federal Constitution empowers Congress exclude certain classes of cases from the appellate jurisdiction of the supreme Court. Defendant argues that the Supreme Court has jurisdiction to issue a writ of certiorari in a case that has been excluded from the jurisdiction of the Supreme Court. Plaintiff disagrees that the Supreme Court has authority to issue a writ in any case in which it does not have any jurisdiction. If a case has been excluded from the Supreme Court's appellate jurisdiction, then the Supreme Court does not have any authority to entertain the matter at all. It may not issue a writ in a matter in which it does not have jurisdiction. If the Supreme Court can issue a writ of certiorari, then it has jurisdiction and if it has jurisdiction the case cannot have been excluded from the jurisdiction of the Supreme Court.

The government's motion to dismiss fails to address the allegation, under III in the complaint, that the Supreme Court and Congress violated the separation of powers. Therefore, the Judiciary Act of 1925 is unconstitutional. This case may not be dismissed for a lack of subject matter jurisdiction.

This action is about statutes or doctrines being unconstitutional. Government counsel has put forth many arguments and the only argument that government counsel seems to have missed is that the doctrine or statutes that the complaint alleges are unconstitutional are not, in fact, unconstitutional. Not one case has been cited that establishes the constitutionality of the doctrine or statues that the complaint alleges are unconstitutional. The arguments advanced by government counsel simply request this court to permit the Federal Government to continue its unconstitutional conduct. None of the arguments put forth by government counsel are for the benefit of the people or in support of the Constitution. Government counsel is reminded of the oath taken, upon entering federal government service, to uphold the Constitution of the United States.

For the foregoing reasons, this Court has jurisdiction over the subject matter in the instant case and the defendant's motion to dismiss should be denied.

The citizen appropriately swears to the response to the Government's motion, so the citizen's response is the equivalent of an affidavit and, therefore, is evidence. The text of Judge Claude M. Hilton's (district court judge) decision dismissing the case follows (footnotes have been omitted):

MEMORANDUM OPINION

This matter came before the Court on Defendant's motion to dismiss. **This action stems from a previous matter in which Plaintiff filed a complaint with the New York legal licensing authorities against a Federal Aviation Administration (FAA) attorney, Mary McCarthy. In that complaint, Plaintiff alleged that McCarthy behaved unethically in some fashion while representing the FAA in a case where the Plaintiff, a non-attorney, represented a co-worker before the Merit Service Protection Board (MSPB). When the Department of Justice defended McCarthy before the licensing board, Plaintiff filed suit to temporarily restrain and preliminarily enjoy it from representing her, although he had no personal stake in either the outcome of the MSPB matter or the outcome of the investigation of McCarthy by the New York licensing authorities. This court denied Plaintiff's motion and dismissed the suit with prejudice for lack of subject matter jurisdiction on the grounds that the government had not waived sovereign immunity. The Fourth Circuit Court of Appeals affirmed the ruling.**

Plaintiff lacks standing to bring this suit. Article III, § 2 of the Constitution, conferred upon federal courts the jurisdiction to hear only matters involving cases or controversies. To satisfy this "case or controversy" requirement, courts have long held that a plaintiff bringing an action in the federal courts must have standing to bring that action. See Lujan v. Defenders of Wildlife, 504 U.S. 555, 559-60 (1992). The standing doctrine has three essential components: injury, causation and damages. See Marshall v. Meadows, 105 F.3d 904, 906 (4thCir. 1997).

In this case, Plaintiff cannot satisfy any of these elements. **The sole injury that Plaintiff alleges is the dismissal of his previous case because the government had not waived sovereign immunity.** Merely alleging that Plaintiff has been injured is insufficient to confer standing. The alleged injuries must be concrete and actual or imminent, not conjectural or hypothetical. See Steel Co. v. Citizens for a Better Environment, 118 S.Ct. 1103, 1016 (1998).

Plaintiff implies **that had the dismissal not been affirmed by the Fourth Circuit, he would otherwise have prevailed on the merits. However, Plaintiff cannot show he would have won his appeal but for the doctrine of sovereign immunity. Moreover, he cannot show that he was harmed in any way by the Supreme Court's denial of his petition for certiorari. Further, he has not alleged, nor can he show, that any other person he seeks to represent as part of a class action was in fact injured as a result of sovereign immunity being asserted in their cases. As such, any injury that** Plaintiff **or the class that he seeks to represent has incurred is merely abstract or hypothetical. However, an abstract injury is insufficient to confer standing upon a litigant.** See **Schlesinger v. Reservists Committee to Stop the War, 418 U.S. 208 (1974).**

Even if Plaintiff could show some type of attenuated injury to satisfy the first element of the standing requirements, Plaintiff **fails to show any causation or redressability**. Plaintiff has failed to establish a fairly traceable connection between his alleged injury and the government's actions, thus failing the second standing requirement. See Steel Co., 118 S.Ct. at 1016. Without a showing that he would have prevailed had his case not been barred by sovereign immunity, Plaintiff cannot show that his alleged injury was caused by the allegedly unconstitutional practice of writ of certiorari or the doctrine of sovereign immunity. See Simon v. Eastern Kentucky Welfare Rights Organization, Inc., 426 U.S. at 42-3.

There is no waiver of sovereign immunity pursuant to which Plaintiff may bring this suit. Waivers of sovereign immunity are strictly construed. The consent of the United States to be sued cannot be implied, but must be unequivocally expressed and strictly construed. See United States v. Testan, 424 U.S. 392, 299 (1976). If such consent is found, it is strictly construed against the person seeking to sue the government. See Research Triangle Institute v. Board of Governors of the Federal Reserve System, 132 F.3d 985 (4thCir. 1997).

Congress has the constitutional right to condition its waiver of immunity in any way it pleases. See <u>United States v. Sherwood</u>, 312 U.S. 584, 586 (1941). Accordingly, even after a plaintiff has overcome the presumption of sovereign immunity and found an express Congressional waiver, he must strictly adhere to any and all conditions and procedures that Congress deems fit to attach to the waiver. See id.

There are several statutes under which a plaintiff may sue the United States. One of the most widely invoked is the Federal Torts Claims Act (FTCA) which provides a limited waiver of sovereign immunity. See <u>United States v. Orleans</u>, 425 U.S. 807 (1976). Congress waived sovereign immunity under the FTCA only for (1) money damages (2) for injury or loss of property (3) caused by the negligent or wrongful acts or omissions of a federal employee acting within the course or scope of his employment; and (4) the act or omission constituted a violation of the law of the state within which the act or omission occurred.

Plaintiff does not seek monetary damages in this litigation. He does not claim an injury to his person or any loss of property. He does not allege that the injuries that he claims he has suffered were caused by the negligent or wrongful acts or omissions of a federal employee. Finally, the court's dismissing his case based upon sovereign immunity in no way constitutes a violation of Virginia or any other state law. Thus, Plaintiff cannot show what there has been a waive of sovereign immunity under the FTCA.

The administrative Procedure Act (APA), 5 U.S.C. §702, authorizes a plaintiff to sue the United States for relief other than money damages. Although Plaintiff seeks declaratory relief in this action, he does not state a cause of action which could be properly brought under the APA. Section 702 only authorizes a suit when a plaintiff has suffered legal wrong because of agency action or has been adversely affected by agency action within the meaning of a relevant statute. Plaintiff complains that the harm he suffered is a result of Congress's passing statutes and the Court's refusing to consider his case in accordance with those statutes. However, neither Congress or the Supreme Court are agencies within the meaning of the APA. <u>See</u> Sections 551(1) and

701(b)(1); J.H. Miles & Co. v. Brown, 910 F.Supp. 1138 (E.D.Va. 1995). Thus, because **there has been no agency action to review, the APA does not apply**.

Finally, Plaintiff fails to state a Little Tucker Act claim. 28 U.S.C. § 1346(a)(2). The Little Tucker Act provides a waiver of sovereign immunity for district courts to hear lawsuits for:

> [a]ny other civil action or claim against the United States, not exceeding $10,000 in amount, founded upon the Constitution, or any Act of Congress, or any regulation of an executive department, or any express or implied contract with the United States . . .

Id. However, the Act has long been construed as authorizing only actions for monetary judgments and not suits for equitable relief against the United States. **See** Richardson v. Morris, **409 U.S. 464, 464-5 (1971). In the instant case, Plaintiff has only sought equitable relief. He has not sought monetary damages. Therefore, he cannot bring this claim under the Little Tucker Act**.

For the above-stated reasons, Defendant's motion to dismiss is granted. An appropriate order shall issue."

Judge Hilton's actual decision does not contain any bold print. The portions above are shown in bold print to show that those portions of Judge Hilton's decision come word for word from the Government's motion to dismiss filed by Sharon L. Parrish, Special Assistant U. S. Attorney.

Lastly, here is the decision from the Court of Appeals:

No. 98-2021

Before Judges Niemeyer, Hamilton, and Butzner

Affirmed by unpublished per curiam opinion.

"Appellant appeals the district court's order dismissing his civil action against the United States. We have reviewed the record and the district court's opinion and find no reversible error. Accordingly, we affirm on the reasoning of the district court."

Here are the important points. **FIRST**, neither Judge Hilton nor Special Assistant U.S. Attorney Parrish can possibly know (1) whether the plaintiff in this case is an attorney because the plaintiff never told the court whether the plaintiff is an attorney (and I haven't figured out what difference it would make if the plaintiff is or is not an attorney, but it must be of some significance to Judge Hilton because Judge Hilton included it in his decision). **SECOND**, neither Judge Hilton nor Special Assistant U.S. Attorney Parrish can possibly know what the plaintiff can and cannot show because plaintiff was never given the opportunity to show anything! **THIRD**, Judge Hilton, obviously, ignored the only evidence that he had before him. That evidence consists of the statements contained in the **COMPLAINT** and **PLAINTIFF'S RESPONSE TO UNITED STATES' MOTION TO DISMISS**. Remember, those are the only documents that are sworn to. The court records do not contain any evidence from the Government or Assistant U.S. Attorney Parrish to support anything that Sharon L. Parrish put forth in her argument to Judge Hilton!! Judge Hilton simply ignored the citizen's evidence and then purposefully echoed the notions of Assistant U.S. Attorney Sharon L. Parrish! Judges are supposed to be unbiased, aren't they??? Yea, they are! They take an oath to administer justice and to discharge their duties faithfully and **impartially**.

If Judge Hilton is impartial and based his decision on the **evidence** before him, then he could not have decided that:

(1) this matter stems from a previous matter in which plaintiff filed a complaint with the New York legal licensing authorities against a Federal Aviation Administration (FAA) attorney, Mary McCarthy because the complaint specifically says that "This action arises under the Constitution of the United States, Article I, Article III, the First Amendment, and the Tenth Amendment" and the response to the Government's motion says "Defendant's counsel incorrectly assumes that the instant case is based entirely on a previous matter regarding Mary McCarthy and the New York legal licensing authorities and that plaintiff filed a petition for writ

of certiorari in the Mary McCarthy matter. Government counsel attempts to support her erroneous assumptions with a citation to 118 S.Ct. 171 in footnote 3 on page 2 of the memorandum of points and authorities. The instant case is not based entirely on the McCarthy matter and plaintiff did not file a petition for writ of certiorari in the McCarthy matter. The allegation, in paragraph 7 of the complaint, that the Supreme Court denied plaintiff's petition for writ of certiorari concerned a matter that in no way involves McCarthy."

(2) "the sole injury that plaintiff alleges is the dismissal of his previous case because the government had not waived sovereign immunity" because the complaint specifically says "This is a class complaint. The class is so numerous that joinder of all members is impracticable, there are questions of law or fact common to the class, the claims or defenses or the representative parties are typical of the claims or defenses of the class," and "The doctrine of sovereign immunity, insofar as the Federal Government asserts the defense against citizens of the United States, is repugnant to the First and Tenth Amendments to the Constitution of the United States. Plaintiff, and others similarly situated, have suffered injury in fact as a result of the doctrine of sovereign immunity being asserted by the Federal Government" and "The Supreme Court's denial of Plaintiff's petition for a writ of certiorari is based on the authority granted by an act or acts that are repugnant to the Constitution of the United States. The Supreme Court's denial of Plaintiff's petition for a writ of certiorari denied Plaintiff rights secured to him by the Federal Constitution. Plaintiff, and others similarly situated, have suffered injury in fact as a result of the Supreme Court's refusal to supervise inferior courts. Plaintiff, and others similarly situated, have suffered injury in fact as a result of the Supreme Court's denial of a petition for a writ of certiorari that alleges that inferior courts have issued decisions contrary to the decisions of the Supreme Court." and "Plaintiff's petition for a writ of certiorari would have been an appeal as of right but for the Act of February 13, 1925, ch. 229, 43 Stat. 936. Plaintiff, and others similarly situated, have suffered injury in fact as a result of the Act of February 13, 1925, ch. 229, 43

Stat. 936. The acts and decisions described herein have been applied in such a way as to deny constitutional rights." Further, the response to the Government's motion says "Defendant's counsel nakedly and contradictorily asserts, in the unsworn and unsupported memorandum of points and authorities in support of defendant's motion to dismiss, that the sole injury that the plaintiff alleges is the dismissal of his previous case because the government had not waived sovereign immunity and that plaintiff has suffered no injury, or at the very most, only an abstract injury. The complaint, in ¶¶ 13, 14, and 22, clearly alleges injuries."

(3) plaintiff cannot show he would have won his appeal but for the doctrine of sovereign immunity because (in addition to it being impossible to see into the future, therefore, this is an impossible standard for a judge to require!) there is no evidence before Judge Hilton on which he can base this decision.

(4) plaintiff cannot show that he was harmed in any way by the Supreme Court's denial of his petition for certiorari because (once again it is impossible for Judge Hilton to see into the future for this one either!) there is no evidence before Judge Hilton on which he can base this decision.

(5) plaintiff has not alleged, nor can he show, that any other person he seeks to represent as part of a class action was in fact injured as a result of sovereign immunity being asserted in their cases because the complaint does allege that other persons have been injured. The complaint says "Plaintiff, and others similarly situated, have suffered injury in fact as a result of the doctrine of sovereign immunity being asserted by the Federal Government."

The lawsuit contains allegations listed under the Roman Numeral 3. Judge Hilton's decision fails to address any of the allegations under Roman Numeral 3 in the complaint! If Judge Hilton graduated from any law school (we will assume for the sake of this discussion that he has), then he must know that when a lawsuit alleges that something is unconstitutional the issue is whether the "thing" that is alleged to be unconstitutional is, in fact, unconstitutional. You don't have to be a graduate of a law school, but you do need some good old common sense to know that the Government may not use sovereign immunity to defend against a lawsuit that alleges that sovereign immunity is unconstitutional. Obviously, the Government can in Judge Hilton's court!! We have another judge to add to the list of judges to be removed!

If Court of Appeals Judges Niemeyer, Hamilton, and Butzner actually reviewed the record as their decision claims, then they would have found all the points that you and I just found, and we aren't appellate court judges! Hey, maybe we should be!! Anyway, they would know that the record does not contain any evidence to support Judge Hilton's decision and they would know also that they could not possibly affirm Judge Hilton's decision based on Judge Hilton's reasoning. The statements in Judge Hilton's decision are either a suspicion or a conclusion (for example, plaintiff lacks standing to bring this suit [conclusion]; the sole injury that plaintiff alleges is the dismissal of his previous case because the government had not waived sovereign immunity [conclusion]; plaintiff cannot show he would have won his appeal but for the doctrine of sovereign immunity [suspicion]; he cannot show that he was harmed in any way by the Supreme Court's denial of his petition for certiorari [suspicion]; nor can he show, that any other person he seeks to represent as part of a class action was in fact injured as a result of sovereign immunity being asserted in their cases [suspicion]) without any reasoning to support them. We can now add three more lying judges to that removal list.

I could go on and on and point out obvious mistake after obvious mistake, but this horse is dead. No need to beat it any further! As you can see for yourself, the facts show that (1) either Judge Hilton does not have a clue about the law, (2) there is collusion between Judge Hilton and the U.S. Attorney's Office, (3) the three judges at the Court of Appeals don't have a clue about the law or their job, (4) the three judges at the Court of Appeals lied and they did not review the record, or (5) the three judges at the Court of Appeals are biased toward the Government. No matter which one is applicable, the facts show that citizens were denied their constitutional rights and four Federal judges have no business being judges! The Constitution provides Congress with the means to remove these judges. However, Congress permits judges such as these to remain judges. And for who's benefit? Can't possibly be for the benefit of the People!!

MORE UNCONSTITUTIONAL PROTECTION FOR THE EXECUTIVE BRANCH

OR

THE DELIBERATIVE-PROCESS PRIVILEGE

Article I of the Constitution

The Congress shall have Power . . . To make all Laws which shall be necessary and proper for carrying into Execution the foregoing Powers, and all other Powers vested by this Constitution in the Government of the United States, or in any Department or Officer thereof.

What is the deliberative-process privilege? During a lawsuit, there is a stage called discovery. Each party gets to ask the other party for information or for evidence. In other words, each party has the opportunity to ask the other party what the other party knows regarding the case or gets to ask the other party to produce a copy of all the evidence the other party has. In a lawsuit against the Government, you can ask the Government to produce all of the documents which show the Government officials involved, what they knew, when they knew it, what they said, etc. Well, federal judges decided that the internal decision making process of the Government needs to be protected in order to safeguard the quality of agency decisions. So, federal judges *invented* the deliberative-process privilege. The Government simply responds to the other party's request for documents or evidence by claiming that the deliberative-process privilege applies to the documents or evidence. The deliberative-process privilege is used by the Government to withhold information or evidence in its possession. Government attorneys use the deliberative-process privilege to inhibit citizens from obtaining redress for the injuries caused by the unconstitutional conduct of Government officials. The deliberative-process privilege is unique to the Government and is not found in the Constitution or based on any law passed by Congress. The following cases contain decisions of federal judges in support of the deliberative-process privilege: NLRB v. Sears, Roebuck & Co., Volume 421 of the United States Reports, page 151; United States v. Board of Educ. of City of Chicago, Volume 610 of the Federal Supplement, page 697; Nadler v. U.S. Dept. of Justice, Volume 955 of the Federal Supplement Second 2d, page 1490.

As discussed earlier, the Constitution vests Congress, and not the federal judges, with the power to decide what laws are necessary for the proper operation, including the internal decision making process, of any Department of the Government. Federal judges cannot substitute themselves for Congress and create the laws they think necessary. Again, federal judges have stepped beyond the power granted in the Constitution and performed the legislative function of creating law. Obviously, the deliberative-process privilege is unconstitutional.

CONGRESS AND THE SUPREME COURT IGNORE THE CHECKS AND BALANCES IN THE CONSTITUTION

OR

THE JUDICIARY ACT OF 1925 IS UNCONSTITUTIONAL

Article I of the Constitution

All legislative Powers herein granted shall be vested in a Congress of the United States, **which shall consist of a Senate and House of Representatives**.

To make all Laws which shall be necessary and proper for carrying into Execution the foregoing Powers, and all other Powers vested by this Constitution in the Government of the United States, or in any Department or Officer thereof.

Article III of the Constitution

The judicial power of the United States, shall be vested in one supreme court, and in such inferior courts as Congress may from time to time ordain and establish.

Article VI of the Constitution

This Constitution, and the Laws of the United States which shall be made in Pursuance thereof; and all Treaties made, or which shall be made, under the Authority of the United States, **shall be the supreme Law of the Land; and the Judges in every State shall be bound thereby**, any Thing in the Constitution or Laws of any State to the Contrary notwithstanding.

We continue our journey and venture deeper into the Supreme Court. In the 1920's, the Justices of the Supreme Court were afraid that the amount of cases brought before the Supreme Court might become more than the Supreme Court could handle, so the Justices brought the matter to the attention of the Judiciary Committees of Congress. Congressional records (Hearing before the Committee on the Judiciary, House of Representatives, 68th Congress, 2nd Session, on H.R. 10479 and Senate Report, No. 362, 68th Congress, 1st Session, Sen. No. 8220) show that:

- Members of Congress suggested that the Justices of the Supreme Court prepare a bill. **THIS WAS MISTAKE #1**.
- The Supreme Court Justices formed a committee and prepared a bill. **THIS WAS MISTAKE #2**.
- The draft of the bill prepared by the Justices of the Supreme Court was introduced into the House and Senate and in hearings held by the House Judiciary Committee. **THIS WAS MISTAKE #3**.
- The Chief Justice of the Supreme Court, instead of a member of Congress, sponsored the legislation. **THIS WAS MISTAKE #4**.
- Senator Cummins, Chairman of the Senate Judiciary Committee, relied on the judicial authorship of the bill. **THIS WAS MISTAKE #5**.
- The Congress clearly understood that the bill was written by the Justices of the Supreme Court and not by members of Congress. Chief Justice Taft and Justices Van Devanter, McReynolds and Sutherland, were afforded the opportunity to render advice and a statement of the Court's views in hearings held on the bill by the House Judiciary Committee. **THIS WAS MISTAKE #6**.
- The Justices sold the bill to the committee by promising to use a sound judicial discretion in deciding which cases they will hear. **THIS WAS MISTAKE #7**.
- The Congress deferred to the prestige of the Supreme Court and its Chief Justice. **THIS WAS MISTAKE #8**.

Quotes from the Statement of William Howard Taft, Chief Justice of the Supreme Court of the United States in the Hearing before the 68th Congress House of Representatives Committee on the Judiciary on March 30, 1922.

"I have been deputed by the Supreme Court *to come here and present to your body this bill*, which, in terms, is a bill to amend the Judicial Code, and to further define the jurisdiction of the circuit courts of appeals, and of the Supreme Court and for other purposes."

"Before I come into the court *a committee had been appointed for its preparation*, consisting of Justice Day, Justice McReynolds, and, I suppose, ex officio, the Chief Justice. It was taken up again and a very careful and very much extended examination of it made by the committee, to which Justice Van Devanter was added. *I suppose we have spent two or three months in its preparation.* The care devoted to it was because of the importance that the court attributed to its passage."

Mr. Michener — "Is it the judgment of each individual member of the Supreme Court that this legislation should be enacted?"

Chief Justice Taft — *"Well, I am told by all the members that I can say that the court is for the bill.* There may be one member — I do not think there are more — who is doubtful about it, or, I should say, doubtful as to its efficacy; but he said to me that I could say the whole court were in favor of the bill. The only question that he has is as how far this will be effective to accomplish all we hope for."

Quotes from the Statement of James C. McReynolds, Associate Justice of the Supreme Court of the United States in the Hearing before the 68th Congress House of Representatives Committee on the Judiciary on December 18, 1924.

I understand that *you asked us to come here and give our views on this bill.*

So *this bill has been framed by the members of the court* that have given the subject special attention with the hope that it would enable the court to eliminate cases of minor importance and devote its attention to things of large importance.

If you will bear in mind the general theory upon which this bill is framed, namely, that cases ought to stop after two Federal courts have passed upon them or after all the State courts have passed upon them, unless they are of particular importance or unless they involve something more than the mere rights of the litigants and concern the public, such as the construction of statutes, the settlement of differences between the different circuit courts of appeal, the settlement of the law upon disputed points, and all that, *you will see why the various provisions have been put in.*

The essence of the legislative authority granted Congress **is the making of laws**. An important part of making a law is the creation of the bill because the bill specifies the details. Congress granted the Justices of the Supreme Court legislative power. The Constitution does not give Congress the authority to grant the Justices of the Supreme Court legislative power. Still, Congress gave the Justices of the Supreme Court what they wanted.

The Framers of the Constitution had the choice of assigning an active share in the process of creating legislation to the Supreme Court, yet they did not do so. The Framers knew of New York's Council of Revision. It had been functioning since 1777. After stating that "laws inconsistent with the spirit of this constitution, or with the public good, may be hastily and unadvisedly passed," the New York State Constitution made the judges of New York part of the law making process by stating that "all bills which have passed the senate and assembly shall, before they become laws," be sent to a Council made up of a majority of judges, "for their revisal and consideration." Pages 21 and 22 of The Records of the Federal Convention of 1787 (edited by Max Farrand 1911) show that during the Federal Convention of 1787, Mr. Randolph proposed a resolution on May 29 that there should be a Council of revision composed of the President and members of the Federal Judiciary. This Council of revision should have authority to examine every act of Congress before it becomes law and that this Council could reject an act of Congress. The Framers of the Constitution did not include this resolution in the Constitution. Therefore, they rejected this proposal and chose not to permit the judges of the Federal Judiciary, including the Justices of the Supreme Court, to render advice concerning pending legislation or to have any part in the making of a law. The Framers did not want the Federal Judiciary involved in writing laws and then ruling on the laws that they wrote!

The Justices of the Supreme Court acknowledge in many decisions that the Justices of the Supreme Court do not have any authority to comment on legislation before the adjudication of a case requires them to do so. Here are some of the Supreme Court cases and the relevant parts:

1885 — Steamship Co. v. Emigration Commissioners, Volume 113 of the United States Reports, page 39, Justice Matthews:

"If, on the other hand, we should assume the plaintiff's case to be within the terms of the statute, we should have to deal with it purely as an hypothesis, and pass upon the constitutionality of an act of Congress as an abstract question. That is not the mode in which this court is accustomed or willing to consider such questions. It has not jurisdiction to pronounce any statute, either of a State or of the United States, void, because irreconcilable with the Constitution, except as it is called upon to adjudge the legal rights of litigants in actual controversies. In the exercise of that jurisdiction, it is bound by two rules, to which it has rigidly adhered, one, never to anticipate a question of constitutional law in advance of the necessity of deciding it; the other never to formulate a rule of constitutional law broader than is required by the precise facts to which it is to be applied. These rules are safe guides to sound judgment. It is the dictate of wisdom to follow them closely and carefully."

1909 — United States v. Evans, Volume 213 of the United States Reports, page 301, Chief Justice Fuller:

"By the constitutions of several of the States the justices of the highest judicial tribunals are obliged to give their opinions on important questions of law upon solemn occasions, when required by either branch of the legislature, or the governor or governor and council, and there are many interesting discussions in the state reports, as well as in articles by the law writers, in respect of such a provision. But no such requirement obtains in Federal jurisprudence. Such a provision was suggested in the Federal Constitutional Convention, but disappeared in the Committee on Detail.

In 1793 President Washington sought to take the opinion of the judges of the Supreme Court of the United States as to various questions arising under our treaties with France, but they declined to respond. Marshall thus speaks of the matter in his Life of Washington: 'About this time it is probable that the difficulties felt by the judges of the Supreme Court in expressing their sentiments on the points referred to them were communicated to the Executive. Considering themselves as merely constituting a legal tribunal for the decision of controversies brought before them in legal form, these gentlemen deemed in improper to enter the field of politics by declaring their opinion on questions not growing out of the case before them.' Story on the Constitution, § 1571."

1911 — Muskrat v. United States, Volume 219 of the United States Reports, page 355, Justice Day:

"In 1793, by direction of the President, Secretary of State Jefferson addressed to the Justices of the Supreme Court a communication soliciting their views upon the question whether their advice to the executive would be available in the solution of important questions of the construction of treaties, laws of nations and laws of the land, which the Secretary said were often presented under circumstances which 'do not give cognizance of them to the tribunals of the country.' The answer to the question was postponed until the subsequent sitting of the Supreme Court, when Chief Justice Jay and his associates answered to President Washington that in consideration of the lines of separation drawn by the Constitution between the three departments of government, and being judges of a court of last resort, afforded strong arguments against the propriety of extrajudicially deciding the questions alluded to, and expressing the view that the power given by the Constitution to the President of calling on heads of departments for opinions 'seems to have been purposely, as well as expressly, united to the executive departments.' Correspondence & Public Papers of John Jay, vol. 3, p. 486.

The subject underwent a complete examination in the case of Gordon v. United States, reported in an appendix to 117 U.S. 697, in which the opinion of Mr. Chief Justice Taney, prepared by him and placed in the hands of the clerk, is published in full. It is said to have been his last judicial utterance, and the whole subject of the nature and extent of the judicial power conferred by the Constitution is treated with great learning and fullness. In that case an act of Congress was held invalid which undertook to confer jurisdiction upon the Court of Claims and thence by appeal to this court, the judgment, however, not to be paid until an appropriation had been estimated therefor by the Secretary of the Treasury; and, as was said by the Chief Justice, the result was that neither court could enforce its judgment by any process, and whether it was to be paid or not depended on the future action of the Secretary of the Treasury and of Congress. 'The Supreme Court,' says the Chief Justice, 'does not owe its existence or its powers to the legislative department of the government. It is created by the Constitution, and represents one of the three great divisions of power in the Government of the United States, to each of which the Constitution has assigned its appropriate duties and powers, and made each independent of the other in performing its appropriate functions. The power conferred on this court is exclusively judicial, and it cannot be required or authorized to exercise any other.'

Concluding his discussion of the subject, the Chief Justice said, after treating of the powers of the different branches of the Government, and laying emphasis upon the independence of the judicial power as established under our Constitution, p. 706: 'These cardinal principles of free government had not only been long established in England, but also in the United States from the time of their earliest colonization, and guided the American people in framing and adopting the present Constitution. And it is the duty of this court to maintain it unimpaired as far as it may have the power. And while it executes firmly all the judicial powers entrusted to it, the court will carefully abstain from exercising any power that is not strictly judicial in its character, and which is not clearly confided to it by the Constitution.' "

1915 — Stearns v. Wood, Volume 236 of the United States Reports, page 78, Justice McReynolds:

"The general orders referred to in the bill do not directly violate or threaten interference with the personal rights of appellant — a Major in the National Guard whose present rank remains undisturbed. He is not therefore in position to question their validity; and certainly he may not demand that we construe orders, acts of Congress, and the Constitution for the information of himself and others, notwithstanding their laudable feeling of deep interest in real controversies, not to discuss abstract propositions."

1931 — White v. Johnson, Volume 282 of the United States Reports, page 373, Justice Roberts:

"This question we need not answer, for the reasons stated as to the two preceding. But it has another fatal defect. An answer would involve merely an examination of the Act and a determination whether on its face it violates the Fifth Amendment. Neither this Court nor the court below is authorized to answer academic questions. The constitutionality of a statute is not drawn into question except in connection with its application to some person, natural or artificial."

1944 — Spector Motor Co. v. McLaughlin, Volume 323 of the United States Reports, page 105, Justice Frankfurter:

" . . . we ought not to pass on questions of constitutionality . . . unless such adjudication is unavoidable."

1945 — Coffman v. Breeze Corporations, Volume 323 of the United States Reports, pages 324-325, Chief Justice Stone:

"In any case, the Court will not pass upon the constitutionality of legislation in a suit which is not adversary, . . . or upon the complaint of one who fails to show that he is injured by its operation, . . . or until it is necessary to do so to preserve the rights of the parties."

1945 — Federation of Labor v. McAdory, Volume 325 of the United States Reports, page 461, Chief Justice Stone:

"This Court is without power to give advisory opinions. It has long been its considered practice not to decide abstract, hypothetical or contingent questions, . . . or to decide any constitutional question in advance of the necessity for its decision, . . . or to formulate a rule of constitutional law broader than is required by the precise facts to which it is to be applied, . . . or to decide any constitutional question except with reference to the particular facts to which it is to be applied."

Some of these decisions are many years before the Judiciary Act of 1925 and some are many years after it. All of these decisions make it clear that the Justices of the Supreme Court do not have the authority to give Congress an advisory opinion concerning the Judiciary Act of 1925. Here is a big kicker! See the decision in the case of Stearns v. Wood in 1915? Notice Justice McReynolds delivered it! He is the very same Justice McReynolds that testified before Congress and gave an advisory opinion on the Judiciary Act of 1925!!

The Constitution does not give Congress the authority to enlarge or diminish the power that the Constitution delegates to the Supreme Court. The congressional records previously mentioned show that Congress, in spite of the Constitution, permitted a committee of Justices of the Supreme Court to draft a bill and that Congress allowed Justices to render an advisory opinion concerning the Judiciary Act of 1925, while the Act was still pending legislation.

Black's Law Dictionary defines *judicial power* as *the authority exercised by that department of government which is charged with declaration of what law is and its construction.* The Supreme Court's judicial power does not include the power to *decide* and *comment* on laws *before* the Supreme Court is called upon to enforce them. The Constitution, in Article I, makes it clear that the task of creating legislation is a task for the elected members of Congress — not for the appointed Justices of the Supreme Court. The framework in the Constitution (1) was intended to separate power so that law making and judicial powers would be in separate hands and (2) prevents the Judicial Branch of the Government from exercising powers delegated to the Legislative Branch.

The Constitution and the facts clearly show that, during the law making process involving the Judiciary Act of 1925, the Justices of the Supreme Court exercised a legislative function when they drafted the bill. When Congress permitted the Justices of the Supreme Court to prepare a bill, Congress substituted the Justices for members of Congress in one of Congress' most important constitutional functions. Confirmation that the Justices of the Supreme Court, not any member of Congress, wrote the bill is found in Chief Justice Taft's testimony before Congress and in his article for the Yale Law Journal. Additional confirmation is found in Associate Justice McReynold's testimony before Congress and in Senate Report No. 362, 68th Congress, 1st Session, Serial No. 8220. In this Senate Report Senator Cummins says "the bill was prepared by a committee of the members of the Supreme Court after a long and careful study of the subject, at the suggestion of the American Bar Association, and has the approval of every member of that Court."

The Justices of the Supreme Court and the members of Congress are bound by the Constitution. The Constitution requires each member of Congress and each Justice of the Supreme Court to take an oath to support the Constitution. Members of Congress acted beyond the bounds of authority granted in the Constitution by permitting the Justices of the Supreme Court to draft the bill and then permitting the Justices of the Supreme Court to comment on the pending legislation. The Justices of the Supreme Court acted beyond the authority granted in the Constitution when they drafted the bill and then commented on the pending legislation. Any law that results from the Justices of the Supreme Court exercising a legislative function is unconstitutional.

In an article for the Yale Law Journal, Vol. XXXV, November 1925, No.1, Mr. William Howard Taft, Chief Justice of the Supreme Court, said "The function of the Supreme Court is conceived to be, not the remedying of a particular litigant's wrong, but the consideration of cases whose decision involves principles, the application of which are of wide public or governmental interest, and which should be authoritatively declared by the final court." Chief Justice Taft wanted to change the function assigned to the Supreme Court by the Constitution to what he personally wanted the Supreme Court's function to be. He believed getting Congress to pass the Judiciary Act of 1925 would accomplish what he wanted. The statement in the Yale Law Journal by Chief Justice Taft sounds like the tyrannical circumstance that the Constitution was written to avoid.

Congress and Chief Justice Taft either forgot or ignored the contents of the Constitution!!!! The Constitution must not be forgotten or ignored because it is the supreme law of the land. The Judiciary Act of 1925 has been used to prevent us from exercising our right to take appeals to the Supreme Court.

In the case of Marbury v. Madison, Mr. Chief Justice Marshall said, "Thus, the particular phraseology of the constitution of the United States confirms and strengthens the principle, supposed to be essential to all written constitutions, that a law repugnant to the constitution is void; and that courts, as well as other departments, are bound by that instrument." Obviously, Congress must repeal the Judiciary Act of 1925 because it is unconstitutional. Any person, who has been denied an appeal based on the Judiciary Act of 1925, has a right to have that appeal heard. Congress must grant any person, who has been denied the right of appeal based on the Judiciary Act of 1925, an appeal. To do otherwise, confirms to the People and indeed to the world, that our Constitution is not the supreme law of the United States and that the branches of the Government may, at their pleasure, disregard the limits that the Constitution places on the exercise of their powers.

OUR RIGHT TO HAVE THE SUPREME COURT REVIEW OUR CASE

OR

THE SUPREME COURT'S PRACTICE OF DISCRETIONARY REVIEW IS UNCONSTITUTIONAL

Preamble to the Constitution

We the People of the United States, **in Order to** form a more perfect Union, **establish Justice**

Article III of the Constitution

The judicial Power of the United States, **shall be vested in one supreme Court, and in such inferior Courts** as the Congress may from time to time ordain and establish.

In all Cases affecting Ambassadors, other public Ministers and Consuls, and those in which a State shall be Party, the supreme Court shall have original Jurisdiction. In all the other Cases before mentioned, **the supreme Court shall have appellate Jurisdiction**, both as to Law and Fact, **with such Exceptions, and under such Regulations as the Congress shall make**.

Article VI of the Constitution

This Constitution, and the Laws of the United States which shall be made in Pursuance thereof; . . . **shall be the supreme Law of the Land** . . . ”

The Senators and Representatives before mentioned, and the Members of the several State Legislatures, and all executive and **judicial Officers, both of the United States** and of the several States, **shall be bound by Oath or Affirmation, to support this Constitution** . . . ”

Quotes from the Statement of William Howard Taft, Chief Justice of the Supreme Court of the United States in the Hearing before the 68th Congress House of Representatives Committee on the Judiciary on March 30, 1922.

I have been deputed by the Supreme Court to come here and present to your body this bill, which, in terms, is a bill to amend the Judicial Code, and to further define the jurisdiction of the circuit courts of appeals, and of the Supreme Court and for other purposes.

Before I come into the court a committee had been appointed for its preparation, consisting of Justice Day, Justice McReynolds, and, I suppose, ex officio, the Chief Justice. It was taken up again and a very careful and very much extended examination of it made by the committee, to which Justice Van Devanter was added. I suppose we have spent two or three months in its preparation. The care devoted to it was because of the importance that the court attributed to its passage.

. . . but it is to change the method by which those cases reach the court, so that there may be promptly winnowed out by the court itself of all the casesd which come those which deserve the court's consideration.

The Supreme Court exercises its discretionary jurisdiction through the writ of certiorari.

A petition for the writ of certiorari is filed, with the record and the briefs on behalf of the petitioner and the opposing party. These are considered by the court.

In every conference on Saturday, the court takes up the cases and discusses them. Of course, it is impossible for the court or any member of the court, in reading the cases not to reach some conclusion, or, at least, a curbstone conclusion, as to whether the case was decided rightly in the court below; but that is not the consideration that determines the action of the court. The question is whether the questions as presented are sufficiently important, considering the function that the Supreme Court has to play — to justify and require the court to let the case into the court for a full hearing on the merits.

No litigant is entitled to more than two chances, namely, to the original trial and to a review, and the intermediate courts of review are provided for that purpose. When a case goes beyond that, it is not primarily to preserve the rights of the litigants. The Supreme Court's function is for the purpose of expounding and stabilizing principles of law for the benefit of the people of the country, passing upon constitutional questions and other important questions of law for the public benefit. It is to preserve uniformity of decision among the intermediate courts of appeal. Whenever a petition for certiorari presents a question on which one circuit court of appeals differs from another, then we let the case come into our court as a matter of course. These being the considerations that govern our allowance of certioraris the question whether the case was rightly decided in the court below as a matter of first impression is one of minor consideration with us.

Only those cases should come to the highest court which are sufficiently important pro bono publico, without regard to the interest of the litigants. As I have said, two chances are enough for any litigated interest . . .

No review is allowed of right from the judgments of the circuit courts of appeals under this bill.

Of course, we can not say certainly how much this will reduce our jurisdiction, but looking over all the cases as they come, we feel very confident that if you give us that authority we can winnow out the cases in such a way that we can catch up with the docket and keep up with it, and that, of course, is most important.

Quotes from the Statement of Willis Van Devanter, Associate Justice of the Supreme Court of the United States in the Hearing before the 68th Congress House of Representatives Committee on the Judiciary on December 18, 1924.

The other is by writ of certiorari, and is commonly spoken of as a discretionary jurisdiction because the court is invested with a discretion to deny a review unless it appears that the questions presented are of public importance or of wide general interest, or that in the interest of uniformity that court should consider and decide them.

When the circuit courts of appeals were created in 1891 (ch. 517, 26 Stat, 826) the Supreme Court was for the first time invested with an extended discretionary jurisdiction.

As to the cases going from the district courts to the circuit courts of appeals, that act provided as to some of them that there should be a right to a further review in the Supreme Court on appeal or writ of error, and as to others that there could be a further review in the Supreme Court on certiorari if upon petition presented therefor that court should find that the case ought to be considered and determined by it, either because the case was of public importance or of wide interest, or because there was a conflict of decision on the questions involved which should be ended by the Supreme Court in the interest of uniformity.

While the authority of the Supreme Court to take cases on petition for certiorari is spoken of as a discretionary jurisdiction, this does not mean that the court is authorized merely to exercise a will in the matter but rather that the petition is to be granted or denied according to a sound judicial discretion.

... if on consideration of the petition therefor the court found the case to be one which by reason of some public or general interest, or some existing diversity of decision, ought to be reviewed by it.

Mr. Montague — Is it the purpose of the court still to exercise very careful scrutiny under the discretionary power in the method you have heretofore indicated?

Justice Van Devanter — It is.

Mr. Montague — Although you ask for discretionary power, you propose to exercise it in the method you have heretofore exercised it.

Justice Van Devanter — Certainly. Of course, we could not maintain the institution and make it accomplish its purpose unless we did, and there is no purpose to do anything else.

Quotes from the Statement of James C. McReynolds, Associate Justice of the Supreme Court of the United States in the Hearing before the 68th Congress House of Representatives Committee on the Judiciary on December 18, 1924.

I understand that you asked us to come here and give our views on this bill.

So this bill has been framed by the members of the court that have given the subject special attention with the hope that it would enable the court to eliminate cases of minor importance and devote its attention to things of large importance.

It is impossible to give cases like that the attention and time that they ought to have if the court is overburdened with matters of much less importance, matters of importance only to the immediate litigant.

All appeals from the district court shall go to the circuit courts of appeals, with certain minor exceptions, and there they shall be final, the theory being that after a man has had two trials in Federal courts, unless his case involves something more than his private interests and is of public importance, it ought to stop.

The problem is whether the time and attention and energy of the court shall be devoted to matters of large public concern, or whether it shall be consumed by matters of less concern without especial general interest, and because the litigant wants the court of last resort to pass upon their rights.

Somebody must determine what cases must come to our court. If you undertake to do it by special enactment, specifically providing what cases shall come and what cases shall not come, you will find that an enormous difficulty arises. It is almost impossible to define it with sufficient accuracy and certainty, and there ought to be some flexibility, and that flexibility is gained by means of the application for certiorari.

If you will bear in mind the general theory upon which this bill is framed, namely, that cases ought to stop after two Federal courts have passed upon them or after all the State courts have passed upon them, unless they are of particular importance or unless they involve something more than the mere rights of the litigants and concern the public, such as the construction of statutes, the settlement of differences between the different circuit courts of appeal, the settlement of the law upon disputed points, and all that, you will see why the various provisions have been put in.

The Supreme Court believes that Congress has granted it the discretionary power to chose which cases, in the Supreme Court's appellate jurisdiction, the Supreme Court will hear. The Supreme Court and Congress believe that the clause in Article Three of the Constitution that reads "with such Exceptions, and under such Regulations as Congress shall make" grants Congress the power to permit the Supreme Court to use discretion in deciding which appellate cases the Supreme Court will hear. This clause in Article III of the Constitution is known as the exceptions clause. Let's take a look into the Constitution and find out, if in fact, it grants Congress the power to permit the Supreme Court to use discretion in deciding which appellate cases the Supreme Court will hear.

Before we get into the body of the Constitution, there are a couple of things that need doing. First, take a moment to examine part of the first sentence of the Preamble to the Constitution. It's at the beginning of this section. There can be no doubt that the Constitution was written to, among other things, establish justice. Now we need to get out Black's Law Dictionary and find out just what it has to say about some words. Black's Law Dictionary defines **justice** as

the proper administration of laws, as well as, **the constant and perpetual disposition of legal matters or disputes to render every man his due**. Notice that this is not just the administration of laws, but the **proper** administration of laws. Black's Law Dictionary defines **discretion** as **the reasonable exercise of a power or right to act in an official capacity**; **involves the idea of choice**. Black's Law Dictionary also says about discretion — **a public officer has discretion whenever the effective limits on his power leave him free to make a choice among possible courses of action or inaction**. Now, let's go to the body of the Constitution.

The Supreme Court's highest functions, as a part of the judicial power granted by the Constitution, are the protection of the Rights guaranteed to every citizen by the Constitution and the supervision of inferior courts. The Constitution defines the jurisdiction of the Supreme Court by stating the cases in which the Supreme Court shall take original jurisdiction, and it states that in all other cases the Supreme Court shall take appellate jurisdiction. We will address only the appellate jurisdiction of the Supreme Court.

At this point we need to get the meaning of the phrase "shall have appellate jurisdiction." So, let's do that. The meaning of **shall** is **command** or **directive**. The meaning of **have** is **to be in possession of** or **take**. The meaning of **appellate jurisdiction** is **the power of a superior court to correct legal errors of an inferior court and to revise the judgments**. *The* Constitution with the phrase "shall have appellate jurisdiction" *commands the Supreme Court to take possession of the power of a superior court to correct legal errors of an inferior court and to revise the judgments.* Thus, the Constitution establishes the appellate jurisdiction of the Supreme Court as obligatory because the Constitution does not give the Supreme Court a choice.

The key to understanding the meaning of the *exceptions* clause is in the definition of the words **except**, **appellate jurisdiction**, **regulations**, and **make**. Well, let's see what those words mean. The definition of **except** is **to leave out** or **exclude**. Remember, the definition of **appellate jurisdiction** is **the power of a superior court to correct legal errors of an inferior court and to revise the judgments**. The definition of **regulation** is **a rule designed for**

controlling or governing behavior. The definition of **make** is to **create**. With these meanings we know that the phrase "with such Exceptions, and under such Regulations as Congress shall make" must mean <u>with such exclusions and under such rules designed for controlling behavior as Congress shall create</u>. The Constitution grants Congress the authority to decide which cases are left out of the power of the Supreme Court to review, and the authority to make the rules that govern the behavior of the Supreme Court. From the definitions of the words in the *exceptions clause*, no other meaning is possible. After reading the exceptions clause with the meanings inserted in the place of the key words, we see that the exceptions clause does not grant Congress the authority to make any of the Supreme Court's jurisdiction discretionary and the exceptions clause does not grant Congress the authority to allow the Supreme Court to exercise discretion in the application of the Supreme Court's appellate jurisdiction.

When Congress excludes a specific group or class of cases from the appellate jurisdiction of the Supreme Court, the Supreme Court does not have **ANY** power to decide **ANYTHING** regarding those cases. **NOTHING AT ALL!** Look at it this way. You and I have separate cases. Our cases fall into the same group or class of cases. If Congress has excluded our group or class of cases from the appellate jurisdiction of the Supreme Court, then the Supreme Court may not chose to hear my case and chose not to hear yours because the Supreme Court no longer has the power to hear either case. Where there is no power there cannot be a choice of which course of action to follow (discretion)!

Now we need to find the meaning for *writ of certiorari*, so let's go back to Black's Law Dictionary. The word **writ** means — **an order issued from a court requiring the performance of a specified act, or giving authority to have it done. A precept in writing, issuing from a court of justice, addressed to a sheriff or other officer of the law, or directly to the person whose action the court desires to command, either as the commencement of a suit or other proceeding or as incidental to its progress, and requiring the performance of a specified act, or giving authority and commission to have it done**. There is no mention of discretion.

Black's Law Dictionary also tells us to see prerogative writs. Let's do that next.

Black's Law Dictionary defines **prerogative writs** as — **those issued by the exercise of extraordinary power of the crown (the court, in modern practice) on proper cause shown; namely, the writs of procedendo, mandamus, prohibition, quo warranto, habeas corpus, and *certiorari***. Still there is no mention of discretion. However, we have found an important phrase here! That phrase being — on proper cause shown. We'll get the definition of certiorari and come back to this important phrase.

Black's Law Dictionary shows us that the word **certiorari** is a Latin term and the word means — **to be informed of. A writ of common-law origin issued by a superior to an inferior court requiring the latter to produce a certified record of a particular case tried therein. The writ is issued in order that the court issuing the writ may inspect the proceedings and determine whether there have been any irregularities**. We still have not seen the word discretion in any definition. A little side note right here. We have found something from the common-law that has been incorporated into our Government by Congress — the writ of certiorari. Congress does know how to incorporate "stuff" from the common-law.

Important point coming up! Black's Law Dictionary, under certiorari, explains that a writ of certiorari is most commonly used to refer to the Supreme Court of the United States, which **uses** the writ of certiorari **as a discretionary device** to choose the cases it wishes to hear. We have the definition of the word writ and the definition of the word certiorari. Neither definition contains the word discretion. By definition a writ of certiorari is **not** a discretionary device.

Just because the Supreme Court uses the writ of certiorari as a discretionary device to choose the cases it wishes to hear does not mean that the Supreme Court is properly using the writ of certiorari. Remember, justice is the **proper** administration of law. The Justices of the Supreme Court are misusing the writ of certiorari for their own self-serving purpose. You have a hammer and chose to drive in a screw with the hammer. The hammer does not become a screwdriver! You have simply misused the hammer. You have used the hammer

129

for a purpose for which the hammer was not intended. The Supreme Court — the writ of certiorari — same thing!! No judge in this country is free to choose to deny justice. A **choice** as to which course of action to follow never enters the picture. No judge in this country has a choice when it comes to correcting a lower court and dispensing justice! The Constitution has seen to that!!

In his article in the Yale Law Journal, Mr. Taft writes "In the Act of 1891, Congress for the first time conferred upon the Supreme Court, in extensive classes of litigation, discretion to decline to review cases if they did not seem to the Court to be worthy of further review." An examination of that Act will show that Mr. Taft is mistaken. The Act of March 3, 1891 is found in Volume 26 of the Statues at Large on page 826. The purpose of this Act reads, "to establish circuit courts of appeals and to define and regulate in certain cases the jurisdiction of the courts of the United States . . ." Section 6 of this Act addresses the Supreme Court and the writ of certiorari. The paragraph reads,

And excepting also that in any such case as is hereinbefore made final in the circuit court of appeals it shall be competent for the Supreme court to require, by certiorari or otherwise, any such case to be certified to the Supreme Court for its review and determination with the same power and authority in the case as if it had been carried by appeal or writ of error to the Supreme Court.

When the Congress wrote the Act of March 3, 1891, the standard for the use of a prerogative writ, including the writ of certiorari, had been set by the Supreme Court 88 years before, in 1803 in the case of Marbury v. Madison. In this case, Mr. Chief Justice Marshall said, *"It is not by the office of the person to whom the writ is directed, but the nature of the thing to be done that the propriety or impropriety of issuing a mandamus, is to be determined."* The standard to be used in deciding to issue a writ of certiorari is the propriety (correctness) or impropriety (incorrectness) of issuing the writ. The correctness or incorrectness of issuing the writ cannot depend on the will of the Justices of the Supreme Court. Why, you ask? Simple, because the will of the Justices of the Supreme Court has nothing to do with the law of the case!

After reading the definition for a writ of certiorari, we see that the standard set by the Supreme Court in 1803 for the use of the writ of certiorari and the current definition for a writ of certiorari agree. We see also that Congress said that in some cases in order to secure a review of their case by the Supreme Court the person must show the Supreme Court proper cause based on the law. In the Act of 1891, Congress did not use the words "at the discretion of the court" or "may at their discretion" or "if it shall appear to the satisfaction of the court" as it did in 1789. With all due respect to Mr. Taft, his interpretation regarding the Act of March 3, 1891 is wrong. Congress did not confer on the Supreme Court discretion to decline to review cases if they did not seem to the Court to be worthy of further review. "It would be a very bold construction to say, that this power could be applied in its appellate form only, to the most important class of cases to which it is applicable." Chief Justice Marshall, Osborn v. Bank of the United States, 1824. He was referring to the judicial power granted by the Constitution.

Now we need to bounce back to that important phrase — *on proper cause shown*. A writ of certiorari is issued *on proper cause shown*. In other words, a person shows the court that there is valid reason **based on the law** to issue the writ of certiorari. The basis for issuing the writ of certiorari must be and is the law, not the feelings or perceptions of any justice or any group of justices about any particular issue! Once a person shows proper cause (i.e., the violation of the Rights guaranteed in the Constitution) the court issues a writ. There is nothing discretionary about it! When Congress said that cases get to the Supreme Court by writ of certiorari, Congress actually said that cases get to the Supreme Court by way of an order issued by the Supreme Court, on proper cause shown, to an inferior court requiring an inferior court to produce a certified record of the case.

The Constitution was written to establish justice. The Supreme Court was created in the Constitution. The powers and responsibilities of the Supreme Court are established by the Constitution, not by Congress and not by the desires of the Justices that are appointed to the Supreme Court. Article VI of the Constitution requires the Justices of the Supreme Court, as judicial officers of the United States, to be bound by oath to uphold the Constitution.

Justice — the **proper** administration of laws and the *constant and perpetual* disposition of legal matters or disputes to render every man his due — is the result when courts apply the principles in the Constitution. Justice requires the Supreme Court to remedy wrongs and to correct the errors of the inferior courts. The Constitution prevents the Supreme Court from refusing justice to anyone. Still, the Justices of the Supreme Court deny justice as a matter of routine!

The Constitution grants:

1. The judicial power of the Government first to the Supreme Court.
2. Congress the authority to ordain and establish courts *inferior* to the Supreme Court.

The word inferior means lower or of lower rank. Thus, inferior courts are lower than or of lower rank than the Supreme Court. The courts created by Congress are not and cannot be replacements for, or equal to, the Supreme Court. The Constitution requires the Supreme Court to supervise the inferior courts created by Congress. If this were not so, then the courts created by Congress could act as equals to the Supreme Court. The Supreme Court of the United States acknowledges that it has supervisory responsibility over the inferior courts. It does so by using the words "call for an exercise of this Court's supervisory power" in subparagraph (a) of Rule 10 of the Rules of the Supreme Court of the United States, adopted January 16, 1997 and effective May 1, 1997. The Constitution assigns the Supreme Court the role of overseer to make certain that all public officials, including the inferior courts, obey the law. The Supreme Court is required to perform this duty all of the time.

When a person alleges a denial of any right secured by the Constitution, or a person alleges that the inferior courts have failed to follow the Supreme Court's decisions, and the case is within the Supreme Court's appellate jurisdiction and is properly brought before the Supreme Court, Article III of the Constitution requires the Supreme Court to hear the case. There can never be a sound judicial reason for refusing to hear any case that alleges a violation of the Constitution if the case is properly brought before the Supreme Court. Still, each year the Supreme Court arbitrarily refuses to hear many such cases.

Supreme Court decisions, that are not contrary to the Constitution, are to be adhered to by the inferior courts until those decisions are reversed. When inferior courts issue decisions that do not conform to lawful Supreme Court decisions, inferior courts act arbitrarily and capriciously. No court may act arbitrarily and capriciously because the Constitution requires proper administration of the law (justice) and any act that is arbitrary and capricious is not proper administration of the law.

Each time an inferior court fails to follow or incorrectly applies decisions of the Supreme Court, the results have overtones of public importance because the uniformity of national law is threatened. The lawful decisions of the Supreme Court are of no importance if those decisions are not followed and are not enforced. The Supreme Court must enforce its decisions, or else its decisions are empty rulings leaving the Rights of the People unprotected. This is one of the reasons that the Constitution does not permit the Supreme Court to exercise any discretion with regard to whether the Supreme Court will correct the errors of inferior courts when those errors are properly brought before the Supreme Court.

We have the constitutional right to have our case decided in accordance with the law of the land. A citizen's constitutional rights cannot be infringed upon simply because members of Congress or the Justices of the Supreme Court choose to do so. Constitutional rights cannot be denied on account of the inadequacy of government resources. The Supreme Court cannot use the Supreme Court's workload to deny or restrict a review. The Supreme Court's workload is real, but it may not be used to justify the denial of citizen rights. The methods used to manage the Supreme Court's workload must be implemented within the framework of the Constitution. The reasons that the Supreme Court's workload is high are largely attributable to the failure of the judicial branch to correctly perform its function.

When an inferior court issues a decision contrary to a decision of the Supreme Court, the Right to have one's case reviewed by the Supreme Court is a Right protected in Article III of the Constitution. The Constitution prevents Congress or Justices of the Supreme Court from tossing aside the Right to have one's case reviewed by the Supreme Court, as if it is of little or no importance. The Constitution forbids the Supreme Court to deny or in any way abridge the rights of the People. The Supreme Court fails to fulfill its constitutional responsibilities and citizens are deprived of the constitutional right to justice each time the Supreme Court refuses to review the case of any person who has properly brought their case before the Supreme Court and the case is within the Supreme Court's appellate jurisdiction.

Whenever an inferior court issues a decision contrary to a decision of the Supreme Court and the Supreme Court refuses to correct the decision of the inferior court, the inferior court is no longer of lower rank, but is elevated to a position equal to the Supreme Court. Article III of the Constitution forbids any of the inferior courts from becoming the equal of the Supreme Court because Article III provides for only one Supreme Court.

The very purpose of the Constitution and the Bill of Rights is to establish legal principles to be applied by the courts — all of the courts, all of the time. The Supreme Court and the inferior courts sit to adjudicate cases involving alleged denials of constitutional rights. The Constitution requires (1) the inferior courts to make decisions consistent with the Constitution, (2) the inferior courts to adhere to the decisions of the Supreme Court, and (3) the Supreme Court to correct the decisions of inferior courts which are contrary to the Constitution or contrary to the laws passed by Congress. Such requirements are essential to the maintenance of an orderly society.

The rights secured by and responsibilities assigned in the Constitution prevent the Supreme Court from denying an individual's petition for review of an inferior court's decision when the petition alleges that the inferior court overlooked, failed to apply, or incorrectly applied Supreme Court decisions. The Constitution has tasked the Supreme Court with an important role in the constitutional system. The Supreme Court's judicial authority, as conferred by the Constitution, imposes the solemn, judicial duty to police the decisions of the inferior courts. The Supreme Court is bound by that judicial obligation and the Supreme Court may not refuse or neglect to perform its duty. In the case of Pierson v. Ray in 1967 the Supreme Court reasoned that it is a judge's duty to decide all cases within his jurisdiction that are brought before him. The judge's duty described by the Supreme Court in Pierson v. Ray must also apply to the Justices of the Supreme Court.

In the case of Butz v. Economou, the Supreme Court based its support of the unconstitutional doctrine of absolute immunity for judicial officers, in part, on one of "the safeguards built into the judicial process" — the correctability of a judge's error on appeal. The Supreme Court said that the "correctability of error on appeal" is just one of the "many checks on malicious action by judges. The safeguards built into the judicial process tend to reduce the need for private damages actions as a means of controlling unconstitutional conduct." The Supreme Court's statement implies that these "safeguards" are in place 100 per cent of the time. Well, let's just test this grand sounding statement in light of the operation of the Supreme Court. There are three levels in the Federal court system. The first level is made up of the district courts. The second level is made up of the courts of appeals. The third level is the Supreme Court. Ok, the Supreme Court's theory is that the errors by the judges in the district courts will be or can be corrected by the judges in the courts of appeals and the errors by the judges in the courts of appeals will be or can be corrected by the Supreme Court. Simple enough, but wait!! A Chief Justice of the Supreme Court said that whether the case was decided rightly in the court below is not the consideration that determines the action of the Supreme Court. It is impossible for the Supreme Court to correct the errors of judges in the courts of appeals when the Supreme Court refuses to hear the cases. It is impossible to have correctability of error on appeal when the Supreme Court arbitrarily decides which cases it will hear. Using the rationale used by the Justices of the Supreme Court, we see that the Supreme Court's practice of discretionary review is destructive to the safeguards in our judicial system. There cannot be any safeguards in a judicial process that permits **the Supreme Court to refuse to hear more than 90 percent of the cases brought before it**. Besides, correction of judicial errors by inferior courts is mandated by the Constitution.

In order for a Government official to have discretion a Government official must have the authority to choose between doing a thing or not doing a thing. If a Government official does not have the authority to choose between doing a thing or not doing a thing, or the Government official is required to follow a specific course of action, then the Government official does not have discretion.

Associate Justice James C. McReynolds, in his statement in the Hearing before the 68th Congress House of Representatives Committee on the Judiciary on December 18, 1924, admits that the Justices of the Supreme Court recognize that "somebody must determine what cases must come to our court." The Constitution places the function of deciding what cases must come to the Supreme Court squarely in the powers granted to Congress. Associate Justice McReynolds, in the same statement admits that the Justices of the Supreme Court also recognize that "if you undertake to do it by special enactment, specifically providing what cases shall come and what cases shall not come, you will find that an enormous difficulty arises. It is almost impossible to define it with sufficient accuracy and certainty . . ." The nail has been hit right on the head!! The Framers recognized that it might be appropriate to exclude some cases from the appellate jurisdiction of the Supreme Court, but that it would be "almost impossible" to define with sufficient accuracy and certainty what cases of the People should be excluded from the appellate jurisdiction of the Supreme Court, and that an enormous difficulty would arise in attempting to do so. However, in the event that the cases that should be excluded from the appellate jurisdiction of the Supreme Court could be defined with sufficient accuracy and certainty, the Framers granted Congress, the elected representatives of the People, the authority to decide what cases of the People should be excluded from the appellate jurisdiction of the Supreme Court. That is precisely why the Constitution is written exactly the way it is. It is almost impossible to decide what cases of the People should be excluded from the appellate jurisdiction of the Supreme Court, but it if can be done, then the representatives of the people should do it. It was not left to the whim of any appointed official of the Government. Remember, the Bill of Rights was added to the Constitution because the Government could not be trusted and the People feared that the Government would disregard their rights. The People did not entrust such an important Right to anyone other than their elected representatives!!!! So, the Framers believed that if Congress could not do it, then it should not be done!!

Suppose the courts of appeals refuse to follow the decisions of the Supreme Court, ought they not to be compelled? Suppose the Executive Branch refuses to follow the Constitution, ought it not to be compelled? Suppose the courts of appeals refuse to protect the rights in the Constitution, ought they not to be compelled? The questions can go on and on. A remedy must be available. Currently, a remedy is not available because of the Supreme Court's practice of arbitrary review.

This Right of ours, yours and mine, to have the Supreme Court review our case was not given to us by Congress, the Supreme Court, or any part of the Government. *We the People* established this right in the Constitution. So, Congress, the Supreme Court, or any part of the Government cannot take the right away. However, Congress and the Supreme Court have failed to honor this Right. Judges, as well as the other Government officials and agencies, are bound by the Constitution. The Constitution says so. In order for Congress or the Supreme Court to find that the Supreme Court has discretion to perform its duties, the Constitution cannot be the supreme law of the land and the Supreme Court's constitutional responsibility to supervise inferior courts and enforce its decisions 100% of the time cannot exist. Of course, neither is possible. For **every** constitutional wrong there **must** be an adequate remedy. In this instance, the remedy for the constitutional wrong committed by Congress and the Supreme Court is that **every** citizen who has been denied a review of an appeal **must be granted a review**.

Now, it wasn't too difficult to understand that the Constitution gives you the Right to have your case heard by the Supreme Court as long as your case falls within the class of cases that come within the Supreme Court's appellate jurisdiction, was it? It is nowhere near as difficult to understand as a judge, a lawyer or a member of Congress would have you believe it is. In fact, it was pretty easy to understand, wasn't it? Congratulations! And you say you don't understand the law or the Constitution! Funny thing though — we have a country full of attorneys. Some of them graduated from our nation's finest law schools. We have hundreds and hundreds of federal judges. Some of them graduated from our nation's finest law schools. I wonder just what our nation's finest law schools *are* teaching with respect to what the Constitution says. *We the People* elect members of Congress in election after election. It seems most of them *are* lawyers. They beg us to send them to Congress. And for what?? Who knows? Whatever their reason for wanting to be in Congress, obviously, they are not interested in protecting our Rights or interested in making sure that the Government functions according to the Constitution.

BLOW AWAY THE SMOKE AND TAKE AWAY THE MIRRORS

OR

THE SAD, UGLY TRUTH ABOUT THE SUPREME COURT

A close examination of the functioning of the Supreme Court reveals a sad, ugly truth. Let's blow away the smoke, take away the mirrors, and examine the exposed facts. The sad, ugly truth will be clear.

President William H. Taft is quoted as saying "No man ought to have, as a matter of right, a review of his case by the Supreme Court. He should be satisfied by one hearing before a court of first instance and one review by a court of appeals." The Justices of the Supreme Court believe the Supreme Court has more work than it can do. The Justices ask Congress to do something about the number of cases brought to the Supreme Court and Congress tells the Justices to draft a bill.

After his Presidency, Mr. Taft is appointed to the Supreme Court. As the Chief Justice of the Supreme Court, Mr. Taft, along with other Justices of the Supreme Court, gives Congress an advisory opinion concerning the bill drafted by the Justices of the Supreme Court even though the Supreme Court has acknowledged that it has no authority to give advisory opinions. Congress relies on the advisory opinion of the Supreme Court and passes the Judiciary Act of 1925. The Judiciary Act of 1925 eliminates the right to the review of a case of the vast majority of citizens. The Supreme Court picks and chooses what work it will or will not perform.

The Congress permits the Supreme Court to make the rules and set the fees for the Supreme Court. The Rules of the Supreme Court say:

If you can afford to pay the $300 docket fee, then the Supreme Court requires:
- the petition to be produced in a booklet that is 6 1/8 and 9 ¼ inches in size.
- the petition to have a cover consisting of 65-pound weight paper.
- the petition to be bound firmly in at least two places along the left margin (saddle stitch or perfect binding preferred).
- that spiral, plastic, metal, and string bindings not be used.
- the text to appear on both sides of the page.
- that you file 40 copies of the booklet.

If you cannot afford to pay the $300 docket fee, then the Supreme Court requires:

- the petition for a writ of certiorari to be produced on 8 ½ by 11 inch paper.
- the petition to be double spaced.
- the petition to be bound at the upper left-hand corner.
- that you file 10 copies.

When we bear in mind that the Constitution was written to establish justice and the Supreme Court is created in the Constitution, it is clear that the only *valid* reason for the Rules of the Supreme Court or anything therein is these Rules must be necessary for the administration of justice. Why do you suppose the Supreme Court requires the $300 fee to be paid whether or not it hears the case? Obviously, the $300 fee is not based on any cost necessary for the administration of justice because you are required to pay the fee when your petition is denied. Why do you suppose the Supreme Court requires the petition to be in a booklet format? Obviously, the booklet format is not necessary for the administration of justice because the Supreme Court does review and grant petitions that are not submitted in the booklet format. Why do you suppose the Supreme Court requires the booklet to be such an unusual size? The fact that the Supreme Court accepts petitions in the 8 ½ by 11 format is proof that the booklet format is not necessary. Why do you suppose the Supreme Court requires 40 copies of the booklet? Obviously, 40 copies of the booklet are not necessary for the administration of justice because that $300 can certainly pay for any reproduction costs associated with the petition. Also, the Supreme Court accepts fewer copies when the petition is submitted in the 8 ½ by 11 format. It certainly appears that the administration of justice and the cost associated with a petition for a writ of certiorari are not the reasons for the required $300 fee, or the required booklet format, or the required 40 copies of the booklet. Then the obvious question is — "What is the purpose of the $300 filing fee, the booklet format, and the 40 copies?" Could the purpose of these requirements be to discourage the filing of a petition for a writ of certiorari? I believe that is exactly the purpose of these requirements!

I decided to write to the Clerk of the Supreme Court and ask some questions. Here is the body of the letter:

William K. Suter, Clerk
Supreme Court of the United States
1 First Street, N.E.
Washington, D.C. 20543

Dear Mr. Suter:

The Supreme Court requires that a fee of $300 be paid to file a petition for a writ of certiorari and that a fee of $200 be paid to file a petition for rehearing. I am requesting to know how the Court arrived at the amounts of $300 and $200, what each fee actually pays for, the actual cost of the items or services covered by each fee, and how the actual cost of the items or services covered by each fee is determined.

The Supreme Court requires a petition for a writ of certiorari be produced in booklet format and on paper that is 6 1/8 by 9 1/4 inches in size. I am requesting to know how and why the Court arrived at the size 6 1/8 by 9 1/4 inches.

Now here is the body of the letter I received:

This is in response to your recent letter asking several questions.

This Court established the docketing fees set forth in the Rules of the Supreme Court of the United States. These fees partially offset some of the costs associated with processing petitions for writs of certiorari and petitions for rehearings. Individuals that qualify for in forma pauperis status under Rule 39 are not required to pay docketing fees.

Other federal courts also charge fees for filing documents. See, for example, 28 U.S. Code § 1914, which establishes docketing fees for U.S. district courts.

The size of the booklet format prescribed in Rule 33.1 was established by the Court many years ago in order to facilitate easy reading and processing. Individuals that qualify for in forma pauperis status are not required to use the booklet format. Pursuant to Rule 12.2, such individuals can submit a petition on 8 1/2 x 11-inch paper as described in rule 33.2.

    Please let me know if you need additional information.

Sincerely,
/s/
William K. Suter
Clerk of the Court

The Clerk wants me to let him know if I need additional information. I would have been satisfied if the Clerk had provided the information I requested! As you can see, the Clerk did not answer a single question in the letter! Writing to the Clerk was useless. Either the Supreme Court does not have answers for the questions or the Supreme Court does not wish to reveal the answers to us.

    What are the "costs associated with processing petitions for writs of certiorari and petitions for rehearings?" Well, there are no copying costs or there shouldn't be any. Not when you are required to submit 40 copies! According to the Clerk's Office, when a petition is received a case analyst checks the petition and if the petition meets the requirements of the Rules, then it is sent to the file room where it waits until the response to the petition is received. After the response to the petition is received, the petition, along with any response, is circulated to the Justices. If the petition does not meet the Rules it is returned to the person filing the petition to be corrected. All of the persons the petition are employees of the Supreme Court and therefore they are employees of the Government. Each one is paid a salary from the Treasury of the United States to perform the functions associated with the petition. Their salaries come from public funds or our tax dollars. The information provided by the Supreme Court does not show any other costs associated with the filing of a petition. The sad, ugly truth is the $300 and the $200 fees are not to offset any costs, but are designed to discourage us from filing a petition with the Supreme Court!

If the size of the booklet is established by the Supreme Court to facilitate easy reading, then the size of the booklet would be 8 1/2 by 11 because the eye strain is less for the 8 1/2 by 11 size. The booklet would certainly be some standard size and not 6 1/8 by 9 1/4 inches. Printers deal in standard sizes like 5 1/2 by 8 1/2 or 9 by 6 or 7 by 10. To print the booklet in a nonstandard size, like 6 1/8 by 9 1/4, is an unnecessary additional cost! What is the purpose of this unnecessary additional cost? The sad, ugly truth is it serves to discourage us from filing a petition with the Supreme Court!

When a petition is filed in a case and the Government is the respondent, the Government can file a response to the petition. However, the Solicitor General, the Government's attorney at the Supreme Court, usually files a waiver that reads:

The Government hereby waives its right to file a response to the petition in this case, unless requested to do so by the Court.

This waiver tells us plenty! It tells us that the Solicitor General and the Supreme Court have established a "relationship." Let me explain. Once the Solicitor General waives the right to respond to a petition, the Government may not later assert the right to respond. Therefore, the Government cannot respond to the petition **and the Supreme Court has no authority to request the Government to do so**. However, after the Justices decide to hear a case, the Supreme Court requests the Government to respond to the petition. The Solicitor General does not bother to read the petition or put forth an argument until the Supreme Court lets him know which cases it will hear! Even though the Solicitor General has waived the right to file a response, the Solicitor General files a response just as soon as his good friends, the Justices of the Supreme Court, tell him to! The citizen must follow the rules and the Government follows none!

The sad, ugly truth is the Supreme Court's primary concern is no longer the protection of the rights of *We the People* or justice. The sad, ugly truth is justice doesn't matter much to the Justices of the Supreme Court. The sad, ugly truth is the law doesn't matter much to the Justices of the Supreme Court. The sad, ugly truth is the Justices of the Supreme Court couldn't care less whether inferior courts obey the Constitution. The sad, ugly truth is the Supreme Court does all it can do to discourage us from filing petitions. The sad, ugly truth is the Justices of the Supreme Court couldn't care less about our rights or justice. The sad, ugly truth is the Justices of the Supreme Court sacrificed our rights and justice in order to have less of a workload for that enormous salary that we pay them to provide justice and protect our rights! The sad, ugly truth is there are only two things that always matter to the Justices of the Supreme Court — their egos and how much work they can get out of doing! They simply want to get paid their enormous salaries and do as they damn well please!

On December 3, 1998 a petition for a writ of certiorari was filed in and placed on the docket of the Supreme Court as No. 98-914. The $300 fee was paid. Below are the important portions of the petition:

QUESTIONS PRESENTED

Important questions for review, not previously decided by this court concerning the constitutionality of the functioning of the Supreme Court, are presented by this case. The questions are:

1. Whether the Justices of the Supreme Court of the United States, during the legislative process that resulted in the passage of the Judiciary Act of 1925, performed a legislative function assigned by the Constitution of the United States to the Congress of the United States.

2. Whether the Congress of the United States, during the legislative process that resulted in the passage of the Judiciary Act of 1925, improperly delegated to the Justices of the Supreme Court of the United States a function assigned to the Congress of the United States by the Constitution of the United States.

3. Whether the Justices of the Supreme Court of the United States, during the legislative process that resulted in the passage of the Judiciary Act of 1925, exercised a power not granted by the

Constitution of the United States when they rendered an opinion, regarding the bill, to the Congress of the United States.

4. Whether the Constitution of the United States grants the Congress of the United States the power to authorize the Justices of the Supreme Court of the United States to base the granting of a petition for a writ of certiorari upon vague, arbitrary, capricious, and other than legal standards, instead of the correctness or incorrectness of granting the petition for a writ of certiorari.

5. Whether the Right of the People to petition the Government of the United States for a redress of grievances, guaranteed in the First Amendment to the Constitution of the United States, includes the right to bring a lawsuit against the Government of the United States, or any official thereof.

    a. Whether sovereign immunity, insofar as the Government of the United States exercises it as a defense against a suit brought by a citizen of the United States, abridges the Right of the People to petition the Government for a redress of grievances.

    b. Whether absolute immunity, insofar as a Government Official of the United States exercises it as a defense against a suit brought by a citizen of the United States, abridges the Right of the People to petition the Government for a redress of grievances.

    c. Whether qualified immunity, insofar as a Government Official of the United States exercises it as a defense against a suit brought by a citizen of the United States, abridges the Right of the People to petition the Government for a redress of grievances.

    d. Whether government contractor immunity, insofar as it is exercised as a defense against a suit brought by a citizen of the United States, abridges the Right of the People to petition the Government for a redress of grievances.

6. Whether the Federal Tort Claims Act, which abridges the Right of the People to petition the Government of the United States for a redress of grievances, is constitutional.

CONSTITUTIONAL PROVISIONS INVOLVED

The First Amendment to the Constitution of the United States provides:

"Congress shall make no law respecting an establishment of religion, or prohibiting the free exercise thereof, or abridging the freedom of speech, or of the press, or the right of the people peaceably to assemble, and to petition the Government for a redress of grievances."

STATEMENT OF THE CASE

Petitioner filed a class complaint, verified in accordance with 28 U.S.C § 1746, in the United States District Court for the Eastern District of Virginia, Alexandria Division, alleging that the doctrine of sovereign immunity, insofar as the Federal Government asserts the defense against lawsuits brought by citizens of the United States, the Act of February 13, 1925, ch 229, 43 Stat. 936 (also known as the Judiciary Act of 1925), and the Federal Tort Claims Act are repugnant to the Constitution of the United States. The complaint also alleges that Petitioner and others similarly situated have suffered injury in fact as a result.

Respondent filed an unsupported motion to dismiss the class complaint. Prior to discovery, the district court granted Respondent's unsupported motion and dismissed the complaint, without hearing oral argument, because the district court believes Petitioner does not have standing to bring this action. The Court of Appeals affirmed the district court's decision.

REASONS FOR GRANTING THE PETITION

This case presents questions, not previously decided by this Court, of grave importance to each and every citizen of this country and to the Government. The questions presented concern:

- The constitutionality of the standards this Court uses to grant or deny a review of an inferior court's decision considering the role that the Constitution mandates for the Supreme Court and the constitutional right to justice.
- The constitutionality of the Act of February 13, 1925 (also known as the Judiciary Act of 1925) when the powers exercised by Congress and the Supreme Court during the creation of this Act are compared to the powers that the Constitution grants Congress and the Supreme Court. This Act is the basis for thousands upon thousands of citizens being denied an appeal as of right.
- The constitutionality of sovereign, absolute, qualified, and the government contractor immunity established by the Federal courts, as well as the constitutionality of the Federal Tort Claims Act, when they are subjected to the prohibition in the First Amendment and considering that common law, which is the basis for the immunities, has not been fully incorporated into the Constitution.

> 1. The Act of February 13, 1925 (also known as the Judiciary Act of 1925) is a result of Congress and the Justices of the Supreme Court exercising powers not granted in the Constitution and it is used to deny citizens the right of appeal.

Congressional records (Hearing before the Committee on the Judiciary, House of Representatives, 68th Congress, 2nd Session, on H.R. 10479 and Senate Report, No. 362, 68th Congress, 1st Session, Sen. No. 8220) show that:

- Members of Congress suggested that the justices of the Supreme Court prepare a bill.

- The Supreme Court Justices formed a committee and prepared a bill.
- The draft of the bill prepared by the Justices of the Supreme Court was introduced into the House and Senate and in hearings held by the House Judiciary Committee.
- The Chief Justice of the Supreme Court, instead of a member of Congress, sponsored the legislation.
- Senator Cummins, Chairman of the Senate Judiciary Committee, relied on the judicial authorship of the bill.
- Congress clearly understood that the bill was written by the justices of the Supreme Court and not by members of Congress. Chief Justice Taft and Justices Van Devanter, McReynolds and Sutherland were afforded the opportunity to render advice and a statement of the Court's views in hearings held on the bill by the House Judiciary Committee.
- Congress deferred to the prestige of the Supreme Court and its Chief Justice.

The essence of the legislative authority granted Congress is the making of laws. An important part of making a law is the creation of the bill because the bill specifies the details. Congress granted the Justices of the Supreme Court legislative power. The Constitution does not give Congress the authority to grant the Justices of the Supreme Court legislative power.

The Framers of the Constitution had the choice of assigning an active share in the process of creating legislation to the Supreme Court, yet they did not do so. The Framers knew New York's Council of Revision. It had been functioning since 1777. Pages 21 and 22 of The Records of the Federal Convention of 1787 (edited by Max Farrand 1911) show that during the Federal Convention of 1787, Mr. Randolph proposed a resolution on May 29 that there should be a Council of revision composed of the President and members of the Federal Judiciary. This Council of revision should have authority to examine every act of Congress before it becomes law and that this Council could reject an act of Congress. The Framers of the Constitution did not include this resolution in the Constitution. Therefore, they rejected this proposal and chose not to permit the judges of the Federal Judiciary, including the Justices of the Supreme Court, to render advice concerning pending legislation or to have any part in the making of a law. The Constitution does not grant the Justices of the Supreme Court any participation in the legislative process.

The Supreme Court has acknowledged that the Justices of the Supreme Court do not have any authority to comment on legislation before the adjudication of a case requires them to do so. See Steamship Co. v. Emigration Commissioners, 113 U.S.33, 39 (1885); United States v. Evans, 213 U.S. 297, 301 (1909); Muskrat v. United States, 219 U.S. 346, 355 (1911); Stearns v. Wood, 236 U.S. 75, 78 (1915); White v. Johnson, 282 U.S. 367, 373 (1931); Spector Motor Co. v. McLaughlin, 323 U.S. 101, 105 (1944); Coffman v. Breeze Corporations, 323 U.S. 316, 324-325 (1945); Asbury Hospital v. Cass County, 326 U.S. 207, 213-214 (1945); Federation of Labor v. McAdory, 325 U.S. 450, 461 (1945). Some of these decisions are many years before the Judiciary Act of 1925 and some are many years after it. All of these decisions make it clear that the Justices of the Supreme Court do not have the authority to give Congress an advisory opinion concerning the Judiciary Act of 1925.

The Constitution does not give Congress the authority to enlarge or diminish the power that the Constitution delegates to the Supreme Court. The congressional records previously mentioned show that Congress, in spite of the Constitution, permitted a committee of justices of the Supreme Court to draft a bill and that Congress allowed Justices to render an advisory opinion concerning the Judiciary Act of 1925, while the Act was still pending legislation.

The Supreme Court's judicial power does not include the power to decide and comment on laws before the Supreme Court is called upon to enforce them. The Constitution, in Article I, makes it clear that the task of creating legislation is a task for the elected members of Congress — not for the appointed justices of the Supreme Court. The framework in the Constitution (1) was intended to separate power so that law making and judicial powers would be in separate hands and (2) prevents the Judicial Branch of the Government from exercising powers delegated to the Legislative Branch.

The Constitution and the facts clearly show that, during the law making process involving the Judiciary Act of 1925, the Justices of the Supreme Court exercised a legislative function when they drafted the bill. When Congress permitted the Justices of the Supreme Court to prepare a bill, Congress substituted the Justices for members of Congress in one of Congress' most important constitutional functions. Confirmation that the Justices of the Supreme Court, not any member of Congress, wrote the bill is found in the testimony of Chief Justice Taft and Associate Justice McReynold before Congress and in the statement of Senator Cummins in Senate Report No. 362, 68th Congress, 1st Session, Serial No. 8220. In this Senate Report Senator Cummins says "the bill was prepared by a committee of the members of the Supreme Court after a long and careful study of the subject, at the suggestion of the American Bar Association, and has the approval of every member of that Court." In the case of <u>American Automobile Ass'n v. United States</u>, 367 U.S. 687, 697, the Supreme Court recognized the impropriety of writing a bill for Congress. In this case Mr. Justice Clark in delivering the opinion of the Court said, "We must leave to the Congress the fashioning of a rule which, in any event, must have wide ramifications." The Justices did not leave the fashioning of the Judiciary Act of 1925 to Congress.

The Justices of the Supreme Court and the members of Congress are bound by the Constitution. The Constitution requires each member of Congress and each Justice of the Supreme Court to take an oath to support the Constitution. Members of Congress acted beyond the bounds of authority granted in the Constitution by permitting the Justices of the Supreme Court to draft the bill and then permitting the Justices of the Supreme Court to comment on the pending legislation. The Justices of the Supreme Court acted beyond the authority granted in the Constitution when they drafted the bill and then commented on the pending legislation. The Judiciary Act of 1925 removed large numbers of appeals as of right and reduced citizens to requesting, rather than demanding, an appeal.

2. This Court uses a standard to select cases to review that is vague, arbitrary, capricious, and denies citizens their constitutional Right to justice.

The Justices do not use any firm standard to control the issuance of a writ of certiorari. They select cases to hear based on vague, arbitrary, and capricious criteria. The reason the Supreme Court gives as the basis for issuing a writ of certiorari is that the Justices of the Supreme Court must think that the case is of some national importance. If a case concerns only the constitutional rights of one citizen, then the petition for a writ of certiorari is routinely denied.

The Constitution does not base the right to have an appeal heard by the Supreme Court on what anyone, including any Justice of the Supreme Court, thinks about the importance of the case. The Constitution does not base the Supreme Court's duties or responsibilities on how the Justices feel about anything. The Constitution says that the violation of a right is enough basis for the Supreme Court to hear a case. The right to secure a review of decisions of the inferior courts does not depend on any discretionary power of the Supreme Court.

The Constitution does not grant the Supreme Court the authority to refuse to hear cases based on how the Justices feel about the case. Congress is not granted the authority to empower the Supreme Court to refuse to hear cases properly brought before it based on arbitrary and capricious standards.

The definition of a writ of certiorari says that it is issued *on proper cause shown*. In other words, a person shows the court that there is valid reason **based on the law** to issue the writ of certiorari. The standard for the use of a prerogative writ, including the writ of certiorari, was set by the Supreme Court in 1803 in the case of Marbury v. Madison, 5 U.S. (1 Cranch) 137. In this case, Chief Justice Marshall said, "*It is not by the office of the person to whom the writ is directed, but the nature of the thing to be done that the propriety or impropriety of issuing a mandamus, is to be determined.*" Thus, the standard to be used in deciding to issue a writ of discretion, including a writ of certiorari, is the propriety (correctness) or impropriety (incorrectness) of issuing the writ. The standard used by the Justices of the Supreme Court is not based on the correctness or incorrectness of issuing the writ. The Supreme Court's stated position is that whether the case was decided rightly in the court below is not the consideration that determines the action of the court.

When Congress said that cases get to the Supreme Court by writ of certiorari, Congress actually said that cases get to the Supreme Court by way of an order issued by the Supreme Court, on proper cause shown, to an inferior court requiring an inferior court to produce a certified record of the case. The Judiciary Act of 1925 does not use contain the words "at the discretion of the court" or "may at their discretion" or "if it shall appear to the satisfaction of the court." The Constitution requires, because it mandates justice, that proper cause and the correctness or incorrectness of issuing the writ must be based on the law of the case; not on what national importance the Justices place on the case. Once a person shows proper cause (i.e., the violation of the Rights guaranteed in the Constitution) the Constitution requires that the Supreme Court issue the writ because the Constitution requires justice. The standard used by the Justices of the Supreme Court is not based on justice or the law of the case.

The powers and responsibilities of the Supreme Court are established by the Constitution, not by Congress and not by the desires of the Justices that are appointed to the Supreme Court. Article VI of the Constitution requires the Justices of the Supreme Court, as judicial officers of the United States, to be bound by oath to uphold the Constitution.

Justice is the **proper** administration of laws and the **constant** and **perpetual** disposition of legal matters or disputes to render every man his due. Justice requires the Supreme Court to remedy wrongs and to correct the errors of the inferior courts. The Constitution prevents the Supreme Court from refusing justice to anyone.

Respectfully, Congress did not confer on the Supreme Court discretion to decline to review cases if they did not seem to the Court to be worthy of further review. *"It would be a very bold construction to say, that this power could be applied in its appellate form only, to the most important class of cases to which it is applicable."* Chief Justice Marshall, Osborn v. Bank of the United States, 1824. The Chief Justice is referring to the judicial power granted by the Constitution.

The Constitution requires the Supreme Court to supervise the inferior courts created by Congress. If this were not so, then the courts created by Congress could act as equals to the Supreme Court.

The Supreme Court of the United States acknowledges that it has supervisory responsibility over the inferior courts. The Constitution assigns the Supreme Court the role of overseer, not only to declare definitively, with final and binding interpretations of the law, what law exists, but also to make certain that all public officials, including the inferior courts, obey the law. The Supreme Court is required to perform all of its duties all of the time.

When a person alleges a denial of any right secured by the Constitution, or a person alleges that the inferior courts have failed to follow the Supreme Court's decisions, and the case is within the Supreme Court's appellate jurisdiction and is properly brought before the Supreme Court, Article III of the Constitution requires that the Supreme Court hear the case. However, the Supreme Court arbitrarily refuses to hear such cases.

Supreme Court decisions, that are not contrary to the Constitution, are to be adhered to by the inferior courts until those decisions are reversed. When inferior courts issue decisions that do not conform to lawful Supreme Court decisions, inferior courts act arbitrarily and capriciously. No court may act arbitrarily and capriciously because the Constitution requires proper administration of the law (justice) and arbitrary and capricious acts are not proper administrations of the law. The Supreme Court's constitutional obligations prevent it from arbitrarily or capriciously refusing to correct injustice.

The detrimental effect of the Supreme Court's practice of choosing which cases it will hear is far reaching and the practice weakens our entire judicial system. Each time an inferior court fails to follow or incorrectly applies decisions of the Supreme Court, the results have overtones of public importance because the uniformity of national law is threatened. The lawful decisions of the Supreme Court are of no importance if those decisions are not followed and are not enforced. The Supreme Court's decisions are to be used by the inferior courts and by the Executive Branch in the performance of their legal duties. The Supreme Court must enforce its decisions; or else its decisions are empty rulings leaving the Rights of the People unprotected. This is one of the reasons that the Constitution does not permit the Supreme Court to exercise any discretion with regard to whether the Supreme Court will correct the errors of inferior courts when those errors are properly brought before the Supreme Court.

Citizens have the constitutional right to have a case decided in accordance with the law of the land. When an inferior court issues a decision contrary to a decision of the Supreme Court, the Right to have one's case reviewed by the Supreme Court is a Right protected in the Constitution. The Constitution prevents Congress or Justices of the Supreme Court to deny or in any way abridge the rights of the People. The Supreme Court fails to fulfill its constitutional responsibilities when it uses vague, arbitrary, and capricious standards to deny a writ of certiorari. Citizens are deprived of the constitutional right to justice each time the Supreme Court refuses based on a vague, arbitrary, and capricious standard to issue a writ of certiorari.

Whenever an inferior court issues a decision contrary to a decision of the Supreme Court and the Supreme Court refuses to correct the decision of the inferior court, the inferior court is no longer of lower rank, but is elevated to a position equal to the Supreme Court. Article III of the Constitution forbids any of the inferior courts from becoming the equal of the Supreme Court because Article III provides for only one Supreme Court.

The very purpose of the Constitution and the Bill of Rights is to establish legal principles to be applied by the courts — all of the courts, all of the time. The Supreme Court and the inferior courts sit to adjudicate cases involving alleged denials of constitutional rights. The Constitution requires (1) the inferior courts to make decisions consistent with the Constitution, (2) the inferior courts to adhere to the decisions of the Supreme Court, and (3) the Supreme Court to correct the decisions of inferior courts. Such requirements are essential to the maintenance of an orderly society. When a petition for a writ of certiorari alleges that the inferior court has decided a case contrary to decisions of the Supreme Court, the rights secured by and responsibilities assigned in the Constitution prevent the Supreme Court from denying an individual's petition simply because the Justices feel that the case is of no great importance.

The Constitution has tasked the Supreme Court with an important role in the constitutional system. The Supreme Court's judicial authority, as conferred by the Constitution, imposes the solemn, judicial duty to police the decisions of the inferior courts. The Supreme Court is bound by that judicial obligation and the Supreme Court may not refuse or neglect to perform its duty. In the case of Pierson v. Ray, 386 U.S. 547 (1967) the Supreme Court reasoned that it is a judge's duty to decide all cases within his jurisdiction that are brought before him. The judge's duty described by the Supreme Court in *Pierson v. Ray* must apply also to the Justices of the Supreme Court.

The Supreme Court supports the doctrine of absolute immunity for judicial officers by declaring that the correctability of a judge's error on appeal is one of "the safeguards built into the judicial process." See Butz v. Economou, 438 U.S. 478, 512. This position requires that these "safeguards" be in place 100 per cent of the time. There are three levels in the Federal court system. The first level is made up of the district courts. The second level is made up of the courts of appeals. The third level is the Supreme Court. The reasoning of the Supreme Court is that the errors by the judges in the district courts will be or can be corrected by the judges in the courts of appeals; and the errors by the judges in the courts of appeals will be or can be corrected by the Supreme Court. It is impossible for the Supreme Court to correct the errors of judges in the courts of appeals when the Supreme Court refuses to hear the cases. It is impossible to have correctability of error on appeal when the Supreme Court arbitrarily decides which cases it will hear. Using the rationale from the Justices of the Supreme Court, the Supreme Court's practice of issuing a writ of certiorari based on vague, arbitrary, and capricious standards is destructive to the safeguards in our judicial system and denies citizens the constitutional right to justice.

The Supreme Court is an officer of the law and cannot at its discretion sport away the vested rights of the people. The Supreme Court's practice of selecting cases to review based on its vague, arbitrary and capricious standard offends the Constitution.

3. Sovereign, absolute, qualified, and the government contractor immunity and the Federal Tort Claims Act abridge the First Amendment Right to petition the Government for a

redress of grievances and are constantly used to deny citizen's this right.

The Government is a government of expressed and limited powers, and all powers from the People not delegated to the Government are retained by the People and by the States. The First Amendment to the Constitution establishes the following rights: (1) <u>freedom of religion</u>, (2) <u>freedom of speech</u>, (3) <u>freedom of the press</u>, (4) <u>the right to peaceably assemble</u>, and (5) <u>the right to petition the government for a redress of grievances</u>. The First Amendment also forbids the making of any law that restricts any of the Rights listed. The last phrase in the series of Rights — the right to petition the government for a redress of grievances — makes it clear that every citizen has the constitutionally protected Right to **petition** the Government for a **redress** of **grievances**. It is one of our most comprehensive Rights; and one of the ways the Constitution guards against Government abuses, in order to prevent Government officials who are vested with authority from becoming oppressors.

The right to petition the Government for a redress of grievances means that a citizen has the right to file a lawsuit against the Government. Since this country was born, a person who files a lawsuit or complaint has been referred to as a petitioner. One of the first governing documents that *We the People* used was the Articles of Confederation. A portion of Article IX of the Articles of Confederation reads:

> The United States in Congress assembled shall also be the last resort on appeal in all disputes and differences now subsisting or that hereafter may arise between two or more States concerning boundary, jurisdiction, or any other cause whatever; which authority shall always be exercised in the manner following: — Whenever the legislative or executive authority or lawful agency of any State in controversy with another shall present a *petition* to Congress *stating the matter in question and praying for a hearing*, notice thereof shall be given by order of Congress to the legislative or executive authority of the other State in controversy, and a day assigned

for the appearance of the parties by their lawful agents, who shall then be directed to appoint, by joint consent, commissioners or judges to constitute a court for hearing and determining the matter in question; but if they cannot agree, Congress shall name three persons out of each of the United States, and from the list of such persons each party shall alternately strike out one, the petitioners beginning, until the number shall be reduced to thirteen . .

In the Articles of Confederation, a State presented its appeal of a dispute against another State in the form of a petition. In the *Marbury v. Madison* opinion at 163, Chief Justice Marshall points out that "In Great Britain the king himself *is sued in the respectful form of a petition*, and he never fails to, comply with the judgment of his court."

There are several methods of petitioning the Government for a redress of grievances. The filing of a lawsuit by a citizen is only **one** method of petitioning the Government for a redress of grievances. The First Amendment protects **all** of the methods that a citizen may use to petition the Government for a redress of grievances. Congress is the only Government body granted law-making power by the Constitution. If Congress is prevented from making a law, then no law can be made.

Sovereign, absolute and qualified immunities are not based on any law passed by Congress. The Supreme Court established sovereign, absolute, and qualified immunity. These immunities are the result of the personal views of the Justices of the Supreme Court based on what the Justices believe the law *should be* — not what the law actually is. The Supreme Court adopted these immunities because the Justices on the Supreme Court believe that these immunities are necessary (1) for the proper functioning of the Government and (2) to protect the Government and Government officials from lawsuits filed by citizens to redress grievances against the Government or Government officials. The Justices of the Supreme Court use "the common-law" as a basis for these immunities.

The Supreme Court uses the following rationale to explain common-law immunities: "Our cases have proceeded on the assumption that common-law principles of legislative and judicial immunity were incorporated into our judicial system and that they should not be abrogated absent clear legislative intent to do so." See Pulliam v. Allen, 466 U.S. 522, 529; Pierson v. Ray, 386 U.S. 547, 554-555 (1967); and Tenney v. Brandhove, 341 U.S. 367 (1951). The first question requiring an answer is "by whom, or by what, and when were these common-law principles of legislative and judicial immunities incorporated into our judicial system?" The second question requiring an answer is "were these immunities incorporated into our judicial system by lawful authority?"

Common-law is not based on the Constitution or any laws passed by Congress. The Constitution is the supreme law of the land and it delegates **the administration of justice** and **the application** of the law of the land to the federal courts. The Constitution does not grant any federal judge the power to decide what laws or immunities are necessary for the proper functioning of the Government. The power to decide what laws or immunities are necessary for the proper functioning of the Government, with some exceptions to that power, is specifically **given to Congress** in Article I of the Constitution. Federal judges, including the Justices on the Supreme Court, may not exercise the power of law-making because they are not granted any law making authority in the Constitution. Deciding what is and what is not going to be a law of the United States is a law making function and the law-making function belongs to Congress.

The problem with the Supreme Court's reasoning is that the common-law of England **IS NOT** a part of the Constitution or the laws of the United States. If the Constitution incorporated any of those common-law principles, then we would find wording in the Constitution similar to "such parts of the common-law . . . as did form the law of . . . on the nineteenth day of April, one thousand seven hundred seventy-five . . ." The New York State Constitution has just such wording in it and it was in existence before the Constitution. The Commonwealth of Virginia, in the Code of Virginia, Title 1, Chapter 2, Section 1-10, also incorporated the common-law into its law by stating "The common law of England, insofar as it is not repugnant to the principles of the Bill of Rights and Constitution of this Commonwealth, shall continue in full force within the same, and be the rule of decision, except as altered by the General Assembly." The Framers could have included the wording from either the New York State Constitution or the Code of Virginia in the Constitution. They chose not to. In Article VI of the Constitution, the Framers included a provision for all debts and engagements entered into *before* the Constitution to be valid under the Constitution, as under the Confederation. The Framers could have included similar wording regarding the common-law. They chose not to. The Constitution does not incorporate any common-law principles of immunity.

Congress has not incorporated any common-law immunity into the laws of this country. Justices of the Supreme Court incorporated these common-law immunities into the laws of the United States, but the Constitution does not grant the Justices of the Supreme Court the power to incorporate common-law immunities into the laws of the United States. Therefore, lawful authority did not incorporate these common-law immunities. Thus, the common-law immunities granted to the Government by the Supreme Court are unconstitutional.

We must remember that the Constitution says that the Constitution is the supreme law of **this** country. Before the Supreme Court can establish any immunity based on the common-law, the Constitution or a law passed by Congress must incorporate the common-law into the federal law. Justice Brandeis points out in the 1938 case of Erie R. v. Tompkins, 304 U.S. 817, 822 that there is no federal common-law. The Constitution requires federal judges to uphold the Constitution and the laws of the United States. The Justices of the Supreme Court are without any authority or basis for sovereign, absolute, and qualified immunity.

In *Marbury v. Madison* at 164-165 and 170, Chief Justice Marshall makes it clear that sovereign, absolute, and qualified immunities cannot be based on common-law and that these immunities do not exist in the United States. He said,

> Is it to be contended that where the law in precise terms, directs the performance of an act, in which an individual is interested, the law is incapable of securing obedience to its mandate? Is it on account of the character of the person against whom the complaint is made? Is it to be contended

that the heads of departments are not amenable to the laws of their country? Whatever the practice on particular occasions may be, the theory of this practice will certainly never be maintained. No act of the legislature confers so extraordinary a privilege, nor can it derive countenance from the doctrines of the common law.

If one of the heads of departments commits any illegal act, under color of his office, by which an individual sustains an injury, it cannot be pretended that his office alone exempts him from being sued in the ordinary mode of proceeding, and being compelled to obey the judgment of the law.

The Constitution explicitly guarantees, in the First Amendment, that each citizen will always have the Right and the opportunity to have his grievance against the Government heard. A United States citizen's Right to sue the Government for wrongs committed is a right retained by the People that has never been surrendered to the Government. Thus, when a citizen of the United States sues the Government, or any Government official, the Constitution forbids the defense of sovereign, absolute, or qualified immunity. These immunities inhibit the exercise of the constitutionally protected Right of a citizen to petition for a redress of grievances. At the very least, they dictate and limit how citizens may petition the Government for redress of grievances. Dictating and limiting how citizens may petition the Government for redress of grievances is also forbidden by the First Amendment to the Constitution.

Federal judges require an express waiver of sovereign immunity by Congress before a citizen may bring a lawsuit against the Government. Before Congress may waive sovereign immunity, there must be something that grants the Government sovereign immunity. Nothing in the Constitution or federal law provides a grant of sovereign immunity. It is the expressed will of the People of the United States, stated plainly and specifically in the First Amendment to the Constitution of the United States, that the Government can be sued by a citizen. Federal judges, by requiring that Congress must first give its permission before a citizen may bring a lawsuit against the Government for a redress of grievances, have built upon a foundation not present in, and indeed contrary to, the Constitution.

In the case of <u>Imbler v. Pachtman</u>, 424 U.S. 422-423, 96 S.Ct. 984, 991, the Supreme Court stated that "public policy" requires absolute and qualified immunity for some Government officials. The "public policy" referred to by the Supreme Court does not exist in the Constitution or in any law written by Congress. In order to establish absolute and qualified immunity for certain Government officials, Justices of the Supreme Court simply decided what the public policy is for our country. The Constitution grants the elected members of Congress the power to decide what "public policy" is. Congress has never established any such "public policy." The Justices of the Supreme Court are not granted the power to decide what public policy is and then decide cases based on their own concept of what that public policy requires. According to the Constitution, the Supreme Court's functions are to decide cases based on what *is* in the Constitution and to interpret the laws based on what Congress has written. It is the duty of the Justices of the Supreme Court to subordinate their own personal views and to subordinate their own ideas of what legislation is wise and what is not.

The First Amendment prevents Congress from establishing such a "public policy." The Framers decided that these immunities are not necessary for the Government to fulfill its governmental functions. "Congress shall make no law . . . abridging . . . the right of the people . . . to petition the Government for a redress of grievances." Establishing such a "public policy" would abridge (restrict) the right of the people to petition the Government for a redress of grievances.

In Article I, Section 6, the Constitution grants members of Congress <u>limited immunity</u> (they are in all cases, except treason, felony and breach of the peace, privileged from arrest during their attendance at, and in going to and from, the session of their respective houses, and they cannot be questioned in any place other than their respective House for any speech or debate in either House). The Framers of the Constitution knew how to grant immunities to the Government. The Framers could have granted the Government or any Government official any immunity they saw fit. However, they decided that sovereign, absolute, and qualified immunities are not necessary for the Government to fulfill its governmental functions. The implementation of immunity defenses by Federal judges for the Government, or for Government officials, to suits brought against the Government by citizens of the United States has caused a tear in the cloth that is the foundation of this nation and infringes on a citizen's constitutional rights and freedoms.

The government contractor immunity was established by federal judges based on the reasoning that a government contractor shares the sovereign immunity of the Government. There is no sovereign immunity for the Government, so the government contractor immunity cannot exist.

In order for any of the immunities discussed above to be constitutional, the Constitution must grant Federal judges the power to create laws and the power to decide what immunities are necessary for the proper execution of the powers vested in the Government or in any department or officer thereof. Of course, this is not so.

The district court's decision, which was affirmed by the Court of Appeals, is that your Petitioner does not have standing to bring this suit. The district court's decision is error. Petitioner alleges in his complaint that he and others similarly situated have suffered injury in fact as a result of (1) the doctrine of sovereign immunity, (2) the Judiciary Act of 1925, and (3) the Supreme Court's arbitrary and capricious denial of a petition for a writ of certiorari. At the pleading stage, the district court decided that your Petitioner cannot prove a variety of issues necessary to this case. The district court's decision is not based on the evidence because the only evidence before the district court was Petitioner's verified complaint and verified response to the Respondent's motion to dismiss. The decisions of the district are based solely on the unsupported assertions of the Respondent. Respondent asserted sovereign immunity as a defense to this suit that challenges the constitutionality of sovereign immunity. This Court has firmly established that your Petitioner need not prove any of the allegations in the complaint at the pleading stage. The district court is not at liberty to speculate on what proof a litigant will be able to produce and then deny him the right to present his case based on that speculation.

CONCLUSION

This case presents important questions concerning the functioning of this Court that ought to be decided by this Court. If the Constitution has any substance, then this Court should issue a writ of certiorari to the United States Court of Appeals for the Fourth Circuit. This Court should use its authority to bring up this entire case for a decision from this Court.

As you can see this petition directly challenges the functioning of the Supreme Court, its authority to pick and choose the cases it will hear, and the constitutionality of the immunities, put in place by the Supreme Court, which prevent you and I from petitioning for a redress of grievances. The Justices of the Supreme Court did not find that the issues raised by this petition are of any importance to this nation. The Justices refused to hear the case.

The Supreme Court's decision to deny this petition was sent via a letter dated January 19, 1999. The body of the letter reads,

The Court today entered the following order in the above-entitled case:

The petition for a writ of certiorari is denied.

Sincerely,

William K. Suter, Clerk

This letter is not signed. Did you notice that this letter does not contain any reason for the denial of the petition? The reason for the denial of the petition must be in the order mentioned in the letter. The following letter was sent to the clerk:

Dear Mr. Suter:

I received your letter of January 19, 1999 advising me that on that date the Court entered an order in Wright v. United States, No. 98-914. A copy of the Court's order does not accompany your letter , so, please send me a copy of the order issued by the Court which contains the Court's decision in my case.

Sincerely,

The Clerk did respond to this letter and sent the following document:

ON PETITION FOR WRIT OF CERTIORARI to the United States Court of Appeals for the Fourth Circuit, No. 98-2021.

ON CONSIDERATION of the petition for a writ of certiorari herein to the United States Court of Appeals for the Fourth Circuit.

IT IS ORDERED by this Court that the said petition be, and the same is hereby, denied.

January 19, 1999

WILLIAM K. SUTER
Clerk of the Supreme Court of the United States

I was surprised to see that this "order" is unsigned and that it has the signature block of the Clerk instead of one of the Justices of the Supreme Court. I read the Rules of the Supreme Court again. I looked for the authority for the Clerk of the Supreme Court to issue an order on behalf of the Court. I telephoned the Office of the Clerk of the Supreme Court and asked one very simple question. "Where can I find the authority for the Clerk of the Supreme Court to issue an order on behalf of the Supreme Court of the United States?' The answer I was given is that after the Court renders a decision it is a part of the Clerk's duties to correspond with the parties. It may be a part of the duties of the Clerk to correspond with the parties, but those correspondence duties do not provide the authority to issue orders. Issuing an order is the equivalent to issuing a decision and only Justices of the Supreme Court are granted the authority to issue decisions.

I'm going to share my suspensions regarding this "order." This order was created so that the Clerk would have something to send in response to the letter requesting a copy of the order entered by the Supreme Court. I mean that orders like this one are not created or entered in the normal course of the Supreme Court's business. If this order was created and entered on January 19, 1999, then there would be no need for the Clerk to create a letter on the same day and send the letter telling about the order. The Clerk doubles his workload by writing the letter.

It's difficult to believe that this order was written by one of the Justices of the Supreme Court because "ON CONSIDERATION of the petition for a writ of certiorari herein to the United States Court of Appeals for the Fourth Circuit" has a period at the end, but it is not a sentence. Surely, each Justice on the Supreme Court knows how to write complete sentences, by maybe not.

I am certain that any one of the Justices on the Supreme Court would tell us that he or she is not above the Constitution. I don't believe that any of them are so arrogant that they would actually *say* that the Constitution is beneath them. Which brings us to the question "If they are not above the Constitution, then why do they not follow the Constitution, or subordinate their views and opinions on how *they* would like things to be to the requirements in the Constitution?" This entire circumstance, including the secret meetings, the secret votes, the unsigned letters, and the unsigned orders, is evidence that the Justices are going to do just as they please, no matter what the Constitution says. The denial of this petition, without comment or explanation, proves that when issues involve the behavior of the Justices or the operation of the Supreme Court the Justices do not and will not acknowledge the sovereignty of *We the People*. The Supreme Court's denial of this petition demonstrates that at least six of the nine Justices have little respect for the Constitution, no respect for the sovereignty that resides within each of us, and no respect for the truth. The facts show that the Congress has failed to watch the Justices and the operation of the Supreme Court. Congress has left the Justices and the Supreme Court to do as they please. Therefore, each member of Congress and each Justice must share equal responsibility for the unconstitutional conduct and decisions of the Justices and for the unconstitutional operation of the Supreme Court.

In the Constitution *We the People* establish a system to insure justice and to provide for a redress of grievances against the Government. Government officials have modified, ruined, and corrupted that system, so that it no longer provides any protection or guarantees for us, the *People*, the true sovereigns of this nation. The system *We the People* established in the Constitution to protect our Rights no longer does so. It now functions to protect the power-mad Government officials and it functions with little and usually no regard for the Rights of the *People*.

According to congressional records, on March 30, 1922 during the hearing on House Resolution 10479 before the Committee on the Judiciary, House of Representatives, Sixty-Seventh Congress, Second Session, the following exchange occurred:

Justice Willis Van Devanter — "But, as to the writ of certiorari, I intended to indicate that the petition must make an affirmative showing of why the case should be taken by our court and the decision below reviewed. The showing must make it plain that there is something substantial — a real question — requiring decision — something that appeals to a sound discretion."

Mr. Christopherson — "I think I have it clear now, and I thank you."

Mr. Montague — "Is it the purpose of the court still to exercise very careful scrutiny under the discretionary power in the method you have heretofore indicated?"

Justice Willis Van Devanter — "It is."

Mr. Montague — "Although you ask for discretionary power, you propose to exercise it in the method you have heretofore exercised it."

Justice Willis Van Devanter — "Certainly. Of course, we could not maintain the institution and make it accomplish its purpose unless we did, and there is no purpose to do anything else."

Mr. Montague — "I think I understand, but I wanted the record to show that."

Clearly, this petition makes it plain "that there is something substantial — a real question — requiring decision — something that appeals to a sound discretion." The Supreme Court has not previously decided the questions presented by this petition. There can be no doubt that the questions presented are of great importance to every citizen of the United States. Still, the Justices refuse to hear this case. Why?

I was extremely curious to see what questions are presented in the petitions granted by the Justices. Considering the magnitude of the questions raised in this petition, surely each of the petitions granted by the Justices raises some monumental questions or constitutional issues of great importance to *every* citizen. I needed to see what the Justices considered "something substantial — a real question — requiring decision — something that appeals to a sound discretion." I telephoned the Supreme Court Clerk's office and ask where I could obtain information that shows me the petitions granted and the questions those petitions present. The young woman was very helpful and told me that I could find the information on the Internet at www.law.cornell.edu/supct. I was off to the Internet. Remember that this petition was denied on January 19, 1999. On the web site, I found that on January 15, 1999 the Justices granted the petition below:

Docket Number 98-0727
Question Presented:
When may an attorney appeal a sanctions order:
not until final judgment (the rule in the Sixth and Tenth Circuits);

immediately, so long as she is no longer participating in the case (the rule in the Fifth Circuit);

immediately, so long as she is so longer participating and the appeal is not intertwined with the merits of the case (the rule in Third Circuit);

immediately, so long as the sanction is "significant" (the rule in the Eleventh Circuit);

or immediately, without conditions (the rule in the Second, Seventh, Eighth, and Night Circuits, but rejected by the First, Fourth, and Federal Circuits?).

Let's review Rule 10 of the Rules of the Supreme Court. Maybe we'll find the reason that this petition was granted and petition No. 98-0914 was denied.

Rules of the Supreme Court
Rule 10. Considerations Governing Review on Certiorari

Review on a writ of certiorari is not a matter of right, but of judicial discretion. A petition for a writ of certiorari will be granted only for compelling reasons. The following, although neither controlling nor fully measuring the Court's discretion, indicate the character of the reasons the Court considers:

(a) a United States court of appeals has entered a decision in conflict with the decision of another United States court of appeals in the same important matter; has decided an important federal question in a way that conflicts with a decision by a state court of last resort; or has so far departed from the accepted and usual course of judicial proceedings, or sanctioned such a departure by a lower court, as to call for an exercise of this Court's supervisory power;

(b) a state court of last resort has decided an important federal question in a way that conflicts with the decision of another state court of last resort or of a United States court of appeals;

(c) a state court or a United States court of appeals has decided an important question of federal law that has not been, but should be, settled by this Court, or has decided an important federal question in a way that conflicts with relevant decisions of this Court.

A petition for a writ of certiorari is rarely granted when the asserted error consists of erroneous factual findings or the misapplication of a properly stated rule of law.

The Supreme Court's Rules state "a petition for a writ of certiorari will be granted only for compelling reasons." Well, the compelling reasons for granting the denied petition are clearly stated in that petition. The granted petition does not contain a single compelling reason for granting it. It does not contend that any of the rules of any Federal Circuit are unconstitutional or that any decision of a Court of Appeals is in conflict with another Court of Appeals. The granted petition does not present a single concerning a constitutional issue, or present any questions concerning violated rights, or any issues of importance to every citizen of this country. In short, the granted petition is not of importance to many people besides the person who filed it. The one question presented by the granted petition can hardly be said to be "something substantial — a real question — requiring decision — something that appeals to a sound discretion." It certainly is not of equal or greater importance to the questions presented by the denied petition. The granted petition simply asks the Justices of the Supreme Court — which rule should I follow? Let's help the Justices out with this question. The answer to the question presented in the granted petition is — you should follow the rule that is applicable to the Federal Circuit that has jurisdiction over your case!

One petition is granted on January 15th and one is denied on January 19th. The Justices must have been considering both petitions at the same time. There isn't a first come first served or quota system in place at the Supreme Court, so neither can be the reason one petition was granted and the other petition denied. A side-by-side comparison of the questions presented by the two petitions shows that the petition the Justices denied must far surpass whatever standards the Justices used to grant the petition concerning sanctions. At the very least, the selection process involving these two petitions proves that the Supreme Court's method of selecting cases to review is absolutely arbitrary!

The Justices' decision not to hear this important case cannot be based on sound discretion or sound reasoning and the Justices no longer, if they ever did, "exercise very careful scrutiny under the discretionary power." Their decision shows that the Justices made a conscious decision to ignore the Constitution, to continue their selfish unconstitutional behavior, and to continue the Government's unconstitutional immunities. Well, I suppose this means, as Justice Willis Van Devanter testified, that the institution (the Supreme Court) is not being maintained and it cannot accomplish its purpose. Could the Justices have a reason for refusing to hear this case? The answer is easy. The Justices read the petition and realize at least two things. First, that their discretionary power **IS** unconstitutional. Second, the Supreme Court functions outside of the Constitution. The Justices refuse to change and submit to the requirements in the Constitution.

In delivering the opinion of the Court in the 1819 Supreme Court case of McCulloch v. Maryland, Volume 17 of the United States Reports, page 316, Mr. Chief Justice Marshall wrote,

"The government proceeds directly from the people; is 'ordained and established,' in the name of the people; and is declared to be ordained, 'in order to form a more perfect union, establish justice, insure domestic tranquillity, and secure the blessings of liberty to themselves and to their posterity.' "

In the same opinion he also wrote,

"The government of the Union, then is, emphatically and truly, a government of the people. In form, and in substance, it emanates from them. Its powers are granted by them, and are to be exercised directly on them, and for their benefit."

I would ask any Justice or any member of Congress to explain the benefit to the *People* for the Supreme Court to operate contrary to the Constitution, but there is no point. There cannot be **any** benefit for the *People* in the Supreme Court's unconstitutional operation, or in the Supreme Court's refusal to determine the constitutionality of the law that forms the foundation for the Supreme Court's operation.

The reason the Justices refused to hear this case is fairly obvious. The Justices refused to hear this case because there is no satisfactory defense to the arguments raised in the petition. The Supreme Court would be forced to change to way it does to conform to the requirements contained in the Constitution! The decision of the Justices not to hear this case is the ultimate proof that the Supreme Court does not follow the Constitution and cares little about protecting our rights.

According to the Office of the Clerk of the Supreme Court, the Supreme Court Justices meet in a secret conference and hold a secret vote to decide to accept or reject a petition for a writ of certiorari. Four of the nine Supreme Court Justices must vote to accept a petition for a writ of certiorari. We know that at least six of the present nine Supreme Court Justices are without honor and lack integrity because the Court refuses to grant this petition, refuses to look at itself and examine the validity of the foundation upon which the Court functions. The facts show that the Supreme Court operates contrary to the Constitution and that the Justices of that Court refuse to correct the Court's unconstitutional behavior. The Supreme Court is an integral part of the system of justice established in the Constitution, but it operates contrary to the Constitution. Therefore, the system of justice established in the Constitution does not exist. The Supreme Court does not exist outside of the system of justice established in the Constitution. The current Supreme Court and the rest of the Federal Judiciary are merely a sham. So, now that we've completed our examination of the Supreme Court let me put this question to you. What are the intent and the real meaning of the words "EQUAL JUSTICE UNDER LAW" that are inscribed on the front of the Supreme Court building?

THE
EXECUTIVE
BRANCH

Article II of the Constitution

The executive Power shall be vested in a
President of the United States of America.

"I do solemnly swear (or affirm) that I will
faithfully execute the Office of President
of the United States, and will to the best of
my Ability, preserve, protect and defend
the Constitution of the United States."

The President shall be Commander in Chief
of the Army and Navy of the United States

" . . . he shall take Care that the
Laws be faithfully executed . . ."

THE GOVERNMENT PERPETUATES & CONDONES DISCRIMINATION

THE EQUAL EMPLOYMENT OPPORTUNITY COMMISSION

Article II of the Constitution provides that the Executive Branch agencies are under the direction and supervision of the President of the United States. The Constitution makes it the first obligation of the President to faithfully execute the Office of President of the United States. Let's see what Black's Law Dictionary has to say about the word faithfully. **Faithfully** is defined as "**conscientious diligence or faithfulness in meeting obligations. Truthfully, sincerely, accurately**." Article II, Section 2 of the Constitution of the United States requires that the President "**shall take care that the laws be faithfully executed**." Let's get the definition from Black's Law Dictionary for the word *care*. The definition reads "**watchful attention; concern; custody; diligence; opposite of negligence or carelessness; prudence; regard; vigilance. To be concerned with, and to attend to, the needs of oneself or another**." The President is required by oath and the Constitution to execute the Office of President of the United States truthfully, sincerely, accurately, and with conscientious diligence and to be vigilant that the laws are truthfully, sincerely, and accurately executed. With regard to discrimination, each President since 1964 has failed to in these responsibilities.

Congress passed the Civil Rights Act of 1964 to **eradicate** discrimination based on race, color, religion, sex, or national origin and declared that its policy should have the "highest priority." Congress created the Equal Employment Opportunity Commission (EEOC) as an agency in the Executive Branch and it was given primary enforcement authority for the Government.

ONCE UPON A TIME

We begin a thorough review of the Equal Employment Opportunity Act of 1972. A review of portions of the Legislative History of the Equal Employment Opportunity Act of 1972 is necessary. "A little more than 6 years ago, Congress enacted Title VII of the Civil Rights Act of 1964, Public Law 88-352, 42 U.S.C. 2000(e)-2000(e-15). That act recognized the prevalence of discriminatory employment practices in the United States and the need for Federal legislation to deal with the problem." "Despite the commitment of

Congress to the goal of equal employment opportunity for all our citizens, the machinery created by the Civil Rights Act of 1964 is not adequate." "The time has come to bring an end to job discrimination once and for all, and to insure every citizen the opportunity for the decent self-respect that accompanies a job commensurate with one's abilities."[1] "It has been the emphasis on voluntariness that has proven to be most detrimental to the successful operation of Title VII." "Administrative tribunals are better equipped to handle the complicated issues involved in employment discrimination cases." "Administrative tribunals are better suited to rapid resolution of such complex issues than are Courts."[2] "The Constitution is as imperative in its prohibition of discrimination in state and local government employment as it is in barring discrimination in Federal jobs." "Although the aggrieved individual may enforce his rights directly in the Federal district courts, this remedy, as already noted, is frequently an empty promise due to the expense and time involved in pursuing a Federal court suit. It is unrealistic to expect disadvantaged individuals to bear the burden." "The Constitution has recognized that it is inimical to the democratic form of government to allow the existence of discrimination in those bureaucratic systems which most directly affect the daily interactions of this Nation's citizens. The clear intention of the Constitution, embodied in the Thirteenth and Fourteenth Amendments, is to prohibit all forms of discrimination."[3] "A critical defect of the Federal equal employment program has been the failure of the complaint process. That process has impeded rather than advanced the goal of the elimination of discrimination in Federal employment. The defect, which existed under the old complaint procedure, was not corrected by the new complaint process. The new procedure, intended to provide for the informal resolution of complaints, has, in practice, denied employees adequate opportunity for impartial investigation and resolution of complaints."

---

[1] Legislative History, Equal Employment Opportunity Act of 1972, House Report Number 92-238, under the heading NEED FOR THE BILL.

[2] Legislative History, Equal Employment Opportunity Act of 1972, House Report Number 92-238, under the heading CEASE AND DESIST ENFORCEMENT POWERS.

[3] Legislative History, Equal Employment Opportunity Act of 1972, House Report Number 92-238, under the heading STATE AND LOCAL GOVERNMENT EMPLOYEES.

CONGRESS CORRECTS THE PROBLEM

"To correct this entrenched discrimination in the Federal service, it is necessary to insure the effective application of uniform, fair and strongly enforced policies. The present law and the proposed statute do not permit industry and labor organizations to be the judge of their own conduct in the area of employment discrimination. There is no reason why government agencies should not be treated similarly. Indeed, the government itself should set the example by permitting its conduct to be reviewed by an impartial tribunal. Because the Equal Employment Opportunity Commission is the expert agency in the field of employment discrimination and because it is an independent agency removed from the administration of Federal employment, it is the most logical place for the enforcement power to be vested." "The Commission is established as a government administrative agency to protect employees against discrimination." "The Equal Employment Opportunity Commission will be authorized by the statute to hear complaints of discrimination in Federal employment and establish appropriate procedures for an impartial adjudication of the complaints."[4]

THE SLIGHT OF HAND BY THE CIVIL SERVICE COMMISSION

In 1972 Congress determined that a critical defect of the Federal equal employment program was the failure of the complaint process used by the Civil Service Commission because the complaint process impeded rather than advanced the goal of the elimination of discrimination. Naturally, now the research focuses on the Civil Service Commission's (CSC) congressionally condemned complaint process. Our inquiry begins with the Federal Register, Volume 34, Number 53, Wednesday, March 19, 1969, page 5367. The CSC's complaint process included:

1. A requirement that a Federal employee seek precomplaint counseling,

---

[4] Legislative History, Equal Employment Opportunity Act of 1972, House Report Number 92-238, under the heading FEDERAL EMPLOYMENT.

181

2. A requirement to file the complaint in writing within 15 days after final interview with EEO Counselor
3. A provision that allows the agency to dismiss a complaint for various reasons, and
4. A provision for a hearing conducted by an appeals examiner who makes a recommended decision to the head of the agency.

After the passage of the Equal Employment Opportunity Act of 1972, the CSC revises Part 713 of the Code of Federal Regulations in the Federal Register, Volume 37, Number 205, page 22727. Numbers 1, 3, and 4 above remain the same. Number 2 changes from "within 15 days" to "within 30 days." In both Federal Register publications, the CSC failed to comply with the notice requirements of the APA. The CSC did not provide a proposed notice of rule making, an opportunity to comment before issuing the final rule, and the rule was not effective thirty days after publication but was effective immediately.

SABOTAGE BY THE U.S EQUAL EMPLOYMENT OPPORTUNITY COMMISSION

The Executive Branch does not transfer the enforcement authority from the CSC to the EEOC until 1978 in Reorganization Plan Number 1. In the Federal Register, Volume 43, Number 251, page 60900, the EEOC publishes a final regulation. In this final regulation the EEOC simply adopts the CSC's regulations for the processing of EEO complaints. The publication date is December 29, 1978 and the effective date is January 1, 1979. The EEOC violated the provisions of the APA because the EEOC, like the CSC, failed to publish a notice of proposed rule making, failed to provide the public with an opportunity to comment before issuing the final rule, and did not publish 30 days in advance. This final regulation is signed by Eleanor Holmes Norton, Chair, EEOC. The EEOC adopted the exact process that Congress determined was a critical defect of the Federal equal employment program and the cause for the failure of the complaint process. In 2003, during the defense of a civil lawsuit filed against the EEOC in United States District Court for the District of Columbia (Civil Case Number1:03CV00837 (CKK)), the Department of Justice (DOJ) and the EEOC proudly boast that the process in use by the EEOC today is the very same process that Congress found unacceptable 30 years ago.

SYSTEM SAFEGUARDS

The administrative justice system safeguards begin with the Administrative Procedure Act- Public Law 404 (APA) passed in 1947. The APA creates the position of hearing examiner. On March 27, 1978 in Public Law 95-251 the hearing examiner position created in the APA is reclassified as administrative law judge (ALJ). The position of administrative judge (AJ) is not created or mentioned. The hearing examiner's decisional independence is protected from undue agency influence. "To insure the independence and impartiality of the administrative process, section 556 of title 5 requires hearing examiners to serve as presiding officers with respect to rule making or adjudicatory hearings (unless the agency itself, or one or more of its members presides)."[5] Additionally, the APA requires a general notice of proposed rule making shall be published in the Federal Register (unless all persons subject thereto are named and either personally served or otherwise have actual notice thereof in accordance with law), after the required notice that the agency shall afford interested persons an opportunity to participate in the rule making through submission of written data, views, or arguments, and the required publication or service of any substantive rule shall be made not less than thirty days prior to the effective date thereof except as otherwise provided by the agency upon good cause found and published with the rule.

ALJ's are an integral part of the administrative tribunal. The Legislative History of the Equal Employment Opportunity Act of 1972, House Report 92-238 shows also that "in an effort to secure an accurate estimate of the projected costs of this legislation to satisfy the requirements of clause 7 of rule XIII the General Subcommittee on Labor, through its chairman, the Honorable John H. Dent, sought

---

[5] Legislative History, Administrative Law Judges-Civil Service, P.L. 95-251, Senate Report No. 95-697, Background,

the views of the Equal Employment Opportunity Commission." The EEOC's response to that inquiry is contained in a letter dated April 22, 1971 and the response proves that the EEOC understood several critical issues. First, Congress intends that the EEOC conduct adjudicatory hearings. Second, Congress intents that a hearing examiner conduct the EEOC hearings. The EEOC response makes clear that the EEOC understood that its adjudicatory hearings required "hearing examiners."[6] The intent of Congress is clear and that is that the EEOC is to conduct impartial adjudications.

ADMINISTRATIVE JUDGE: A FICTIONAL CHARACTER

The EEOC conducts hearings. However, the EEOC does not use ALJ's to conduct its hearings. Instead the EEOC employs an individual whom the EEOC refers to as an Administrative Judge (AJ). However, the AJ position does not actually exist. It is not an official title or position. What is an AJ really? An AJ is actually an attorney-examiner. The position description for each attorney-examiner position shows that the position is in the GS-0905 classification series.

THE MAKING OF THE ADMINISTRATIVE JUDGE

Congress created the ALJ position, but did not create the AJ position. So, who created the AJ position and when and how? Here is what is known. In the Federal Register Volume 51 dated July 10, 1986 the Merit Systems Protection Board (MSPB) issues final regulations. The summary reads, "The Merits Systems Protection Board is republishing its entire rules of practice and procedure in this Part to eliminate any confusion because of improper structure or text resulting from previous piecemeal changes and temporary pilot programs." On page 25149 § 1201.4 General definitions (a) Presiding official reads "Any person authorized by the Board to preside over any hearing or to make a decision on the record, including an attorney-

---

[6] Hearing examiner positions were created 26 years earlier in the APA. On March 27, 2978, Congress changed the hearing examiner title to Administrative Law Judge, P.L. 95-251.

examiner, an administrative judge, an administrative law judge, the Board, or any of the Members of the Board." The MSPB mentions the AJ for the first time in a final regulation. The APA requires that the first reference to AJ be in the notice of proposed rulemaking and that the public has a chance to comment.

In the Supplementary Information on page 25146 the MSPB writes "On June 29, 1979, the Board published final regulations of practice and procedure (44 FR 38842) implementing its adjudicatory responsibilities under the Civil Service Reform Act of 1978 (Pub. L. 95-454)." The final regulations of practice and procedure published on June 29, 1979 are not found on page 38842, but on page 38342 of Volume 44 of the Federal Register. General definitions are found on page 38350 and read, "(a) Presiding official. Any person designated by the Board to preside over any hearing or to make a decision on the record, including an appeals officer, an administrative law judge, the Board, or any of the Members of the Board." There is no reference to AJ.

The EEOC introduces the AJ into its regulations in the same unlawful manner. On August 18, 1986 in Federal Register Volume 51 beginning on page 29482 the EEOC issues a notice of proposed rulemaking. On page 29487 is § 1613.218 Hearing. Subparagraph (a) reads "Complaints examiner. The hearing shall be conducted by a Commission complaints examiner, except in instances where the Commission finds it is practical to delegate this responsibility to a Complaints Examiner from another agency who shall not be an employee of the agency in which the complaint arose." There is no mention or reference to the use of an AJ. On October 30, 1987 in Federal Register Volume 52 beginning on page 41920 the EEOC issues a Final Rule. On page 41921 the EEOC writes "In response to the comments on § 1613.218, the Commission made a number of clarifying revisions. Three significant changes were made. First, the authority of Administrative Judges, in response to a party's request, to order production of evidence or witnesses was clarified."

In 1986 the MSPB fails to follow the provisions of the APA and introduces the AJ for the first time in a final regulation. One year later the EEOC follows the MSPB's lead and pulls the same unlawful stunt. Coincidence?

THE WRONG PERSON FOR THE JOB

Information published by the Office of Personnel Management (OPM) gives the series definition for the GS-0905 General Attorney Series. It may only adjudicate *cases arising under contracts or under the regulations of a Federal Government agency when such regulations have the effect of law, and rendering decisions or making recommendations for disposition of such cases*." **Federal employee EEO complaints do not involve hearings arising under contracts or under the regulations of a Federal Government agency when such regulations have the effect of law**. Therefore, it is inappropriate for the EEOC's and the MSPB's attorney-examiners to adjudicate Federal employee EEO complaints. Also, the GS-905 attorney-examiner position may not adjudicate administrative procedure act hearings because the attorney-examiner is not the agency, one or more members of the body which comprises the agency, or examiners appointed as provided in the APA.

When a Federal employee files an appeal of an agency's final decision with the EEOC an attorney in the GS-905 series decides the appeal. The EEOC's official title for the position is General Attorney. "The incumbent processes and renders decisions on a variety of cases, a substantial number of which involve highly complex or unusual novel issues, for which there is unsettled or no Commission policy or precedent. The incumbent, through the decision writing process (which includes participating in Special Assistant's meetings and making oral presentations at Commission meetings), will assist the Commissioners in formulating policy and precedent designed to resolve such issues and thereafter provide guidance to ensure the development of a consistent body of law concerning such issues."[7] Can an individual responsible for formulating EEOC policy enjoy decisional independence regarding that policy? Regardless, the individual who is deciding appeals at the EEOC is in the wrong job series and not an ALJ.

---

[7] Position Description, dated April 27, 1999, General Attorney (Civil Rights) GS-0905, Appeals Division, Appellate Review Programs, Office of Federal Operations, Office of the Chairwomen, Equal Employment Opportunity Commission.

A PROPERLY TRAINED ADJUDICATOR
IS ESSENTIAL FOR A FAIR TRIAL

The U.S. Code Title 5, Part III, Subpart C, Chapter 41, Section 4103(a) requires that the EEOC train its employees. The EEOC admits that it does not provide standard training to newly hired attorney-examiners. In a letter, dated November 2, 2001, A. Jacy Thurmond, Jr., Assistant Legal Counsel at the EEOC, writes "The EEOC does not provide standard training to newly hired Administrative Judges or Supervisory Administrative Judges." If somehow the EEOC could justify the use of AJ's, then the EEOC still fails to provide training to them.

DISREGARD THE LAW JUST DO WHAT I TELL YOU

The EEOC's attorney-examiners are subject to undue agency influence and do not enjoy decisional independence. For example, Chapter 2, paragraph III, of the U.S. EEOC Handbook for Administrative Judges, dated July 1, 2002, states "AJ's must follow Commission policy and precedent in adjudicating their cases. When there is a conflict between the Commission's position and that of the Circuit Court in the jurisdiction where the AJ sits, an AJ must follow Commission policy."

WILL THE REAL JUDGE ENTER AND SIGN IT PLEASE

The EEOC actually contracts private attorneys to represent themselves as administrative judges and adjudicate Federal employee EEO complaints.[8] Of course, there is no authority that establishes an AJ or that authorizes the EEOC to contract out its adjudication function. After all, adjudication of EEO complaints is an inherently governmental function because the authority to adjudicate stems from the U.S. Constitution and the laws of the United States. The EEOC has not promulgated any regulations that permit a private

---

[8] Letter dated March 17, 2003 from Donald J. Names, Director, Special Services Staff, EEOC to Melvin Hirshman, Bar Counsel, Attorney Grievance Commission of Maryland.

citizen to adjudicate Federal employee EEO complaints. Congress has appropriated no funds for this expense, but the EEOC spends appropriated funds for it.

DON'T CALL ME THAT

Title 5 Section 5105 of the United States Code contains the standards for classification of positions. Paragraph (c) requires that the use of official class titles. The last sentence of this paragraph provides that "this requirement does not prevent the use of organizational or other titles for internal administration, public convenience, law enforcement, or similar purposes." The use of the title administrative judge does not serve a law enforcement purpose and is not for public convenience or any similar purpose. Federal law prohibits the use of the title administrative judge outside of the organization. Such a restriction does not restrain the EEOC or the MSPB.

The use of the title of AJ outside of the agency has detrimental consequences. First, AJ's are believed to be the same as ALJ's. Of course, they are not the same. Second, Congress refers to the position of attorney examiner as AJ in the NO FEAR legislation. Congressional use of the title adds credibility to a position that was established contrary to the APA and is used to prevent the impartial adjudication of complaints filed with the EEOC and the MSPB.

THE HIDDEN JEWEL IN EXECUTIVE ORDER 11478

On August 8, 1969 President Richard M. Nixon signs Executive Order 11478. It reads, in relevant part, "Section 1. It is the policy of the Government of the United States to provide equal opportunity in Federal employment for all persons, to prohibit discrimination in employment because of race, color, religion, sex, or national origin, and to promote the full realization of equal employment opportunity through a continuing affirmative program in each executive department and agency. This policy of equal opportunity applies to and must be an integral part of every aspect of personnel policy and practice in the employment, development, and advancement, and treatment of civilian employees of the Federal Government." On December

28, 1978 the President of the United States issues Executive Order 12106. This Executive Order amends the first sentence of Section 1 of Executive Order No. 11478 by substituting "national origin, handicap, or age" for "or national origin." Executive Order 11478 does not limit nondiscrimination to personnel actions, but clearly mandates nondiscrimination in every aspect of the employment, development, advancement, and treatment of Federal employees.

Title VII Section 2000e-16 [Section 717] (a) reads, in relevant part, "All personnel actions affecting employees or applicants for employment . . . in military departments as defined in section 102 of title 5 [United States Code], in executive agencies . . . as defined in section 105 of title 5 [United States Code] in the United States Postal Service and the Postal Rate Commission, in those units of the Government of the District of Columbia having positions in the competitive service, and in those units of the legislative and judicial branches of the Federal government having positions in the competitive service, and in the Library of Congress shall be made free from any discrimination based on race, color, religion, sex, or national origin." Section 2000e-16(c) reads, in relevant part, "a complaint of discrimination based on race, color, religion, sex or national origin, brought pursuant to subsection (a) of this section, Executive Order 11478, or any succeeding Executive orders, or after one hundred and eighty days from the filing of the initial charge with the department . . ."

The EEOC does not recognize a Federal employee's right to bring an EEO complaint pursuant to Executive Order 11478. The EEOC's regulations governing the Federal sector EEO process are found in 29 C.F.R. § 1614. A list of the complaints of discrimination covered these regulations is found in 29 C.F.R. § 1614.103. Executive Order 11478 is not in the list. In the preface of the EEOC's annual report to the President and to Congress for fiscal year 2002, the period from October 1, 2001 through September 30, 2002, the EEOC writes "In the federal sector, the EEOC enforces Title VII of the Civil Rights Act of 1964 (Title VII), which prohibits employment discrimination on the basis of race, color, religion, sex, and national origin; the Age Discrimination in Employment Act of 1967 (ADEA), which prohibits employment discrimination against individuals 40 years of age and older; the Equal Pay Act of 1963 (EPA), which prohibits discrimination on the basis of gender in compensation for substantially similar work under similar conditions; and Sections 501 and 505 of the Rehabilitation Act of 1973 (Rehabilitation Act), which prohibit employment discrimination against federal employees and applicants with disabilities." Executive Order 11478 is not listed among the mandates enforced by the EEOC. The EEOC consistently holds that a Federal employee is not protected in every aspect of his or her "treatment."

FEDERAL EMPLOYEES WITHOUT CONSTITUTIONAL PROTECTION

In an effort to correct the deficiencies noted above, the aforementioned lawsuit was filed. The lawsuit was assigned to United States District Judge Colleen Kollar-Kotelly. She issued a Memorandum Opinion dismissing the lawsuit against the EEOC. In her memorandum opinion, Judge Kollar-Kotelly writes that Title VII provides no cause of action against the EEOC for failing to provide the process designed by Congress, that the APA provides no cause of action for claims under the APA because the EEOC's final order is not in the legal sense of the word a final order, that the EEOC, as an agency in the Federal Government, has sovereign immunity for violations of the Fifth Amendment, and that the EEOC cannot be sued for a failure to comply with Executive Order 11478. Time and time and time again the Supreme Court of the United States decided that the Constitution of the United States applies to prisons and to the inmates therein. Is it possible that Federal employees do not enjoy the same protections that the U.S. Constitution provides to inmates? Of course, the answer is no.

To support her decision to dismiss the APA claims Judge Kollar-Kotelly relies on the process that Congress established for the private sector in Section 706 of Title VII of the Civil Rights Act of 1964, as amended. Of course, the Federal sector process is found in Section 717, not in Section 706. When the Federal courts determine that the Federal Government may violate the Constitution of the United States and citizens have no recourse in the Federal courts the U.S.

Constitution becomes a worthless piece of paper. The fact that the APA specifically provides recourse to the Federal courts from final actions of Federal agencies is no protection when a Federal Judge decides that a final order of an agency is not really a final order, in spite of the fact that the document says final order. In Section 717 of Title VII of the Civil Rights Act of 1964, as amended, Congress decided that Federal employees have recourse for complaints brought pursuant to Executive Order 11478. Judge Kollar-Kotelly decided otherwise.

THE END OR A NEW BEGINNING

The facts establish that the complaint process used by the EEOC is substantially flawed. It is not the process designed by Congress and it is the process condemned by Congress. Remember, the CSC's use of this process is the reason Congress transferred enforcement authority to the EEOC. FED discovered many other flaws in the process. Only the most outrageous ones are included in this article. Judge Kollar-Kotelly's decision proves two important points beyond any doubt. First, as Congress noted in House Report Number 92-238 in the Legislative History of the Equal Employment Opportunity Act of 1972, "although the aggrieved individual may enforce his rights directly in the Federal district courts, this remedy, as already noted, is frequently an empty promise due to the expense and time involved in pursuing a Federal court suit." Indeed, this is an empty promise. Second, the deficiencies in the Federal sector EEO process cannot be corrected by proceeding to Federal court. Judge Kollar-Kotelly's decision establishes that even though Federal courts require that Federal employees must proceed through the Federal sector EEO process (exhaustion of administrative remedies) Federal courts will not require that the EEOC provide the process mandated by Congress. In the conclusion of the memorandum opinion, Judge Kollar-Kotelly writes "However, what Plaintiff is not entitled to do is bring a suit against the EEOC in federal court disputing the procedures the EEOC chooses to implement in hearing those claims brought before it, regardless of the subject of the complaint raised before the EEOC."

It is clear to any reflective thinker that Congress must act quickly and decisively. The solution is simple. Appropriating more funds to the EEOC is not the answer. Congress must correct the deficiencies, leave nothing open to the discretion of the Executive Branch, and hold Government officials personally accountable or stop wasting the American taxpayer's money on the sham known as the Federal EEO process.

After the Civil Rights Act of 1964 was passed, several government regulations concerning equal employment opportunity were written. We will be discussing Title 29 of the Code of Federal Regulations (CFR) parts 1613 and 1614. 29 CFR 1613 was created in 1972 (Federal Register, Volume 37, page 22717, 1972) and 29 CFR 1614 (the successor to 29 CFR 1613) became effective October 1, 1992. 29 CFR 1614.102 mandates that each Government agency shall:

- Maintain a continuing affirmative program to promote equal opportunity and to identify and eliminate discriminatory practices and policies.

- Provide sufficient resources to its equal employment opportunity program to ensure efficient and successful operation.

- Conduct a continuing campaign to eradicate every form of prejudice or discrimination from the agency's personnel policies, practices and working conditions.

- Review, evaluate and control managerial and supervisory performance in such a manner as to insure a continuing affirmative application and vigorous enforcement of the policy of equal opportunity.

- Take appropriate disciplinary action against employees who engage in discriminatory practices.

- Establish a system for periodically evaluating the effectiveness of the agency's overall employment opportunity effort.

- Appraise its personnel operations at regular intervals to assure their conformity with its program.

29 CFR part 1613, the predecessor to 29 CFR part 1614, contained the same requirements.

On August 12, 1969 President Richard Nixon issued Executive Order 11478, EQUAL EMPLOYMENT OPPORTUNITY IN THE FEDERAL GOVERNMENT. It reads, "It has long been the policy of the United States Government to provide equal opportunity in Federal employment on the basis of merit and fitness and without discrimination because of race, color, religion, sex, or national origin. All recent Presidents have fully supported this policy, and have directed department and agency heads to adopt measures to make it a reality . . . NOW, THEREFORE, under and by virtue of the authority vested in me as President of the United States by the Constitution and statutes of the United States, it is ordered as follows: Section 1. It is the policy of the Government of the United States to provide equal employment in Federal employment for all persons, to prohibit discrimination in employment because of race, color, religion, sex, or national origin, and to promote the full realization of equal employment opportunity through a continuing affirmative program in each executive department and agency. This policy of equal opportunity applies to and must be an integral part of every aspect of personnel policy and practice employees of the Federal Government. Section 2. The head of each executive department and agency shall establish and maintain an affirmative program of equal employment opportunity for all civilian employees and applicants for employment within his jurisdiction in accordance with the policy set forth in section 1. It is the responsibility of each department and agency head, to the maximum extent possible, . . . provide for a system within the department or agency for periodically evaluating the effectiveness with which the policy of this Order is being carried out. Section 4. * * * Procedures for the consideration of complaints shall include at least one impartial review within the executive department or agency and shall provide for appeal to the Civil Service Commission."

Not one agency in the Executive Branch complies with the seven requirements contained in 29 CFR part 1614 outlined above. The EEOC does not regularly force agencies to comply with its regulations, so it is not surprising that the EEOC does not force agencies to comply with the law! In spite of the fact that there is a requirement for each agency to have EEO regulations, some Government agencies do not have EEO regulations. The Department of Labor is an example of a Government agency that does not have the required EEO regulations.

Government officials are permitted to lie to Congress and in the courts without penalty. In front of the EEOC, Government attorneys defend the unlawful decisions of Government officials regardless of the truth. In the courts, the Department of Justice defends Government agencies and Government officials regardless of the truth. Government officials intentionally sabotage the civil rights laws by using their agency's civil rights office as a tool of management to support decisions that violate the law.

Government officials do not comply with the law of the land, they do not comply with applicable regulations, and they suffer no consequences for their failure to comply. When Government agencies are presented with evidence of violations of the civil rights law, the agencies fail to properly investigate. Government agencies condone violations of the civil rights law by Government officials and, in fact, Government officials who practice discrimination are promoted. When you want to stop people from robbing banks, you don't ignore them, you don't reward them, and you don't ask them if they understand that it is wrong to rob banks. **YOU PUNISH THEM**. The same is true if you want to stop Government officials from violating the civil rights law. Obviously, our President's do not wish to stop violations of the civil rights law during their respective administrations!!

Some things are pretty plain. The civil rights law has no priority in the Executive Branch, in contrast to the "highest priority" as mandated by Congress. Each President failed to uphold his oath and failed to take care that the laws are faithfully executed. The EEOC does not perform the mission assigned to it by Congress with regard to the Government. None of our representatives needs a degree in rocket science to know that the EEOC fails to comply with its congressional mandate or that the agencies of the Executive Branch fail to comply with the law or the EEOC's regulations.

Of course, if any of our representatives really do want to know just what is actually going on at the EEOC or in the EEO programs in the agencies in the Executive Branch, then he or she simply needs to get out of his or her office and visit the EEOC or the EEO offices of the Executive Branch agencies. History teaches us that expecting our Senators and Congressmen to actually do so is too much to expect. In July 2003, I wrote a letter, regarding the EEOC's and MSPB's failures concerning discrimination, to the Representatives and Senators listed below:

Representatives

Tom DeLay
Dan Burton
Mark E. Souder
Ron Lewis
Chris Cannon
John J. Duncan, Jr.
Candice S. Miller
John Carter
John L. Mica
Edolphus Towns
Carolyn B. Maloney
Danny K. Davis
Diane E. Watson
Linda T. Sanchez

Eleanor Holmes Norton
Rick Boucher
Bob Goodlatte
Frank Wolf
Artur Davis
Wayne Gilchrest
Roy Blunt
Eddie Bernice Johnson

Thomas M. Davis, III
Ileana Ros-Lehtinen
Steven C. LaTourette
Jo Ann S. Davis
Adam H. Putnam
John Sullivan
Tim Murphy
William Janklow
Henry A. Waxman
Paul E. Kanjorski
Elijah E. Cummings
John F. Tierney
Stephen F. Lynch
C.A. Dutch Ruppersberger
Chris Bell

Randy Forbes
Jim Moran
Alcee Hastings
Roscoe Bartlett
Steny H. Hoyer
Albert Wynn

Christopher Shays
John M. McHugh
Doug Ose
Todd Russell Platts
Edward L. Schrock
Nathan Deal
Michael Turner
Marsha Blackburn
Tom Lantos
Bernard Sanders
Dennis J. Kucinich
William Lacy Clay
Chris Van Hollen
Jim Cooper

Eric Cantor

Virgil H. Goode, Jr.
Robert C. Scott
Sheila Jackson-Lee
Benjamin L. Cardin
Major R. Owens
Barbara Lee

Senators

Bill Frist	Tom Daschle	Mitch McConnell
Susan M. Collins	Ted Stevens	George V. Voinovich
Norm Coleman	Arlen Specter	Robert F. Bennett
Peter G. Fitzgerald	John E. Sununu	Richard C. Shelby
Joseph I. Lieberman	Carl Levin	Daniel K. Akaka
Richard J. Durbin	Thomas R. Carper	Mark Dayton
Frank Lautenberg	Mark Pryor	Chuck Grassley
Harry Reid	George Allen	Paul Sarbanes
Barbara Mikulski	John Warner	

Not one of these representatives of the people did anything. In February 2005, I wrote a letter to the Congressional Black Caucus requesting its assistance to secure hearings on the EEOC and MSPB. I received no response and as far as I know the Congressional Black Caucus took no action.

In the summer of 2005, I visited the office of newly elected Senator Barack Obama. I had a meeting with his staffers and during that meeting I requested his assistance in addressing and changing the operation of the EEOC and MSPB. Senator Obama was not interested in changing anything regarding the ongoing discrimination within the Federal Government. Now, his platform is one of change?

On May 12, 2006, I wrote a letter concerning the EEOC's and MSPB's failures to Tom Davis, Chairman, Committee on Government Reform, Jon C. Porter, Chairman, Subcommittee on the Federal Workforce and Agency Organization, Susan Collins, Chairman Committee on Homeland Security and Government Affairs, and George V. Voinovich, Chairman, Subcommittee on Oversight of Government Management, the Federal Workforce, and the District of Columbia. Not one of these representatives of the people did anything.

May 1, 2007 at 2:30 p.m. I met with Congressman Danny K. Davis, Chairman of the House of Representatives Subcommittee on Federal Workforce, Postal Service, and the District of Columbia. During our meeting, I passed along to Congressman Davis all of the information you just read and asked him to hold a hearing on the EEOC and the MSPB. His reply to my request for a hearing was to say, "I don't see a problem with that." Congressman Davis never held the hearing. Why didn't he you ask? I sincerely believe that Congressman Davis did not hold the hearing in order to protect Eleanor Holmes Norton who is a fellow Democrat and Clarence Thomas, an associate justice on the U.S. Supreme Court.

Ms. Norton was the seventh Chair of the EEOC. She served from June 1977 to February 1981. Holding a hearing on the EEOC will, of course, result in Ms. Norton being exposed as a contributor of what is currently wrong with the EEOC. Congressman Davis was not going to have that! It is interesting to note that Clarence Thomas followed Ms. Norton as Chair of the EEOC. He served as Chair from May 1982 to March 1990. He, too, is responsible for the mess known as the EEOC and now he is an associate justice on the U.S. Supreme Court!

In November 2007, news sources reported that, during argument in the case of Federal Express Corp. v. Holowecki, Justices of the U.S. Supreme Court (except Justice Thomas – I wonder why Justice Thomas had nothing to say!) severely criticized the EEOC for its failures. For example, Justice Scalia is reported saying, "Mr. Heytens, let me tell you going in that my . . . main concern in this case, however the decision comes out, is to do something that will require the EEOC to get its act in order, because this is nonsense. This whole situation can be traced back to the agency, and . . . whoever ends up bearing the burden of it, it's the agency's fault, and this scheme has to be revised."

Year after year our representatives in Congress permit the EEOC and Government officials in the Executive Branch to ignore congressional mandates! And who is getting hurt? Not any member of Congress! Not any presidential appointee at the EEOC! *We the People* are the ones footing the bill and being hurt!

THE MERIT SYSTEMS
PROTECTION BOARD

Congress established the U.S. Merit Systems Protection Board (Board) in the Civil Service Reform Act of 1978. It is an agency in the Executive Branch and it is suppose to serve as a guardian of Government employees. The Board's mission is to ensure that Government employees are protected against abuses by management of Government agencies. When a Government employee believes that an agency has violated one of the areas within the jurisdiction of the Board, the Government employee may file an appeal with the Board. An administrative judge of the Board hears the employee's appeal and the administrative judge issues an initial decision in the case. If the employee does not agree with the administrative judge's initial decision, then the employee may file a petition for review of that decision with the Board.

This procedure sounds pretty good, but you probably already suspect that if the Board is in this book — well. You see a big problem with the Board is this — when a petition for review of an administrative judge's initial decision is filed with the Board, the members of the Board are required to review the record in the employee's case, to review what the administrative judge did, to review the decision issued by the administrative judge, and then to issue a final decision. Indications are that the members of the Board do not fulfill their responsibilities.

The Board's decision too often reads *"After full consideration, we DENY the appellant's petition for review of the initial decision issued on (the date is inserted here), because it does not meet the criteria for review set forth in 5 C.F.R. 1201.115. This is the Board's final order in this appeal. The initial decision in this appeal is now final. 5 C.F.R. 1201.113(b)."* The criteria for review set forth in 5 C.F.R. 1201.115 is "The petition for review must state objections to the initial decision that are supported by references to applicable laws or regulations and by specific references to the record." In 1998 a person, who received the Board's "does not meet the criteria for review" decision, took the petition for review, which was filed with the Board, to Mr. Peter Broida, Esquire. Mr. Broida is an attorney who is considered to be an authority on practice before the Board. He was paid for his time and asked to read the petition for review and explain just what is wrong with it. After Mr. Broida read the petition, he responded that he does not know what is wrong with the petition. He also stated that about 70% of all petitions for review to the Board receive the same response. If an attorney who is an authority on practice before the Board does not know, then who would?? The point here is that the Board's "does not meet the criteria for review" is obviously too vague and ambiguous to be of any value.

A federal employee may appeal the Board's "does not meet the criteria for review" to a court of appeals. In the overwhelming majority of cases that are appealed to the court of appeals, judges at the court of appeals uphold the Board's "does not meet the criteria for review" decision. A judge on any court of appeals should never uphold such a vague and ambiguous ruling. There are two reasons for a judge on the court of appeals not upholding such a vague and ambiguous ruling. The first reason is —(this is just too simple) the judge or judges on the court of appeals would be unable to determine the basis for the Board's decision because the Board does not indicate its reasoning for the determination that the petition does not meet the criteria for review. A decision without any reasoning to support the decision is arbitrary and capricious. An arbitrary and capricious decision is reason enough for the court of appeals to overturn the Board's decision.

Two federal court decisions will help to adequately explain this point. In the case of Missouri Broadcasting Corp. v. Federal C. Commission, 94 F.2d 623, 626 the federal court says,

"because no commission exercising the judicial function ought to give a decision without knowing the grounds therefor, and the statement of those grounds necessarily must be drawn from the facts found . . . What we have said, we hope sets a sufficient standard to prevent the recurrence of this question on future appeals."

Also, in the case of Saginaw Broadcasting Co. v. Federal C. Com'n, 96 F.2d 554, 559 the federal court says,

"The requirements that courts, and commissions acting in a quasi-judicial capacity, shall make findings of fact, is a means provided by

Congress for guaranteeing that cases shall be decided according to the evidence and the law, rather than arbitrarily or from extralegal considerations; and findings of fact serve the additional purpose, where provisions for review are made, of apprising the parties and the reviewing tribunal of the factual basis of the action of the court or commission, so that the parties and the reviewing tribunal may determine whether the case has been decided upon the evidence and the law or, on the contrary, upon arbitrary or extralegal considerations. When a decision is accompanied by findings of fact, the reviewing court can decide whether the decision reached by the court or commission follows as a matter of law from the facts stated as its basis, and also whether the facts so stated have any substantial support in the evidence. In the absence of findings of fact the reviewing tribunal can determine neither of these things. The requirement of findings is thus far from a technicality. On the contrary, it is to insure against Star Chamber methods, to make certain that justice shall be administered according to facts and law. This is fully as important in respect of commissions as it is in respect of courts . . . The language of Mr. Justice Butler in Atchison, T. & S. F. Ry. Co. v. United States, 295 U.S. 193, 55 S.Ct. 748, 79 L.Ed. 1382, that: 'This court will not search the record to ascertain whether, by use of what there may be found, general and ambiguous statements in the report intended to serve as findings may by construction be given a meaning sufficiently definite and certain to constitute a valid basis for the order. In the absence of a finding of essential basic facts, the order cannot be sustained.' 295 U.S. 193, at pages 201, 202, 55 S.Ct. 748 at page 752, 79 L.Ed. 1382. seems pertinent. It is not the duty of the court to make findings for the Commission and when the Commission has failed in its duty to make such findings, it is impossible for the court to review its conclusion. This too we regard as reversible error."

The Board, like a commission, performs a quasi-judicial function. The standards set forth in these cases apply equally to the Board's decisions because the standards apply to decisions by a court and a commission. The argument that the Board is not a commission is irrelevant because the Board is lower than (inferior to) a court! These federal court decisions show that the Board may not simply say that a petition "does not meet the criteria for review." The statement "does not meet the criteria for review" is a conclusion and does not contain any reasoning for the conclusion. Therefore, the statement does not serve to apprise the party or the reviewing tribunal (court of appeals) of the factual basis of the Board's decision that the petition "does not meet the criteria for review." The party and the judges on the court of appeals cannot determine whether the Board based its decision on the contents of the petition for review and the regulation, or, on the contrary, upon arbitrary or extralegal considerations. Extralegal considerations can be the Board's WORKLOAD!!! Obviously, if the Board based its decision that a petition for review does not meet the criteria for review on the Board's workload, then the Board's decision is arbitrary! Who knows what the Board based its decision on? I don't know. Do you know? The judges on the court of appeals cannot possibly know because the Board never explains the basis of its decision!

Does the phrase "does not meet the criteria for review" mean that no part of the petition for review meets the criteria for review, only part of the petition for review meets the criteria for review, or not enough of the petition for review meets the criteria for review? If the phrase means that no part of the petition for review meets the criteria for review and a recognized authority like Mr. Broida cannot see that no part of the petition meets the criteria for review, then a Government employee does not stand a chance of receiving justice before the Board because the Government employee's attorney would have no idea what to put in the petition for review. If the phrase means something other than no part of the petition for review meets the criteria for review, then a Government employee does not stand a chance of receiving justice before the Board because the Government employee's attorney would have no idea what to put in the petition for review. There is that magical word **justice** again! You remember, **justice** is one of the reasons *We the People* wrote the Constitution!!

The Board has great power over the cases brought before it, yet it acts arbitrarily and capriciously, in a summary manner, and it acts according to vague criteria, without explaining the reasons for its actions. (I call this behavior *Supreme Court Fallout* or *Supreme*

Court Syndrome because the Supreme Court behaves exactly the same way concerning the issuance of a writ of certiorari.) The federal courts condone the Board's denying justice to many Government employees.

In its annual reports to the Congress, the Board tells Congress that the federal courts condone its behavior and that the federal courts also deny justice to Americans. Now let's see what action Congress has taken to correct these unconstitutional actions. Checking . . . still checking . . . still checking . . . still checking . . . still checking . . . still checking . . . done checking . . . Congress has done **NOTHING!** I am sure that you are surprised! Yea, right. Once again, the members of Congress who have **ASKED** and **PLEADED** with us to elect them to Congress, so that they can look out for our rights, **HAVE FAILED TO DO SO!!!**

PROTECT YOUR RIGHTS, PLEASE DON'T MAKE ME LAUGH

OR

THE JUSTICE DEPARTMENT

Congress established the Department of Justice to investigate and prosecute violations of federal laws. A federal law passed by Congress to guard against the deprivation of citizens rights by persons exercising governmental authority is found in the Title 18 Part I Chapter 13 Section 242 of the U.S. Code. This section of federal law reads,

"Whoever, under color of any law, statute, ordinance, regulation, or custom, willfully subjects any person in any State, Territory, Commonwealth, Possession, or District to the deprivation of any rights, privileges, or immunities secured or protected by the Constitution or laws of the United States, or to different punishments, pains, or penalties, on account of such person being an alien, or by reason of his color, or race, than are prescribed for the punishment of citizens, shall be fined under this title or imprisoned not more than one year, or both; and if bodily injury results from the acts committed in violation of this section or if such acts include the use, attempted use, or threatened use of a dangerous weapon, explosives, or fire, shall be fined under this title or imprisoned not more than ten years, or both; and if death results from the acts committed in violation of this section or if such acts include kidnapping or an attempt to kidnap, aggravated sexual abuse, or an attempt to commit aggravated sexual abuse, or an attempt to kill, shall be fined under this title, or imprisoned for any term of years or for life, or both, or may be sentenced to death."

The Department of Justice refuses to investigate and prosecute violations of this federal law when whites in power deprive blacks of their constitutional rights! When a person of color complains to the Department of Justice that constitutional rights were violated the response from the Department of Justice is the Department of Justice only investigates and prosecutes allegations involving deprivation of constitutional rights caused by the use of excessive force. Now, read the above section of the federal law again. Do you see the words "excessive force" in the section? Of course you don't. So, as long as persons in power deprive you of your constitutional rights without using excessive force it is quite all right with the Department of Justice! Please, don't take my word for it. Pick up the telephone and call your local FBI office and simply ask the question.

In June 2007 I wrote to Senator Jim Webb regarding this very issue. In the letter I demanded that Senator Webb demand that the Department of Justice enforce this section of the U.S. Code because several deputies of Loudoun County Virginia Sheriff broke into my home, without a warrant or any authority at all, and assaulted me. Senator Webb did not bother to even respond to my letter. He did nothing! During his campaign for the U.S. Senate, Senator Webb ran on the platform that our representatives in Congress fail to represent us! Now he is one of those representatives in Congress who fails to represent or, at least, Senator Webb doesn't stand up for the constitutional rights of persons of color!

The Department of Justice investigated and prosecuted Mr. Michael Vick and Mr. Barry Bonds. Mr. Vick was prosecuted for dog fighting and Barry Bonds for perjury regarding steroids in baseball. The Department of Justice will not prosecute whites for breaking the law and depriving persons of color of their constitutional rights, but will prosecute a person of color for mistreating a dog. Apparently, in this country a dog's rights are more important that the constitutional rights of a person of color!

White federal managers perjury themselves every day during proceedings in federal court, and in proceedings before the EEOC and the MSPB. Yet, I know of no federal manager prosecuted for perjury by the Department of Justice. Major league baseball is a GAME! A game which is of less importance that the proper functioning of the federal government! The money spent by the Department of Justice investigating who took what substance in order to better his performance in baseball would have been much better spent repairing the damage caused by Katrina, or repairing America's infrastructure, or feeding and housing the homeless in America, or paying for health care for America's children, or paying down the national debt! Who's taking what performance enhancing substance in baseball is a subject for major league baseball and not a subject that the funds of the taxpayer ought to be spent investigating. Spending taxpayer money investigating the happenings in baseball before repairing the damage caused by Katrina, or repairing America's infrastructure, or feeding and housing the homeless in America, or paying for health care for America's children, or paying down the national debt places baseball ABOVE all of these!

I know the argument that youth look up to professional sports figures. The very same youth need better schools, need health care, need food and clothing and shelter! The officials in the Federal Government must believe that the integrity of baseball it is more important to homeless and hungry youth that shelter or food or clothing or good schools! The very same youth look up to the President of the U.S., lawyers, judges, and many other high profile persons in government. What does the Department of Justice do when these people lie? You know the answer – and it is NOTHING! It doesn't take a degree in rocket science to figure out why these two black men were prosecuted by the Department of Justice when the same or greater violations of federal law by whites in power are ignored by the Justice Department.

Let me provide you with another outrageous example of the Justice Department's failure to protect the constitutional rights of a person of color. I know that the Department of Justice is aware of the situation that follows because I traveled to Atlanta and had a face-to-face with two agents of the Federal Bureau of Investigation in the Atlanta Office of the FBI and explained it all and showed them all of the documents involved. The Department of Justice did not investigate and did not prosecute one single white person for the deprivation of constitutional rights under the color of law. Here is the circumstance.

In **August 2005**, the Department of Transportation, Federal Highway Administration (FHWA) publishes vacancy announcement number FHWA.LK-2005-0079, Program Analyst (Info & Mgmnt Team Leader). Under "QUALIFICATION REQUIREMENTS" the vacancy announcement reads, in relevant part, "The specialized experience must include experience which has equipped the applicant with expert ability and experience with various software packages/ programs for data manipulation and analysis." An African-American female, and a Caucasian female, both apply for the position. Agency documents establish that the African-American female meets the experience with various software packages/programs requirement, but the Caucasian female fails to meet this requirement. In spite of not qualifying for the position, a FHWA Human Resources Office places the Caucasian female's name on the list of qualified candidates.

In **September 2005**, interviews are conducted and the interview sheets also confirm that the Caucasian female does not meet the experience with various software packages/programs requirement. Nevertheless, the FHWA Resource Center Director, a Caucasian female, with the approval of both the FHWA Executive Director, a Caucasian male, and the FHWA Director of Field Services – West, a Caucasian female, the Caucasian female for the position.

The African-American female contacts an EEO counselor on November 1, 2005 and on **December 14, 2005** she files a complaint of discrimination regarding the selection. This EEO complaint is sent to the Regional Director, Atlanta Regional Office, Departmental Office of Civil Rights (DOCR), Department of Transportation (DOT). It is assigned complaint number 2006-20065-FHWA-03. An investigation was conducted and at the conclusion of the investigation a Report of Investigation (ROI) was sent to FHWA. Up to this point **nine** DOT and FHWA people in either management or EEO had the opportunity to review the selection. Yet, it appears that the fact that the Caucasian female was not qualified for the position was either not noticed or ignored.

After the African-American female filed the complaint of discrimination, the Caucasian female selected for the position, who is now the supervisor of the African-American female, and the Caucasian female responsible for making the selection open an investigation alleging that the African-American female misused government funds.

They seized her personal property without proper authority. Obviously, the **seizure of each item of personal property**, without a shred of evidence to support the assertion that any of it was property of the U.S. Government, as well as the **seizure of each item of personal property** is a separate and clear **violation of constitutional rights guaranteed by the Fourth Amendment of the U.S. Constitution** (unreasonable seizures). According to agency documents, **there are at a minimum six separate Fourth Amendment violations**. The

Office of the Inspector General (OIG) is called in to investigate the allegation regarding misused of government funds.

The Inspector General Act of 1978 mandates that the **OIG report expeditiously to the Attorney General** of the United States whenever the OIG has reasonable grounds to believe there is a violation of Federal criminal law. There is no authority that permits the OIG to do anything other than to report to the Attorney General.

According to the Special Agent-in-Charge of the investigation, documents developed during the OIG and FHWA investigations were taken by him and handed over to the District Attorney's Office in Fulton County, Georgia. The purpose was to have the State of Georgia prosecute the African-American female for stealing funds from the FHWA. The Fulton County DA's Office secured an indictment based on testimony of at least one employee of the DOT. The African-American female was tried and convicted of theft of monies in excess of $500.00 from FHWA. Judge Bedford sentenced her to ten (10) years in prison. The African-American female was incarcerated on April 30, 2007.

Now, we'll examine the multitude of obvious violations in this scenario. First, and for most, obviously the owner of the property in funds in question is the FHWA. The FHWA is an operating administration within the DOT and the DOT is a Department within the Executive Branch of the Federal Government. The United States Code, Title 28, Part II, Chapter 31, Section 516. Conduct of litigation reserved to Department of Justice reads, "Except as otherwise authorized by law, the conduct of litigation in which the United States, **an agency**, or officer thereof is a party, **or is interested**, and **securing evidence therefor, is reserved to officers of the Department of Justice,** under the direction of the Attorney General." Thus, Federal law clearly prohibits **Paul L. Howard, Jr., District Attorney for Fulton County**, Georgia or any other official in the State of Georgia from seeking an indictment or prosecuting the African-American female for theft of any amount of money from FHWA! The African-American female should never been subjected to a trial by the State of Georgia. FHWA attorneys, who are Federal government attorneys, are paid to know Federal law, or, at least, know how to look it up.

So, one must presume some insidious motive on the part of the OIG and FHWA.

Second, the State of Georgia obtained an indictment and a conviction against the African-American female based wholly on testimony and documents given by employees of DOT and FHWA to the Fulton County District Attorney's Office in violation of the Code of Federal Regulations (CFR), Title 49, Volume I, Part 9, §§ 9.1, 9.2, 9.3, 9.9, 9.13, and 9.15. The U.S. Supreme Court held in Chrysler Corp. v. Brown, 441 U.S. 281 (1979) "that properly promulgated, substantive agency regulations have the 'force and effect of law.'" Thus, these properly promulgated, substantive agency regulations have the force and effect of law. The OIG and FHWA are mentioned in Title 49, Volume I, Part 9, § 9.3 Definitions. Therefore, the employees of the OIG and FHWA are bound and restricted by the contents of these regulations. These sections of the CFR prohibit the actions taken by all of the DOT and FHWA employees involved.

Third, the words **"DEPARTMENT OF TRANSPORTATION-OFFICE OF INSPECTOR GENERAL. FOR OFFICIAL USE ONLY. (Public availability to be determined under 5 U.S.C. 552)"** come into play here. Each document that was turned over to the Fulton County DA's office violated the provisions of 5 U.S.C. § 552! Court transcripts indicate that dozens upon dozens of documents fall into this category. Each violation carries a maximum penalty of Five Thousand Dollars ($5,000.00).

Fourth, during his investigation, the OIG learned that **that no crime was committed within the boundaries of Georgia**. Yet, they went forward with the lie and in violation of Federal law.

Fifth, nothing offered during the trial indicates or suggests that any payments of Federal funds were made contrary to Federal law. The United States Code, Title 31, Subtitle III, Chapter 33, Subchapter II, Section 3332 reads, in relevant part, "(f)(1) Notwithstanding any other provision of law (including subsections (a) through (e) of this section and sections 5120(a) and (d) of title 38), except as provided in paragraph (2) all Federal payments made after January 1, 1999, **shall be made by electronic funds transfer**." The Federal Acquisition Regulations, Subpart13.3, Section 13.302 Purchase orders reads, in relevant part, "(c) **In accordance with 31 U.S.C. 3332, electronic** funds transfer (EFT) is required for payments except as provided in 32.1110." **Before the prosecution began, the Fulton County DA had the document in his office that establishes the EFT's for FHWA are processed in Oklahoma, and not in Georgia!** The crime for which the African-American female was charged requires the disbursement of funds and **any disbursement of funds did not occur within the boundaries of Georgia.** Thus, **nothing that the African-American female was accused of doing violated any Georgia law.**

Sixth, the members of FHWA who testified during the trial had no authority to present themselves as representatives of the U.S. Government and then speak on behalf of the FHWA.

Seventh, since Federal law prohibits the Fulton County District Attorney from prosecuting the African-American female in this circumstance and the result of that wrongful prosecution is the imprisonment of the African-American female, the State of Georgia, the U.S. Government, the OIG, and members of FHWA management are guilty of wrongful imprisonment. For the record, the African-American female stole no money from FHWA!

The Fulton County District Attorney's actions were taken unlawfully under the color of law. The African-American female lost her "liberty" as a result of the unlawful acts described herein. The following information was downloaded from the Federal Bureau of Investigation's web site at http://www.fbi.gov/hq/cid/civilrights/color.htm.

> Preventing abuse of this authority, however, is equally necessary to the health of our nation's democracy. That's why it's a federal crime for anyone acting under "color of law" willfully to deprive or conspire to deprive a person of a right protected by the Constitution or U.S. law. "Color of law" simply means that the person is using authority given to him or her by a local, state, or federal government agency. **The FBI is the lead federal agency for investigating color of law abuses,** which include acts carried out by government officials operating both within and beyond the limits of their lawful authority.

False arrest and fabrication of evidence: The Fourth Amendment of the U.S. Constitution guarantees the right against unreasonable searches or seizures. A law enforcement official using authority provided under the color of law is allowed to stop individuals and, under certain circumstances, to search them and retain their property. It is in the abuse of that discretionary power—such as an unlawful detention or illegal confiscation of property—that a violation of a person's civil rights may occur.

Fabricating evidence against or falsely arresting an individual also violates the color of law statute, taking away the person's rights of due process and unreasonable seizure. In the case of deprivation of property, the color of law statute would be violated by unlawfully obtaining or maintaining a person's property, which oversteps or misapplies the official's authority.

The Fourteenth Amendment secures the right to due process. The person accused of a crime must be allowed the opportunity to have a trial and should not be subjected to punishment without having been afforded the opportunity of the legal process.

All of this occurred because an African-American woman employed by the FHWA spoke up because an unqualified Caucasian woman was promoted! Clearly, multiple violations of 18 U.S.C. § 242 occurred in Ms. Hill-Brown's circumstance and the FBI and the Department of Justice did absolutely nothing! One of the most precious rights that we enjoy as citizens of these United States is Liberty. The Preamble to the Constitution of the United States declares it. The abuses that the African-American female suffered at the hands of the U.S. Government and the State of Georgia ought to offend anyone.

I wrote detailed letters and sent them via facsimile to Mary E. Peters, Secretary of Transportation, to Michael Chertoff, Secretary of the Department of Homeland Security, to Calvin L. Scovel, DOT Inspector General, to Congressman Henry Waxman, and to

Congressman Danny K. Davis. None of the high placed officials took any action at all!

Here is one final note about this circumstance. The FHWA gave the State attorney an award for this illegal prosecution!

THE FEDERAL RESERVE

RESERVE

AND

ELECTRONIC CHECK CONVERSION

Businesses are using a practice referred to as electronic check conversion. What is electronic check conversion? Electronic check conversion occurs when a business takes the personal check that you write to a business and uses the information on the check to send your bank an electronic debt transaction for your checking account instead of depositing the check in the bank. This electronic transaction is called an electronic funds transfer. The problem with electronic check conversion is it is AGAINST THE LAW!! Now I'll prove that electronic check conversion is unlawful and that the Federal Reserve System is aware of this unlawful practice and condones it!

The US. Code in Title 15 Chapter 41 Subchapter VI Electronic Fund Transfers Section 1693a Definitions reads,

As used in this subchapter -
(1) the term "accepted card or other means of access" means a card, code, or other means of access to a consumer's account for the purpose of initiating electronic fund transfers when the person to whom such card or other means of access was issued has requested and received or has signed or has used, or authorized another to use, such card or other means of access for the purpose of transferring money between accounts or obtaining money, property, labor, or services;
(2) the term "account" means a demand deposit, savings deposit, or other asset account (other than an occasional or incidental credit balance in an open end credit plan as defined in section 1602(i) of this title), as described in regulations of the Board, established primarily for personal, family, or household purposes, but such term does not include an account held by a financial institution pursuant to a bona fide trust agreement;
(3) the term "Board" means the Board of Governors of the Federal Reserve System;
(4) the term "business day" means any day on which the offices of the consumer's financial institution involved in an electronic fund transfer are open to the public for carrying on substantially all of its business functions;
(5) the term "consumer" means a natural person;

(6) the term "electronic fund transfer" means any transfer of funds, other than a transaction originated by check, draft, or similar paper instrument, which is initiated through an electronic terminal, telephonic instrument, or computer or magnetic tape so as to order, instruct, or authorize a financial institution to debit or credit an account. Such term includes, but is not limited to, point-of-sale transfers, automated teller machine transactions, direct deposits or withdrawals of funds, and transfers initiated by telephone. Such term does not include-

(A) any check guarantee or authorization service which does not directly result in a debit or credit to a consumer's account;

(B) any transfer of funds, other than those processed by automated clearinghouse, made by a financial institution on behalf of a consumer by means of a service that transfers funds held at either Federal Reserve banks or other depository institutions and which is not designed primarily to transfer funds on behalf of a consumer;

(C) any transaction the primary purpose of which is the purchase or sale of securities or commodities through a broker-dealer registered with or regulated by the Securities and Exchange Commission;

(D) any automatic transfer from a savings account to a demand deposit account pursuant to an agreement between a consumer and a financial institution for the purpose of covering an overdraft or maintaining an agreed upon minimum balance in the consumer's demand deposit account; or

(E) any transfer of funds which is initiated by a telephone conversation between a consumer and an officer or employee of a financial institution which is not pursuant to a prearranged plan and under which periodic or recurring transfers are not contemplated; as determined under regulations of the Board;

(7) the term "electronic terminal" means an electronic device, other than a telephone operated by a consumer, through which a consumer may initiate an electronic fund transfer. Such term includes, but is not limited to, point-of-sale terminals, automated teller machines, and cash dispensing machines;

(8) the term "financial institution" means a State or National bank, a State or Federal savings and loan association, a mutual savings bank,

a State or Federal credit union, or any other person who, directly or indirectly, holds an account belonging to a consumer;

(9) the term "preauthorized electronic fund transfer" means an electronic fund transfer authorized in advance to recur at substantially regular intervals;

(10) the term "State" means any State, territory, or possession of the United States, the District of Columbia, the Commonwealth of Puerto Rico, or any political subdivision of any of the foregoing; and

(11) the term "unauthorized electronic fund transfer" means an electronic fund transfer from a consumer's account initiated by a person other than the consumer without actual authority to initiate such transfer and from which the consumer receives no benefit, but the term does not include any electronic fund transfer (A) initiated by a person other than the consumer who was furnished with the card, code, or other means of access to such consumer's account by such consumer, unless the consumer has notified the financial institution involved that transfers by such other person are no longer authorized, (B) initiated with fraudulent intent by the consumer or any person acting in concert with the consumer, or (C) which constitutes an error committed by a financial institution.

An electronic check conversion is an electronic funds transfer. Remember two important points. First, the term "electronic fund transfer" means any transfer of funds, **other than a transaction originated by check**, draft, or similar paper instrument. Second, the term "unauthorized electronic fund transfer" means an electronic fund transfer from a consumer's account initiated by a person other than the consumer without actual authority to initiate such transfer and **from which the consumer receives no benefit**. There you have it! An electronic fund transfer cannot be originated by the check you write and **you** receive no benefit from the business turning your check into an electronic fund transfer! No part of the law that governs electronic fund transfer permits a business to simply tell you that if you write the business a check, then the business has permission to transform the check into an electronic fund transfer.

How do banks and businesses get away with doing this? Simple. The Federal Reserve System permits and condones the practice in spite of the law!! I know that the Federal Reserve System knows about this practice and condones it because I personally wrote to Chairman Greenspan in summer of 2005. Nothing was done to stop this illegal practice.

WE GET TO MAKE
THE RULES SO WE
THINK WE CAN DO
ANYTHING WE WANT

OR

THE

CONGRESS

Article I Section 1 of the Constitution

All legislative Powers herein granted shall be vested in a Congress of the United States, which shall consist of a Senate and House of Representatives.

Now that's a pretty plain and simple statement. The Constitution vests in Congress all legislative posers that are written in the Constitution. So, let's examine the Constitution and see just what powers and authorities are granted to Congress.

Article I Section 2[5]- "The House of Representatives shall chose their Speaker and other Officers, and shall have the sole Power of Impeachment."

Article I Section 3[6]- "The Senate shall have the sole Power to try all Impeachments."

Article I Section 8[1]- "The Congress shall have Power To lay and collect Taxes, Duties, Imposts and Excises, to pay the Debts and provide for the common Defence and general Welfare of the United States; but all Duties, Imposts and Excises shall be uniform throughout the United States"

Article I Section 8[2]-"To borrow Money on the credit of the United States."

Article I Section 8[3]-"To regulate Commerce with foreign Nations, and among the several States, and with the Indian Tribes."

Article I Section 8[4]- "To establish an uniform Rule of Naturalization, and uniform Laws on the subject of Bankruptcies throughout the United States."

Article I Section 8[5]- "To coin Money, regulate the Value thereof, and of foreign Coin, and fix the Standard of Weights and Measures."

Article I Section 8[6]- "To provide for the Punishment of counterfeiting the Securities and current Coin of the United States."

Article I Section 8[7]- "To establish Post Offices and post Roads."

Article I Section 8[8]- "To promote the Progress of Science and useful Arts, by securing for limited Times to Authors and Inventors the exclusive Right to their respective Writings and Discoveries."

Article I Section 8[9]- "To constitute Tribunals inferior to the supreme Court."

Article I Section 8[10]- "To define and punish Piracies and Felonies committed on the high Seas, and Offences against the Law of Nations."

Article I Section 8[11]- "To declare War, grant Letters of Marque and Reprisal, and make Rules concerning Captures on Land and Water."

Article I Section 8[12]- "To raise and support Armies, but no Appropriation of Money to that Use shall be for a longer Term than two Years."

Article I Section 8[13]- "To provide and maintain a Navy."

Article I Section 8[14]- "To make Rules for the Government and Regulation of the land and naval Forces."

Article I Section 8[15]- "To provide for calling forth the Militia to execute the Laws of the Union, suppress Insurrections and repel Invasions."

Article I Section 8[16]- "To provide for organizing, arming, and disciplining, the Militia, and for governing such Part of them as may be employed in the Service of the United States, reserving to the States respectively, the Appointment of the Officers, and the

Authority of training the Militia according to the discipline prescribed by Congress."

Article I Section 8[17]- "To exercise exclusive Legislation in all Cases whatsoever, over such District (not exceeding ten Miles square) as may, by Cession of particular States, and the Acceptance of Congress, become the Seat of the Government of the United States, and to exercise like Authority over all Places purchased by the Consent of the Legislature of the State in which the Same shall be, for the Erection of Forts, Magazines, Arsenals, dock-Yards, and other needful buildings."

Article I Section 8[18]- "To make all Laws which shall be necessary and proper for carrying into Execution the foregoing Powers, and all other Powers vested by this Constitution in the Government of the United States, or in any Department or Officer thereof."

Article IV Section 3[2]- "The Congress shall have Power to dispose of and make all needful Rules and Regulations respecting the Territory or other Property belonging to the United States; and nothing in this Constitution shall be so construed as to Prejudice any Claims of the United States, or of any particular State."

Amendment IX- "The enumeration in the Constitution, of certain rights, shall not be construed to deny or disparate others retained by the people."

Amendment X- "The powers not delegated to the United States by the Constitution, nor prohibited by it to the States, are reserved to the States respectively, or to the people."

Amendment XIII Section 1 –"Neither slavery nor involuntary servitude, except as a punishment for crime whereof the party shall have been duly convicted, shall exist within the United States, or any place subject to their jurisdiction."

Section 2-"Congress shall have power to enforce this article by appropriate legislation."

Amendment XIV Section 1 "All persons born or naturalized in the United States, and subject to the jurisdiction thereof, are citizens of the United States and of the State wherein they reside. No State shall make or enforce any law which shall abridge the privileges or immunities of citizens of the United States; nor shall any State deprive any person of life, liberty, or property, without due process of law; nor deny to any person within its jurisdiction the equal protection of the laws."

Section 2- "Representatives shall be apportioned among the several States according to their respective numbers, counting the whole number of persons in each State, excluding Indians not taxed. But when the right to vote at any election for the choice of electors for President and Vice President of the United States, Representatives in Congress, the Executive and Judicial officers of a State, or the members of the Legislature thereof, is denied to any of the male inhabitants of such State, being twenty-one years of age,\15\ and citizens of the United States, or in any way abridged, except for participation in rebellion, or other crime, the basis of representation therein shall be reduced in the proportion which the number of such male citizens shall bear to the whole number of male citizens twenty-one years of age in such State."

Section 3-"No person shall be a Senator or Representative in Congress, or elector of President and Vice President, or hold any office, civil or military, under the United States, or under any State, who, having previously taken an oath, as a member of Congress, or as an officer of the United States, or as a member of any State legislature, or as an executive or judicial officer of any State, to support the Constitution of the United States, shall have engaged in insurrection or rebellion against the same, or given aid or comfort to the enemies thereof. But Congress may by a vote of two-thirds of each House, remove such disability."

Section 4-"The validity of the public debt of the United States, authorized by law, including debts incurred for payment of pensions and bounties for services in suppressing insurrection or rebellion, shall not be questioned. But neither the United States nor any State shall assume or pay any debt or obligation incurred in aid of insurrection or rebellion against the United States, or any claim for the loss or emancipation of any slave; but all such debts, obligations and claims shall be held illegal and void."

Section 5-"The Congress shall have power to enforce, by appropriate legislation, the provisions of this article."

Amendment XV Section 1-"The right of citizens of the United States to vote shall not be denied or abridged by the United States or by any State on account of race, color, or previous condition of servitude."

Section 2-"The Congress shall have power to enforce this article by appropriate legislation."

Amendment XVI-"The Congress shall have power to lay and collect taxes on incomes, from whatever source derived, without apportionment among the several States, and without regard to any census or enumeration."

Amendment XIX-"The right of citizens of the United States to vote shall not be denied or abridged by the United States or by any State on account of sex. Congress shall have power to enforce this article by appropriate legislation."

Amendment XX Section 4- "The Congress may by law provide for the case of the death of any of the persons from whom the House of Representatives may choose a President whenever the right of choice shall have devolved upon them, and for the case of the death of any of the persons from whom the Senate may choose a Vice President whenever the right of choice shall have devolved upon them."

Amendment XXIII Section 1-"The District constituting the seat of Government of the United States shall appoint in such manner as the Congress may direct: A number of electors of President and Vice President equal to the whole number of Senators and Representatives in Congress to which the District would be entitled if it were a State, but in no event more than the least populous State; they shall be in addition to those appointed by the States, but they shall be considered, for the purposes of the election of President and Vice President, to be electors appointed by a State; and they shall meet in the District and perform such duties as provided by the twelfth article of amendment."

Section 2-"The Congress shall have power to enforce this article by appropriate legislation."

Amendment XXIV Section 1-"The right of citizens of the United States to vote in any primary or other election for President or Vice President, for electors for President or Vice President, or for Senator or Representative in Congress, shall not be denied or abridged by the United States or any State by reason of failure to pay any poll tax or other tax."

Section 2-"The Congress shall have power to enforce this article by appropriate legislation."

Amendment XXVI Section 1-"That right of citizens of the United States, who are eighteen years of age or older, to vote shall not be denied or abridged by the United States or by any State on account of age."

Section 2-"The Congress shall have power to enforce this article by appropriate legislation."

The Constitution grants Congress quite a bit of power, but the Constitution grants Congress **ONLY** the powers and authorities stated in the Constitution. Congress has no powers or authorities other than the powers and authorities granted in the Constitution.

Congress has the power and authority to deal with the out of control federal judiciary. Various members of Congress have complained over the years about Federal judges legislating from the bench. Well, members of Congress do not need to complain about such behavior. The Constitution grants Congress the authority and power to deal with such behavior.

The Constitution grants Congress the power to remove judges. Mr. Hamilton, in one of his letters to the people of New York, Federalist Number 89, explains the safeguards the Framers placed in the Constitution concerning the federal judiciary. Mr. Hamilton says, "There can never be danger that the judges, by a series of deliberate usurpations on the authority of the legislature, would hazard the united resentment of the body intrusted with it, while this body was possessed of the means of punishing their presumption, by degrading them from their stations." The danger Mr. Hamilton speaks of is no longer a phantom, but has become a terrible reality! So, let's ask Congress some questions. Who do the members of the House and Senate think the responsibility falls upon to protect the Rights of the people and to make sure all courts and judges function according to the Constitution? Why haven't you done anything about the unconstitutional behavior of judges? What are you going to do to correct the unconstitutional behavior of judges? What are you going to do to correct the affects of the unconstitutional behavior of Federal judges? When will the first removal hearing for a judge begin? Congress holds lots of hearings on subject matter that is absolutely none of the business assigned to Congress in the Constitution, but Congress does not deal appropriately with the federal judiciary.

Speaking of Congress holding hearings on subject matter that is not any of its business. It is looooong past time that someone point out to members of Congress that the Constitution of these United States gives Congress no power or authority regarding steroid use by a professional athlete! You read all of the powers and authorities granted to Congress in the Constitution. Did you see anything that remotely refers to or implies to steroid use by a professional athlete? I concede that this is an issue of concern to parents, their children, medical practitioners, coaches, team owners, sports sponsors, etc. At this moment in this country there are much higher priorities for the Congress to spend the Peoples' monies on (i.e. rebuilding after disasters like Katrina, better schools, improved infrastructure, health care for all Americans, securing America's borders, better care, benefits, and salary for our military men and women, better pay for teachers, firefighters, and police officers, addressing hate crimes, discrimination, and the deprivation of civil rights, etc.). The list goes on and on, but the list DOES NOT include ANYTHING with regard to who took steroids to better his or her athletic performance. What ought to be news worthy is the fact that members of Congress are spending the Peoples' hard earned tax dollars on what, according to the Constitution, is none of the business of Congress! Whatever happened to the oath of SUPPORT and DEFEND THE CONSTITUTION??

The current annual salary for each member of Congress is reported to be a minimum of $168,000. Let's see what we get for that hefty salary we pay members of Congress.

We've seen how useless it was to file a lawsuit to correct the unconstitutional behavior of the Supreme Court. We've seen also how all those unconstitutional governmental immunities that the federal judiciary legislated from the bench keep us from filing a lawsuit to alter the unconstitutional behavior of the Government! If you want to appeal the lower court's rulings and go on to the Supreme Court, then the Supreme Court simply takes your money and refuses to hear your case. So, YOU see how YOUR First Amendment Right to petition the Government for a redress of a grievance is being trampled upon and the members of Congress that beg us to elect them and pay them to protect our Rights do nothing.

The Government has gone to great lengths to make sure that the Constitution is inoperative. The arrogance and the "I am so important" attitude of Government officials, judges, and members of Congress make it seem like they are all are doing us a favor when they take our money (that paycheck they receive from the public treasury). Each one of them is constantly crying that they need more money. They don't earn the paycheck the get!! What do We the People get for our money? We get our Rights trampled upon, we get the Constitution ignored, and we get hearings on steroid use in major league baseball!!!

SEPARATION OF CHURCH AND STATE

THE DECLARATION OF INDEPENDENCE

When in the Course of human events, it becomes necessary for one people to dissolve the political bands which have connected them with another, and to assume among the Powers of the earth, the separate and equal station to which the Laws of Nature and of **Nature's God** entitle them, a decent respect to the opinions of mankind requires that they should declare the causes which impel them to the separation.

We hold these truths to be self-evident, that all men are created equal, that they are **endowed by their Creator** with certain unalienable Rights, that among these are Life, Liberty, and the pursuit of Happiness. That to secure these rights, Governments are instituted among Men, deriving their just powers from the consent of the governed.

We, therefore, the Representatives of the United States of America, in General Congress, Assembled**, appealing to the Supreme Judge of the world for the rectitude of our intentions**, do, in the Name, and by Authority of the good People of these Colonies, solemnly publish and declare, That these United Colonies are, and of Right ought to be Free and Independent States; that they are Absolved from all Allegiance to the British Crown, and that all political connection between them and the State of Great Britain, is and ought to be totally dissolved; and that as Free and Independent States, they have full Power to levy War, conclude Peace, contract Alliances, establish Commerce, and to do all other Acts and Things which Independent States may of right do. And for the support of this Declaration, **with a firm reliance on the Protection of Divine Providence**, we mutually pledge to each other our Lives, our Fortunes and our sacred Honor.

Article VI of the Constitution
" . . . no religious Test shall ever be required as a Qualification to any Office or public Trust under the United States."

Amendment I to the Constitution of the United States

Congress shall make no law respecting an establishment of religion,
or prohibiting the free exercise thereof

Law of the United States

Title 5 of the United States Code, Part III, Subpart B, Chapter 33,
Section 3331 requires each member of Congress, every employee in
the civil service, and every person in the military service to take the
following oath:

"I,   , do solemnly swear (or affirm) that I will support and
defend the Constitution of the United States against all enemies,
foreign and domestic, that I will bear true faith and allegiance to
the same; that I take this obligation freely, without any mental
reservation or purpose of evasion, and that I will well and faithfully
discharge duties of the office on which I am about to enter. **So help
me God**."

Law of the United States

Title 28 of the United States Code, Part I, Chapter 21, Section 453
requires each justice or judge of the United States to take the following
oath:

"I,   , do solemnly swear (or affirm) that I will administer justice
without respect to persons, and do equal right to the poor and to the
rich, and that I will faithfully and impartially discharge and perform
all the duties incumbent upon me as   according to the best
of my abilities and understanding, agreeably to the Constitution and
laws of the United States. **So help me God**."

Our country is founded on the belief that we have some
unalienable Rights. The belief in these unalienable Rights resulted
in a war. Our Declaration of Independence concedes that the source
of these unalienable Rights is our Creator. In our Declaration of

238

Independence we first acknowledge that there is a Supreme Judge of this world and then we appeal to the Supreme Judge of the world for the correctness of our independence. Our Declaration of Independence declares that the United States is founded on a firm reliance on the **protection** of Divine Providence. Indeed our country's founding documents concede that without the Creator *THIS* United States cannot exist. The majority of State Constitutions in the Preamble contain a reference to a Creator or a statement similar to "grateful to Almighty God." Our way of life is firmly rooted in the belief that we have unalienable Rights and without the Creator or Almighty God there are no unalienable Rights. After all, we got those precious unalienable Rights from the Creator or Almighty God.

Remember that the Bill of Rights (the first ten amendments to the Constitution) was written because the Government could not be trusted to restrain itself and the Framers of the Constitution wanted to make it absolutely clear that certain rights are beyond the reach of the Government. The first right mentioned is religion. The Constitution says that Congress shall make no law respecting an establishment of religion, or prohibiting the free exercise thereof. There is nothing in the Constitution that requires a separation of church and state.

We can hardly have a separation of church and state when the oaths that we require members of Congress, all the employees in the civil service, all the members of the military service, and our judges to take includes the request for God's help. All of our money carries the words "In God We Trust." Our Presidents have clergy to the White House, a government building, for prayer. We acknowledge a Creator, we ask that Creator to judge our intentions, we rely on Divine Providence for protection, we ask God to help Congress and our judges, and our Presidents pray in the White House.

Look at what our schools have become since we excluded the Creator from the schools. How can we separate the Creator from any aspect of the way of life that we acknowledge the Creator has given us? Can America, indeed, should America, expect the protection of Divine Providence? America acknowledges that America is based on what the Creator has given. but America chooses to exclude the Creator from aspects of American life. If America continues to exclude the Creator, then what kind of judgment should America expect from the Supreme Judge of the world?

SO NOW WHAT?

Well, now you know. The facts show just how unconstitutional the Government is. The facts also show that Government officials, whose jobs are to protect our rights, constantly ignore our rights. The Supreme Court, Congress, and the Executive Branch are all out of control. Government officials hope you would never learn what you know now. It is time for the really tough questions. Can this mess be fixed? If so, how? If not, why not?

I believe it can be fixed, but in order to fix this mess each of us, **ME, YOU,** and other Americans must stand up and say **ENOUGH IS ENOUGH** and **THE GOVERNMENT IS OUT OF CONTROL!**

The fix for this mess is — the Government must be brought inline with the Constitution and the members of Congress do not honor their oath to support and defend the Constitution must not be re-elected! What does support and defend the Constitution mean? That's an easy question. The answer is it means acting accordance with what is written in the Constitution!

In order to bring the Government inline with the Constitution, Congress does not need to hold any hearings, order any reports, or receive any testimony. The factual information currently available to each member of Congress establishes that it is past time for the members of Congress to hold the Executive and Judicial Branches accountable for not complying with the Constitution and the law of the land. It is not difficult for Congress to hold the other two Branches accountable and bring the Government inline with the Constitution because the Constitution gives Congress the tools to do what is necessary! Those Government officials who fail to comply must be removed (i.e. impeached). The Constitution says that Congress makes the rules and laws for the operation of the Government. For starters, to bring the Government inline with the Constitution and to prevent any further oppression of the People by any part of the Government, Congress must pass laws that state the following:

1. There is no federal common-law.
2. The Government does not have sovereign immunity to suits brought by a citizen.

3. Government officials do not have absolute immunity to suits brought by a citizen.
4. Government officials do not have qualified immunity to suits brought by a citizen.
5. The government contractor immunity does not exist because sovereign immunity does not exist.
6. The deliberate-process privilege does not exist.
7. The administrative exhaustion doctrine is abolished because it is contrary to the Constitution.
8. No law may be used as an exclusive remedy for a redress of grievances against the Government.
9. The restrictions in the Federal Tort Claims Act are repealed because such restrictions are unconstitutional.
10. There is no limit on the amount one can recover for a redress of grievances (i.e. Civil Rights Act of 1991) because Congress' establishment of such a limit on the redress of grievances is unconstitutional.
11. All cases denied a review because of the Judiciary Act of 1925 or because of the Supreme Court's vague, arbitrary and capricious standard are reinstated.
12. Appellate judges who do not perform the required review are guilty of a high misdemeanor.
13. Courts will not issue per curiam decisions.
14. In all meetings, conferences, or discussions, for the conduct of court business, in every Federal court, there shall be a court reporter and the court reporter shall make a verbatim record of the meeting, conference or discussion.
15. When two federal courts of appeals disagree on the law, one of the federal court of appeals must ask the Supreme Court to resolve the issue and the Supreme Court must hear the case.
16. A judge will sign all decisions issued by Federal courts.
17. Equal Employment Opportunity time frames will be the same for the Government and the private sector.
18. The Merit Systems Protection Board must include a factual basis for "does not meet the criteria for review."
19. The Department of Justice shall include in their decision to represent a Government employee the specific reasons that

form the basis for the decision and forward a copy to the plaintiff and the Congress.

20. All bills and laws shall contain the specific portion of the Constitution granting Congress the authority for the act.

21. Any Government employee who commits perjury or persuades another to commit perjury, in any proceeding, shall be removed from federal service and shall be subject to criminal and/or civil action.

The Preamble to the United Nations Universal Declaration of Human Rights reads "Whereas it is essential, if man is not to be compelled to have recourse, as a last resort, to rebellion against tyranny and oppression, that human rights should be protected by the rule of law." The Government's behavior proves that the Government has become the Tyrant that the Constitution is constructed to prevent. EVERY Federal judge, justice, member of Congress, and Government employee takes an oath to support and defend the Constitution. Yet, our Constitution or the law no longer protects our Rights because Government officials wield power and ignore the Constitution and the law, and Congress permits their behavior. There are no longer adequate remedies for correcting the unconstitutional behavior of the Government because the Judicial Branch, instead of applying the law, creates law that only serves to protect the unlawful behavior of Government officials. Have we as a People come to the last resort against the tyranny and oppression of the Government? Some Americans may think so. The task at hand is enormous. The members of Congress should move swiftly to correct their unconstitutional behavior and the unconstitutional behavior of the Executive and Judicial Branches. It's long past the time for us to hold them accountable for everything they do and everything they don't do!!! They work for us!! WE PAY THEM!!! The founding fathers started the **FIRST** Congress. Surely, we can continue our nation with a mostly new Congress. I say mostly new Congress because we may not have to replace all of them.

A member of Congress' political party membership is irrelevant because every member of Congress takes an oath to do what we have found that they fail to do — uphold the Constitution. Political parties are not mentioned in the Constitution or in the oath taken by the members of Congress. The members of Congress who have integrity and honor will immediately correct the problems identified in this book, so that the Government is operating according to the Constitution and each member of Congress who is without integrity and honor should not be re-elected. If *We the People* re-elect any member of Congress who fails to support and defend the Constitution, thereby demonstrating a lack of honor and integrity, then *We the People* cannot be surprised or complain when there are **NO RIGHTS REMAINING**.

The freedom and citizenship we enjoy comes
with a very important responsibility!
That responsibility is eternal vigilance!
***We the People* must be ever watchful!**

I will restate the offer found in the beginning of this book. I will be happy to meet any Supreme Court Justice, any member of Congress, or any Government official in the public forum of his or her choice and defend anything written in this book.